"Over and over again people have [illegible] Protestants are suddenly a public force to be reckoned with on political and social issues. Madison Trammel's convincing and insightful *Fundamentalists in the Public Square* prompts us to rethink the premise behind such surprise. In light of this valuable revisionist study, we can start to see the Scopes Trial of 1925, the Moral Majority of the 1980s, and today's Culture Wars as all part of one continuous way of being Christian in America."

—Timothy Larsen,
McManis Professor of Christian Thought, Wheaton College

"In this creatively researched study, Madison Trammel makes a good case for modifying parts of the standard picture of American fundamentalism in the 1920s and 1930s. Through intensive scrutiny of local newspapers, he shows that fundamentalist leaders long sustained active commentary on questions surrounding alcohol and evolution, two concerns that both antedated and postdated the much-publicized 'Monkey Trial' of 1925 involving William Jennings Bryan and the question of evolution. Trammel follows Matthew Sutton and a few others who improve the history of earlier fundamentalism by fleshing out complexities in a story with ongoing as well as historical significance."

—Mark A. Noll,
research professor of history, Regent College

"The fundamentalists who censured theological modernism in the 1920s are often supposed to have been inactive in the public square because they believed in concentrating on saving souls. However, in *Fundamentalists in the Public Square*, Madison Trammel clearly demonstrates that they were strongly engaged in opposition to evolution and in support of prohibition. By drawing on a wealth of evidence from the press of four states, he also shows that they suffered less condemnation at the hands of public opinion than might be expected."

—David Bebbington,
emeritus professor of history, University of Stirling

"Seldom does a volume decisively propose a new interpretation that dislodges an 'everyone knows given' in historical accounts. But Madison Trammel's *Fundamentalists in the Public Square* does just that. It has been widely assumed the Scopes Trial of 1925 marked a watershed event in the history of American fundamentalism. The famous trial allegedly so gravely discouraged fundamentalists that they lost much of their zeal to advance their cause. Through careful research of contemporary newspapers, Trammel demonstrates that neither the Scopes Trial nor the negative fallout from Prohibition decisively crippled fundamentalists' desire to promote their beliefs to the nation. This book may change the way the story of American fundamentalism in the Twenties is told."

—John Woodbridge,
research professor of church history and the history of
Christian thought, Trinity Evangelical Divinity School

"A solid and deft study that contributes to the new interpretive paradigm concerning fundamentalists and the public square. Trammel makes a compelling case that during the post-Scopes Roaring Twenties and beyond, fundamentalists never left the building."

—Barry Hankins,
professor of history, Baylor University

FUNDAMENTALISTS *in the* PUBLIC SQUARE

Evolution, Alcohol, and Culture Wars
after the Scopes Trial

FUNDAMENTALISTS
in the PUBLIC SQUARE

Evolution, Alcohol, and Culture Wars
after the Scopes Trial

MADISON TRAMMEL

STUDIES IN HISTORICAL AND SYSTEMATIC THEOLOGY

LEXHAM
ACADEMIC

Fundamentalists in the Public Square: Evolution, Alcohol, and Culture Wars after the Scopes Trial
Studies in Historical and Systematic Theology

Copyright 2023 Madison Trammel

Lexham Academic, an imprint of Lexham Press
1313 Commercial St., Bellingham, WA 98225
LexhamPress.com

Print ISBN 9781683597186
Digital ISBN 9781683597193
Library of Congress Control Number 2023935085

Lexham Editorial: Todd Hains, Allisyn Ma, Katy Smith, Mandi Newell
Cover Design: Joshua Hunt
Typesetting: Katy Smith, Abigail Stocker

To Asher and Kai

CONTENTS

ACKNOWLEDGMENTS

—

This project started as a dissertation, accompanied by all the pain, uncertainty, and joy common to that endeavor, before settling more comfortably into its current form. Those who shepherded me through the dissertation phase deserve much thanks, especially Jason Duesing and John Woodbridge, my supervisors, who pointed me in the fruitful direction of newspaper studies and offered helpful corrections along the way. Any weaknesses in the book are uniquely mine, of course, and remain despite their best efforts.

I must also acknowledge fellow PhD students in historical theology at Midwestern Baptist Theological Seminary who both encouraged me and challenged me with the quality of their research and writing. Many of them have since published their own dissertations or other works of scholarship. To name just a few, Jesse Payne, Geoff Chang, Mark Fugitt, Jenny-Lyn de Klerk, Ronni Kurtz, Sam Parkison, and Camden Pulliam, I appreciate your work and am grateful for the opportunity to study alongside you for a time.

Devin Maddox, my director at B&H Publishing, granted me salaried, non-vacation time to complete this book, for which I will forever be grateful. His commitment to fostering a healthy work-life balance for others is both admirable and worthy of imitation.

Finally, I want to thank my wife, Regina, and sons, Asher and Kai, for the good cheer, opinionated conversation, and consistent love and support they bring to our home. May the Lord lead you in joy and gladness. You are always a joy to me.

INTRODUCTION

This book is as much about a common narrative of fundamentalist-evangelical history as it is about fundamentalists themselves. The narrative, shaped by historians like George Marsden and Joel Carpenter, among many others, suggests that fundamentalists withdrew from cultural engagement following the 1925 Scopes Trial, leaving behind evangelicalism's otherwise consistent tradition of such efforts. Carl Henry's post–World War II call to fundamentalists to renew their commitment to Christian social responsibility, captured in his 1947 book *The Uneasy Conscience of Modern Fundamentalism*, seems to confirm this narrative.

Yet there is reason to question it. Despite its facility in explaining fundamentalism's increasing marginalization during the interwar period and in grounding a trajectory of neo-evangelical emergence beginning in the mid-1940s, the narrative suffers two weaknesses. First, it asserts a more complete fundamentalist retreat from social action than can be observed in the historical record. Second, it creates an arbitrary point in time for the beginning of this retreat, one tied to the highly publicized Tennessee Scopes Trial. This study aims to document these two weaknesses more thoroughly than has been done previously, relying primarily on evidence drawn from newspaper reporting. In so doing, it confirms and adds detail to an alternative narrative of fundamentalist-evangelical history.

A few key definitions, as well as a brief summary of evangelical history, will be helpful upfront.

DEFINING EVANGELICALISM

With all the diversity of thought observable throughout evangelical history, it is worth asking whether the term "evangelical" has any specific meaning. What is an evangelical? How may the movement, evangelicalism, best be defined?

Historians usually categorize evangelicalism as a branch of Protestantism unified not by denominational ties but rather by a shared adherence to the gospel's centrality.[1] Randall Balmer characterizes it as a "vast and diverse religious movement" that includes "fundamentalists, Pentecostals, holiness people, charismatics, the sanctified tradition, neoevangelicals, various ethnic groups and on and on. Evangelicalism is anything but homogenous—racially, theologically, or politically."[2] The common thread among this diverse group is an experience of rebirth by the gospel and a priority to share the gospel with others.

As Timothy George summarizes, "Evangelicals are a worldwide family of Bible-believing Christians committed to sharing with everyone everywhere the transforming good news of new life in Jesus Christ, an utterly free gift that comes through faith alone in the crucified and risen Savior."[3] Evangelicals' understanding of the gospel is thus not doctrinal alone, but also experiential; it requires a response and motivates action. Faith is viewed as a "living, personal trust in the Lord," and this faith "is the basis of our fellowship across so many ethnic, cultural, national, and denominational divides."[4]

Bruce Hindmarsh identifies the seventeenth-century Anglican emphasis on "one thing needful," referring to a purity of intention in spiritual matters, as a key precursor to evangelicalism, which "turned [the emphasis] into something more explosive."[5] Rather than referring simply to unity of doctrine and devotion, "one thing needful" became a call that was "renewed, heightened, and addressed to all. And it was linked with a promise as preachers held out the prospect of an immediate experience of God's forgiveness and the felt presence of the Holy Spirit."[6]

1. See, for instance, Randall Balmer, *The Making of Evangelicalism: From Revivalism to Politics and Beyond* (Waco, TX: Baylor University Press, 2010), 2; David Bebbington, *Evangelicalism in Modern Britain: A History from the 1730s to the 1980s* (Grand Rapids: Baker Book House, 1992), 1; Douglas A. Sweeney, *The American Evangelical Story: A History of the Movement* (Grand Rapids: Baker Academic, 2005), 17.

2. Balmer, *Making of Evangelicalism*, 2–3.

3. Timothy George, "If I'm an Evangelical, What Am I?" *Christianity Today* (August 9, 1999): 9.

4. George, "If I'm an Evangelical," 9.

5. Bruce Hindmarsh, *The Spirit of Early Evangelicalism: True Religion in a Modern World* (New York: Oxford University Press, 2018), 2.

6. Hindmarsh, *The Spirit of Early Evangelicalism*, 2.

In *Who Is an Evangelical?*, Thomas S. Kidd defines evangelicalism concisely as "the religion of the born again."[7] He unpacks this definition as follows:

> Evangelicals are born-again Protestants who cherish the Bible as the Word of God and who emphasize a personal relationship with Jesus Christ through the Holy Spirit. This definition hinges upon three aspects of what it means to be an evangelical: being born again, the primacy of the Bible, and the divine presence of God the Son and God the Holy Spirit.[8]

Kidd notes that evangelicalism has become identified with Republican politics in recent years and that current evangelical believers might more commonly refer to themselves as "Bible-believing" or "born again," or even as a member of their church or denomination rather than with the word "evangelical."[9] Still, the historic beliefs and practices of evangelicalism have remained consistent from the Great Awakening to the present day.

Furthermore, while evangelicals have always stressed the Bible's inspiration and authority, this emphasis did not strongly distinguish them from broader Protestantism until the fundamentalist-modernist controversy during the early twentieth century. As modernists "questioned the reliability of the Bible ... the doctrine of the Bible's 'inerrancy' (its entire veracity in all details) became an evangelical hallmark."[10] The fundamentalists under investigation in this study may, therefore, be credited with bringing evangelicalism's emphasis on the Bible to the fore and with defining it more carefully in opposition to views that would accommodate the possibility of scientific or historic errors in Scripture.

Theologian Roger Olson describes "evangelical" as a fraught term, often contested, and he identifies seven possible ways of defining it: (1) as an aspect of authentic Christianity focused on the good news, or "evangel," rather than on legalism or moralism; (2) as a Reformation-derived synonym for Protestant; (3) as the Protestant-leaning wing or impulse within the Anglican church; (4) as the "movement of 'heart Christianity' that arose out of German

---

7. Thomas S. Kidd, *Who Is an Evangelical?* (New Haven, CT: Yale University Press, 2019), 4.
8. Kidd, *Who Is an Evangelical?*, 4.
9. Kidd, *Who Is an Evangelical?*, 1–2.
10. Kidd, *Who Is an Evangelical?*, 5.

Pietism"; (5) as a reference to the conservative Protestant, or fundamentalist, reaction to theological liberalism in the late nineteenth and early twentieth centuries; (6) as the neo-evangelicalism that emerged out of this early
twentieth-century fundamentalism and sought to distance itself from its
perceived separatism; and (7) as a broad descriptor of any religious group
that is particularly "aggressive" or committed to missionary outreach.[11]

Though the word "evangelical" contains a wide range of possible mean-
ings, Olson asserts that it remains a historically useful designator to describe
"a loose affiliation (coalition, network, mosaic, patchwork, family) of mostly
Protestant Christians" who affirm the following:

> a supernatural worldview; the unsurpassable authority of the Bible
> for all matters of faith and religious practice; Jesus Christ as unique
> Lord, God, and Savior; the fallenness of humanity and salvation pro-
> vided by Jesus Christ through his suffering, death, and resurrection;
> the necessity of personal repentance and faith (conversion) for full
> salvation; the importance of a devotional life and growth in holiness
> and discipleship; the urgency of gospel evangelism and social trans-
> formation; and the return of Jesus Christ to judge the world and estab-
> lish the final, full rule and reign of God.[12]

Some evangelicals may affirm a greater number of central beliefs, according to Olson, but none will affirm less. Nor will any deny these doctrines.[13]

Other scholars have suggested slightly different lists of characteristics to
define evangelicalism. Douglas Sweeney surveys several possible definitions,
while highlighting the challenge of describing such a diverse movement:
"When viewed from the perspective of our multiplicity, we evangelicals hold
hardly anything in common. We are a people more remarkable for our differences than our union."[14] Yet he, too, concludes that evangelicalism remains

---

11. Roger E. Olson, *Pocket History of Evangelical Theology* (Downers Grove, IL: InterVarsity
Press, 2007), 7–13. Olson observes further that "defining *evangelical, evangelicalism*, and *evangelical theology* has become something of a cottage industry in the waning years of the twentieth
century and early years of the twenty-first century. ... Entire scholarly conferences and symposia
have devoted great effort and energy to the cause of investigating and finally comprehensively
describing evangelicalism."

12. Olson, *Pocket History of Evangelical Theology*, 14–15.

13. Olson, *Pocket History of Evangelical Theology*, 15.

14. Sweeney, *American Evangelical Story*, 20.

a coherent and concrete phenomenon—that "there is still such a thing as a definite and definable evangelical movement today."[15] For a historical definition, he spotlights the work of British scholar David Bebbington, whose approach will be considered ahead. For a theological definition, he summarizes another British scholar, Alister McGrath, in suggesting six "fundamental convictions" that hold evangelicalism together.

1. The supreme authority of Scripture as a source of knowledge of God and a guide to Christian living.

2. The majesty of Jesus Christ, both as incarnate God and Lord and as the Savior of sinful humanity.

3. The lordship of the Holy Spirit.

4. The need for personal conversion.

5. The priority of evangelism for both individual Christians and the church as a whole.

6. The importance of the Christian community for spiritual nourishment, fellowship, and growth.[16]

Sweeney's own, one-sentence definition is somewhat unusual but still useful: "Evangelicals comprise a movement that is rooted in classical Christian orthodoxy, shaped by a largely Protestant understanding of the gospel, and distinguished from other such movements by an eighteenth-century twist."[17] This definition stresses evangelicalism's connection to historic orthodoxy, the Reformation, and the revivalist Great Awakening era out of which it was born.

Randall Balmer echoes Sweeney's outlook in viewing evangelicalism as uniquely shaped by the eighteenth century. In particular, he highlights three precursors to the movement that formed it as it emerged from the Great Awakening: "Scots-Irish Presbyterianism, Continental Pietism, and the vestiges of New England Puritanism."[18] The lack of a single denominational

15. Sweeney, *American Evangelical Story*, 23.
16. Sweeney, *American Evangelical Story*, 18.
17. Sweeney, *American Evangelical Story*, 23–24.
18. Balmer, *Making of Evangelicalism*, 2.

identity, along with a sometimes negative view of tradition, also bequeathed a kind of "malleability" to evangelicalism, enabling "evangelical leaders to speak to the idiom of the culture, whether embodied in the open-air preaching of George Whitefield in the eighteenth century, the democratic populism of Peter Cartwright and Charles Finney on the frontier, or the suburban, corporate-style megachurches of the twentieth century."[19] Balmer simplifies the defining features of evangelicalism to three: "an embrace of the Holy Bible as inspired and God's revelation to humanity, a belief in the centrality of a conversion or 'born again' experience, and the impulse to evangelize or bring others to the faith."[20] While he leaves out Sweeney's and McGrath's emphases on the Holy Spirit, Jesus, and the community of faith, he similarly highlights conversion, evangelism, and the Bible's authority.

The most widely cited list of evangelical characteristics, however, was suggested by David Bebbington, who affirms Balmer's three features and adds an emphasis on the cross. Bebbington's list is concise, as it can be expressed in four words, and its characteristics together provide a set of boundaries within which most Protestant believers could be considered evangelicals and outside of which most would be either Christians of another tradition or persons of another faith or no faith. Bebbington's characteristics, his "quadrilateral of [evangelical] priorities," include conversionism, activism, biblicism, and crucicentrism.[21]

By conversionism, Bebbington means "the belief that lives need to be changed" by people responding to the gospel and being spiritually born again;[22] by activism, "the expression of the gospel in effort," which is often vigorous endeavors intended both to spread the gospel message and to better society;[23] by biblicism, "a particular regard for the Bible" stemming from a belief "that all spiritual truth is to be found in its pages";[24] and by crucicentrism, "a stress on the sacrifice of Christ on the cross" that views the doctrine of atonement as holding central and foundational importance.[25] Like other

---

19. Balmer, *Making of Evangelicalism*, 3.
20. Balmer, *Making of Evangelicalism*, 2.
21. Bebbington, *Evangelicalism in Modern Britain*, 3.
22. Bebbington, *Evangelicalism in Modern Britain*, 3, 5–10.
23. Bebbington, *Evangelicalism in Modern Britain*, 3, 10–12.
24. Bebbington, *Evangelicalism in Modern Britain*, 3, 13–14.
25. Bebbington, *Evangelicalism in Modern Britain*, 3, 14–17.

historians, Bebbington acknowledges that evangelicalism has flowered in many different denominations and changed over time. However, he concludes that its "common features ... have lasted from the first half of the eighteenth century to the second half of the twentieth."[26]

Every definition of evangelicalism surveyed above holds explanatory power and common threads run throughout. Indeed, some may see the many definitions offered by theologians and historians as nearly fungible, since they are alike in so many respects. Scholars universally acknowledge the unity-in-diversity that marks evangelicalism, for instance, along with its singular focus on responding to the gospel. However, this book will rely most heavily on Bebbington's definition because it is widely affirmed and because its brevity affords it a shorthand usefulness. Evangelicals broadly, including the fundamentalists of the 1920s, will be understood to be essentially conversionist, activist, biblicist, and crucicentric.

DEFINING FUNDAMENTALISM AND CULTURAL ENGAGEMENT

Two other key terms warrant definitions: "fundamentalism" and "cultural engagement." In its broadest and often least complimentary usage, fundamentalism can refer not only to specifically Protestant believers but to extremism found within any religious group. As Malise Ruthven summarizes:

> The F-word has long since escaped from the Protestant closet in which it began its semantic career around the turn of the 20th century. ... It may [now] be described as a religious way of being that manifests itself in a strategy by which beleaguered believers attempt to preserve their distinctive identities as individuals or groups in the face of modernity and secularization.[27]

In this handling of the term, Muslim terrorist groups are sometimes referred to as fundamentalist, as are devout Jewish, Buddhist, and Hindu believers.

A second usage of the term remains focused on Protestantism, but does so with a wide-angle lens, seeing fundamentalism as a strain or emphasis

---

26. Bebbington, *Evangelicalism in Modern Britain*, 2.

27. Malise Ruthven, *Fundamentalism: A Very Short Introduction* (New York: Oxford University Press, 2007), 5–6.

present throughout evangelical history. Ernest Sandeen adopts this understanding of the term in his noteworthy 1970 book, *The Roots of Fundamentalism*:

> The primary function of this study has been to provide historical evi-
> dence for the argument that Fundamentalism existed as a religious
> movement before, during, and after the controversy of the twenties.
> This involves, in the first place, the separation of the Fundamentalist
> *movement* and the Fundamentalist *controversy*. ... The Fundamentalist
> movement was a self-conscious, structured, long-lived, dynamic
> entity with recognized leadership, periodicals, and meetings.[28]

In this second way of using the term "fundamentalism," Protestant believers
from the nineteenth century until the present day are included—nearly any
believer or group that has self-identified as fundamentalist—but no follow-
ers of other religious traditions.

A third usage of the term focuses narrowly on the conservative evangelicalism that took shape in the years leading up to the American religious disputes of the 1920s, then emerged in full during those disputes,
coming to represent arguably a majority of US evangelicals until the rise
of neo-evangelicalism in the mid-to-late 1940s. George Marsden defines
this fundamentalism succinctly as "militantly anti-modernist Protestant
evangelicalism ... the movement that for a time in the 1920s created a national
sensation with its attempts to purge the churches of modernism and the
schools of Darwinism."[29]

All three definitions of fundamentalism can be helpful, and Sandeen's
effort to trace fundamentalism throughout modern Protestant history
remains instructive. Yet this book will use the term in its third, most historically specific sense, adopting the definition offered by Marsden. No other
term better describes the conservative, anti-modernist Protestants of the
1920s, giving this meaning continued usefulness for studies of evangelicalism

28. Ernest R. Sandeen, *The Roots of Fundamentalism: British and American Millenarianism, 1800-1930* (Grand Rapids: Baker Books, 1978), xiii.

29. George M. Marsden, *Fundamentalism and American Culture: The Shaping of Twentieth-Century Evangelicalism, 1870-1925* (New York: Oxford University Press, 1980), 4-5.

in the years following the Moody era and preceding the neo-evangelical shift in outlook and priorities.

Cultural engagement may also be defined in more than one way. Christian cultural engagement, most broadly, refers to any attempt to influence the thoughts, actions, and structures of a society in order to better align them with Christian virtues and values. Such engagement seeks to relate the City of God to the City of Man. While big-picture influence is normally in view, individuals within society need not be overlooked. As Joshua Chatraw and Karen Swallow Prior observe, "Engaging culture, rightly conceived, includes studying the world around us—to understand its aspirations, longings, institutions, artifacts, ideas, and issues—in order to better engage the *people* within cultures."[30]

This book will use as synonyms of cultural engagement terms like "social action" and "public action." The broad understanding of cultural engagement above will undergird all such terms but with a more definite application to fundamentalists at the fore.

This specific application comes from Bebbington. One of the pillars of his quadrilateral definition of evangelicalism is activism, which he defines to include both spiritual activities and social activities. Bebbington attributes the social side of evangelical activism to the movement's "philanthropic urge" and characterizes it as "attempts to enforce the ethics of the gospel" in the world.[31] Because Bebbington's definition is grounded in evangelical distinctives, it is directly applicable to a study of fundamentalism's social action and, thus, to fundamentalism's place within the arc of evangelical history. When this book uses "cultural engagement" or "social action" or similar terms, it will therefore refer to "attempts to enforce the ethics of the gospel" within society.

---

30. Joshua D. Chatraw and Karen Swallow Prior, *Cultural Engagement: A Crash Course in Contemporary Issues* (Grand Rapids: Zondervan Academic, 2019), 22.

31. Bebbington, *Evangelicalism in Modern Britain*, 12. For a classic exploration of the connection between evangelism and cultural engagement, spiritual activities and social activities, in evangelical history, see also Timothy L. Smith, *Revivalism and Social Reform: American Protestantism on the Eve of the Civil War* (Nashville: Abingdon Press, 1957).

THE STORY OF EVANGELICALS IN NORTH AMERICA

Evangelicalism began in the early to mid-eighteenth century with the First Great Awakening, a period of transatlantic revivals led by preachers such as John Wesley, George Whitefield, and Jonathan Edwards.[32] These revivals involved Anglicans, Methodists, Baptists, Congregationalists, and Presbyterians. Though some objected to the methods of the revivalists and doubted the fruits of their efforts, defenders such as Edwards made a strong case for the validity of the awakening in works like *The Distinguishing Marks of a Work of the Spirit of God* (1741), *Some Thoughts Concerning the Present Revival of Religion* (1742), and *A Treatise on Religious Affections* (1746).[33] Ultimately, despite its attendant controversies, the Great Awakening brought together many Protestants who had hitherto focused primarily on their disagreements with one another. Douglas Sweeney describes this result of the Great Awakening as follows:

> In the wake of the Reformation, Protestant leaders began *infighting* in much the same way as they fought the Catholics. ... But during and after the Great Awakening, much of this changed for good—not overnight, and never completely, but considerably and noticeably. In a work of amazing grace and by the power of the Holy Spirit, untold numbers of Protestant leaders began to join hands across these boundaries and to collaborate in the work of gospel ministry. They did not establish a new church. Rather, they labored ecumenically—*inter*-denominationally and *pan*-geographically—cosponsoring revivals, concerts of prayer, and common fasts.[34]

---

32. Evangelicalism's origin in the Great Awakening is widely attested. Randall Balmer (cited previously), David Bebbington, and Doug Sweeney (cited ahead) begin their histories with the Great Awakening. See also the preface to Thomas Kidd, *The Great Awakening: A Brief History with Documents* (Boston: Bedford/St. Martin's Press, 2008), which states that the "Great Awakening gave birth to American evangelical Christianity," and Mark Hutchinson and John Wolffe, *A Short History of Global Evangelicalism* (New York: Cambridge University Press, 2012), 32, which distinguishes between earlier religious movements and the revivals of the Great Awakening: "What happened in the 1730s and 1740s was more than a gradual confluence of streams of influence and connection. It was a point of vigorous new departure, in which the Holy Spirit was manifestly at work in the world." Virtually every historian of evangelicalism views the Great Awakening similarly as the genesis of evangelicalism.

33. All of Jonathan Edwards's extant works, including both published books and unpublished notebooks and sermons, can be found at *The Works of Jonathan Edwards Online*, Jonathan Edwards Center at Yale University, http://edwards.yale.edu.

34. Douglas A. Sweeney, *The American Evangelical Story* (Grand Rapids: Baker Academic, 2005), 28–29.

A recent set of volumes published by IVP Academic divides the history of evangelicalism following the Great Awakening into distinct, recognizable eras. After the series' book on the Awakening period itself comes *The Expansion of Evangelicalism: The Age of More, Wilberforce, Chalmers and Finney* by John R. Wolffe. This volume highlights what is commonly called the Second Great Awakening, another period of revivals extending from the late eighteenth century through the early decades of the nineteenth century, along with the "new measures" revivals that followed it, which extended to the middle of the nineteenth century.[35]

Next in the series is *The Dominance of Evangelicalism: The Age of Spurgeon and Moody* by David Bebbington, which surveys the middle to late nineteenth century, during which time evangelical beliefs and practice achieved a broad level of acceptance, and evangelical leaders had a high level of influence in the United States. This cultural consensus favoring evangelicalism began to break down, as detailed in *The Disruption of Evangelicalism: The Age of Mott, Machen and McPherson* by Geoff Treloar, during a period roughly spanning the early to mid-twentieth century. It was during the period of disruption that many evangelicals became known as fundamentalists, a term that stemmed in part from the 1910 to 1915 publication of a series of essays entitled *The Fundamentals*. This new name distinguished theological conservatives from religious modernists who attempted to adapt traditional Christian understandings of miracles, the Bible, Jesus, and salvation to Enlightenment challenges and modern science.

The IVP Academic series ends with *The Global Diffusion of Evangelicalism: The Age of Graham and Stott* by Brian Stanley, which charts the emergence of neo-evangelicalism in the middle of the twentieth century. Neo-evangelicals self-consciously sought to distance themselves from what they saw as fundamentalism's separatism and isolationism and to recapture the evangelical ethos of earlier eras. The neo-evangelical era extends until the current day when evangelicals are once again simply called evangelicals.[36]

---

35. Some evangelical historians would investigate the Second Great Awakening as a distinct era, but Wolffe prefers to study all the revivalism from 1790 to 1850 together, as these years combined to spur great growth in the movement, propelling it to a position of cultural prominence in the United States. Other books, such as Nathan Hatch, *The Democratization of American Christianity* (New Haven, CT: Yale University Press, 1989), take a similar approach.

36. Stanley places particular emphasis on evangelicalism's increasingly global identity; indeed, the term "evangelical" has become as much an identifier of conservative Protestants

The overall progression charted in IVP's series on evangelical history is commonly used, and many historians of evangelicalism recount the movement's eras similarly. Some identify the eras with slightly different emphases.[37] Others flesh out the story line by paying greater attention to what could be seen as intra-era developments. In Heath Carter and Laura Rominger Porter's *Turning Points in the History of American Evangelicalism*, for instance, separate chapters are devoted to evangelicalism's relationship to the Enlightenment, an aspect of the Great Awakening era; the shaping of American ideals of domesticity, one development of the Civil War and Moody era; the emergence of urban Pentecostalism, arguably an outgrowth of modernism-denying fundamentalism; and Lausanne '74, a key event within evangelicalism's modern era of global growth.[38] Yet in nearly every history of evangelicalism, the shape, main events, and key influencers of the movement remain consistent.

One notable aspect of the evangelical story is its internationalism. Never confined by national borders, the evangelical movement began simultaneously in England and the British colonies, and broader missionary efforts marked it from the turn of the nineteenth century.[39] As the title of Stanley's book, *The Global Diffusion of Evangelicalism* suggests, evangelicalism matured into a genuinely global phenomenon in the modern era, when missionary efforts bore fruit in mature churches and denominations that were both influenced by American evangelicalism and thrived independently of its oversight.

---

in Latin America and Africa as of English-speaking believers in the United States and England. See Brian Stanley, *The Global Diffusion of Evangelicalism: The Age of Billy Graham and John Stott* (Downers Grove, IL: IVP Academic, 2013), 14–16.

37. See, for example, the Table of Contents of Darren Dochuk, Thomas S. Kidd, and Kurt W. Peterson, *American Evangelicalism: George Marsden and the State of American Religious History* (Notre Dame, IN: University of Notre Dame Press, 2014), vii–ix, which labels the Great Awakening a Puritan period, the Second Great Awakening and Moody/Spurgeon era "Protestantism's Century," fundamentalism a protest of modernity, and neo-evangelicalism a partial rejection and partial embrace of pluralism. Even in a progression such as this, geared toward intellectual history, the same basic story line of evangelical growth and development is reflected.

38. Heath W. Carter and Laura Rominger Porter, *Turning Points in the History of American Evangelicalism* (Grand Rapids: Eerdmans, 2017), vii–viii.

39. Andrew Walls describes modern-day missions as the "autumnal child" of evangelical revivals: "Fifty years separate the great events of Northampton and Cambuslang from the formation of the earliest of the voluntary societies to promote Christian activity in the non-Christian world; yet, without the revival, the societies would have been inconceivable." See Andrew Walls, *The Missionary Movement in Christian History: Studies in the Transmission of Faith* (Maryknoll, NY: Orbis Books, 1996), 79.

Melani McAlister writes, "That is why the history of American evangelical-ism cannot be fully understood through a domestic lens."[40] Evangelicalism's commitment to a global outlook has shaped its history.[41]

A second notable aspect of the evangelical story is its intellectual cur-rents. While a handful of shared doctrinal commitments have given the move-ment unity, evangelicalism also birthed and nurtured a variety of sometimes contradictory theological emphases. Bruce Hindmarsh identifies a strain of devotion at the heart of early evangelical thought, a devotion that centered on "earnestness" and experiencing and "spreading a more directly personal experience of Christianity."[42] Yet evangelical thought was also shaped by the Enlightenment era in which it was born, particularly by new ideas in sci-ence, law, and art. "There was an epochal change from the authority of the ancients to that of the moderns. ... Evangelicalism arose, quite precisely, in the middle of this transition."[43] Early evangelicals disputed predestination among themselves: as early as 1739, Methodists had split into Calvinist and Arminian factions.[44] Nineteenth-century evangelicals, though generally shar-ing in Republican political ideals and a confidence in common sense moral reasoning, divided over the interpretation of Scripture and, more point-edly, its application to slavery.[45] "The intellectual resources that evangelical Protestants had so eagerly embraced ... were powerless in the face of division over slavery."[46] More recently, evangelicals have differed over eschatology, women's roles, charismatic gifts, and much else, with theologian Roger Olson drawing on George Marsden and Donald W. Dayton to identify two overar-ching impulses, a "Puritan-Princeton paradigm" focused on doctrine and a "Pietist-Pentecostal paradigm" focused on spiritual experience.[47]

---

40. Melani McAlister, *The Kingdom of God Has No Borders: A Global History of American Evangelicals* (New York: Oxford University Press, 2018), 3.

41. For an overview of evangelical history that traces its international connections in nearly every era of its development, see also Hutchinson and Wolffe, *A Short History of Global Evangelicalism*.

42. Hindmarsh, *Spirit of Early Evangelicalism*, 1, 3.

43. Hindmarsh, *Spirit of Early Evangelicalism*, 4.

44. Hindmarsh, *Spirit of Early Evangelicalism*, 235.

45. Mark Noll, *America's God: From Jonathan Edwards to Abraham Lincoln* (New York: Oxford University Press, 2002), 209, 367–69, 386.

46. Noll, *America's God*, 386.

47. Roger E. Olson, *The Story of Christian Theology: Twenty Centuries of Tradition and Reform* (Downers Grove, IL: InterVarsity Press, 1999), 594.

THE CENTRAL QUESTION

With key definitions and a survey of evangelical history in mind, we now turn our attention to the specific, central question this study seeks to answer: Did American interwar fundamentalists disengage from social concerns following the 1925 Scopes Trial, or did they continue to wield influence in the public square, particularly in support of Prohibition and in opposition to the teaching of evolution? Throughout evangelical history, born-again believers have been marked by conversionism, activism, biblicism, and crucicentrism. The activism leg of these four characteristics always included both spiritual and social endeavors. Therefore, if fundamentalists did not engage in social action, they would be unique in the history of evangelicalism. Such a retreat would have put them at odds with their evangelical forebears and descendants alike.

Alcohol and evolution will be in focus because both were leading social issues during the early interwar period—issues that fundamentalists had actively engaged with before the trial. If fundamentalists continued to oppose alcohol and evolution after the trial, then the Marsden-Carpenter narrative about withdrawal from cultural engagement cannot be true.

Theologically, the fundamentalists' doctrine was indisputably evangelical, Bible-centered, and in contrast to progressive theology. No scholar or critic doubts this commitment. J. Gresham Machen's *Christianity and Liberalism*, published in 1923, captured well the conflict between fundamentalism and modernism, portraying modernism as another religion altogether.

> The great redemptive religion which has always been known as Christianity is battling against a totally diverse type of religious belief, which is only the more destructive of the Christian faith because it makes use of traditional Christian terminology. This modern non-redemptive religion is called "modernism" or "liberalism."[48]

Much of the theological conflict of the 1920s centered on the authority of Scripture, and on this point, the neo-evangelicals who came after the interwar fundamentalists agreed with their predecessors. J. I. Packer's *"Fundamentalism" and the Word of God*, published in 1956, demonstrates the importance of Scripture's inspiration and inerrancy for both groups.[49]

---

48. J. Gresham Machen, *Christianity and Liberalism* (Grand Rapids: Eerdmans, 1923), 2.

49. See J. I. Packer, *"Fundamentalism" and the Word of God* (Grand Rapids: Eerdmans, 1958), 9–23.

Socially, however, some neo-evangelicals viewed fundamentalists as having engaged in a shameful retreat from cultural action. Carl F. H. Henry's *Uneasy Conscience of Modern Fundamentalism* critiqued interwar fundamentalists for possessing "no social program calling for a practical attack on acknowledged world evils. ... The great majority of Fundamentalist clergyman, during the past generation of world disintegration, became increasingly less vocal about social evils."[50]

This study will demonstrate that Henry's portrayal of fundamentalists was inadequate. Though his motivation for painting such a picture is not in focus, modest suggestions about why he did so, despite counterevidence of which he would have been aware, will be offered in the pages ahead.

RESEARCH METHODOLOGY

Newspapers are not the only lens through which to observe the Scopes Trial's effect on fundamentalism; magazine articles, books, and public talks can be assessed as well. However, newspapers were the dominant medium of the 1920s, at a time when radio had not yet penetrated most households and magazines and books reached far fewer readers. A credible case that the Scopes Trial embarrassed fundamentalists and prompted their public retreat cannot therefore be made apart from newspapers. In addition, reporters in the 1920s covered fundamentalists with some regularity; any defeat or wide-scale disengagement that left no trace in newspaper coverage cannot be considered consequential.

Newspapers are also a worthwhile primary source for this study because press coverage of fundamentalists has been little researched. The writings of nationally known columnists such as H. L. Mencken appeared in relatively few publications, and blistering critiques of fundamentalists such as those he wrote were the exception rather than the norm. Much remains to be discovered about everyday reporting on fundamentalists, the kind many readers in America would have encountered with regularity.

Evolution was a growing concern for fundamentalists throughout the early 1920s, and the decade was simultaneously deeply shaped by Prohibition—arguably the most significant social legislation of the era.

---

50. Carl F. H. Henry, *The Uneasy Conscience of Modern Fundamentalism* (Grand Rapids: Eerdmans, 1947), 16, 18.

Fundamentalists were an active faction of the dry movement that led to
Prohibition; key fundamentalist leaders such as Billy Sunday spoke loudly
against alcohol in the early 1920s, and fundamentalists were early supporters
of the full national ban on the sale and consumption of alcohol. Any diminishment in their efforts to oppose evolution and alcohol following the Scopes
Trial would have been noteworthy.

The specific years this study covers are 1920 to 1933. These years sur-
round the Scopes Trial and span roughly the first half of the interwar period,
including the full era of Prohibition. For a reconsideration of whether interwar fundamentalists withdrew from cultural engagement, or what activities they engaged in if they did not disengage, the years of 1920 to 1933 are
thus pivotal in shedding light on the trajectory of interwar fundamentalism.

One key tool makes this study possible. Previously, research of newspaper reporting would have involved travel to various libraries and long
hours spent in microfiche rooms. A broad study of newspaper reporting
spanning multiple publications and states would have been logistically chal-
lenging, to say the least. This study relies on the fully searchable, digital
newspaper database NewspaperArchive.com. The database went online in
1999 and has been adding newspapers to its collection steadily since then. It
currently catalogs more than thirteen thousand publications over a period
of nearly four hundred years.[51] For the purposes of this study, searches in
the database are built on combinations of keywords such as "fundamentalist," "Prohibition," "alcohol," "Scopes," and "evolution." The database is large,
however, such that a full national search would yield too many articles for a
single study: more than 5,400 pieces related to fundamentalists and evolution
or alcohol between 1920 and 1933. Attention is therefore restricted to articles
from newspapers in the nation's four most populous states in the 1920s: New
York, Pennsylvania, Illinois, and Ohio.[52] Major cities such as New York City
and Philadelphia hosted many more newspapers throughout the 1920s than
they do today,[53] and the residents of these states comprised about 25 percent

---

51. See the "About Us" page at NewspaperArchive.com: https://newspaperarchive.com/
about-us/.

52. See U.S. Bureau of the Census, *Historical Statistics of the United States: Colonial Times to
1970, Part 1*, William Lerner (Washington, DC, 1975), Chapter A, 24–37.

53. A comparison of active newspapers in every major metro area of the United States during
the 1920s and the 2010s can be made at NewspaperArchive.com: https://newspaperarchive.com/.

of the country's population throughout the decade.[54] NewspaperArchive.com has cataloged hundreds of newspapers published in New York, Pennsylvania, Illinois, and Ohio between 1920 and 1933. For a full list of the newspapers included in this study, see the chart located in the Appendix.[55]

One limited study of newspaper reporting on the Scopes Trial has already been conducted and should be mentioned. Initiated by the historian of science, Ronald L. Numbers, the study is difficult to locate, though Edward Larson and Barry Hankins, among others, cite it.[56] Numbers surveyed five metropolitan newspapers' coverage of the trial, concluding that none published proclamations of an evolutionist victory or a fundamentalist defeat. Yet Numbers looked only at reporting on the trial itself, rather than reporting during the years preceding and following the trial, and his scope was limited to just the five cities. This study will survey a wider range of years and many more publications to provide a fuller view of newspaper reporting on the cultural engagement of interwar fundamentalists.

CHAPTER SUMMARIES

Finally, at the close of this introduction, here is a chapter-by-chapter breakdown of how this study's argument will unfold.

Chapter 1: "Fundamentalist Historiography and the Peculiarity of Fundamentalism" examines the secondary literature on fundamentalist history, identifying two main streams of historiography. One views the interwar era as a time of retreat from public action, while the other suggests this interpretation may be incomplete. The rest of the book will build a case in support of the second interpretation.

---

54. *Historical Statistics of the United States*, Chapter A, 24–37.

55. More than five hundred publications are included in the NewspaperArchive.com database for New York, Pennsylvania, Illinois, and Ohio between 1920 and 1933. Some were published for part, but not the whole, period under investigation, while others featured little or no coverage of fundamentalism. In addition, the database is extensive but not comprehensive. Not every newspaper published during the period is cataloged. Still, articles on fundamentalists and evolution or Prohibition can be found in dozens of publications digitized by NewspaperArchive.com across the four states.

56. See Edward J. Larson, *Summer for the Gods: The Scopes Trial and America's Continuing Debate over Science and Religion* (New York: Basic Books, 1997), 206, and Barry Hankins, "The (Worst) Year of the Evangelical: 1926 and the Demise of American Fundamentalism," *Fides et Historia* 43, no. 1 (2011): 5. This researcher has been unable to find the original study. Larson notes that he viewed a copy prior to publication, which may indicate the study has not yet been published.

Chapter 2: "Fundamentalism, Evolution, and Newspaper Reporting, 1920–1933," explores the tenor, extent, and content of newspaper reporting on fundamentalists and evolution between those years, focusing on activities fundamentalists were reported to have undertaken in opposition to evolution and the attitudes of newspaper reporters toward those actions whenever evident.

Chapter 3: "Fundamentalism, Alcohol, and Newspaper Reporting, 1920–1933," follows a similar pattern, exploring the tenor, extent, and content of newspaper reporting on fundamentalists and alcohol between those years, focusing on those activities fundamentalists were reported to have undertaken in opposition to alcohol or in support of Prohibition and on the attitudes of newspaper reporters toward those actions.

Following the demonstration of continued fundamentalist social concern in chapters 2 and 3, chapter 4, "Fundamentalist Social Action and Dispensational Theology," evaluates interwar fundamentalists' nascent or implicit theology of cultural engagement. A better understanding of the theological rationale, or lack of theological rationale, underpinning their public engagement is useful in further fleshing out the picture of social action undertaken by interwar fundamentalists. Chapter 4 thus complements chapters 2 and 3 as a theological assessment.

Most of the interwar fundamentalist leaders who emerge in chapters 2 and 3, such as William Bell Riley, John Roach Straton, Paul Rader, and J. Frank Norris, were committed dispensationalists. Others, like Aimee Semple McPherson and Billy Sunday, were influenced by dispensationalism. Chapter 4 compares the tactics and stated aims of fundamentalist social activists with key tenets of dispensational theology, particularly dispensational views on the Bible, sin, salvation, anthropology, and the church and eschatology—the doctrinal loci most relevant to cultural engagement. The writings of theologians such as Harry A. Ironside, Arno C. Gaebelein, C. I. Scofield, and, especially, Lewis Sperry Chafer are relied upon in charting the dispensational outlook of the interwar era.

Finally, chapter 5: "Conclusions," synthesizes the discoveries of the previous three chapters, analyzes their significance, and suggests key takeaways. Interpretations of interwar fundamentalists' social engagement, fundamentalist alignment within broader evangelical history, and the historiography of fundamentalism are proposed. A better understanding of neo-evangelical critiques of fundamentalists—critiques such as those found in Henry's *Uneasy Conscience of Modern Fundamentalism*—is also suggested.

1
—

FUNDAMENTALIST HISTORIOGRAPHY AND THE PECULIARITY OF INTERWAR FUNDAMENTALISM

The Scopes Trial's significance revolves around it being more than simply a notable event in the history of fundamentalism. It certainly was a notable event, both at the time and in its later memorializing in popular culture. As has been mentioned already, though, the trial has been assessed in two very different ways in fundamentalist historiography, and therein lies its deeper significance. These differing assessments contribute to diverging narratives of the fundamentalist movement.

In one view of fundamentalist history, the Scopes Trial of 1925 represents a turning point. Before the trial, fundamentalists are seen as having engaged in social action, including efforts against evolution, alcohol, and various expressions of public immorality. After the trial, which in this view represented a Pyrrhic victory, with fundamentalists winning the court case but losing in the court of public opinion, fundamentalists withdrew from social engagement and focused on building up their own institutions. An era of separatist fundamentalism ensued, ending with the mid-1940s emergence of neo-evangelicals like Carl Henry, Billy Graham, and Harold John Ockenga.

A second view of the Scopes Trial sees it as relatively inconsequential in the arc of fundamentalist history, resulting neither in a widespread sense of internalized shame among fundamentalists nor in their public withdrawal. The narrative of a fundamentalist retreat is questioned in this interpretation. Perhaps fundamentalists never did withdraw. Perhaps they found their ability to influence the public square gradually diminished throughout the interwar period, focusing on their own institutions more out of necessity

1

than a disregard for the importance of "enforc[ing] the ethics of the gospel" in the world.[1] This chapter surveys fundamentalist historiography, tracing the development of these two contrasting views of the Scopes Trial.

A DIVERGENCE IN FUNDAMENTALIST HISTORIOGRAPHY

Fundamentalist histories can be roughly separated into those published before Ernest Sandeen's 1970 book, *The Roots of Fundamentalism*, and those published after, with those published prior to his book tending toward less nuanced or even biased portrayals. Sandeen himself criticizes much of the fundamentalist historiography preceding him, writing that "the fate of Fundamentalism in historiography has been worse than its lot in history."[2]

The first noteworthy study of fundamentalism was Stewart G. Cole's *The History of Fundamentalism*, published in 1931 during the interwar period. Cole includes a lot of good information about the roots of fundamentalism and about fundamentalist-modernist debates within various denominations. While he accurately describes fundamentalism as an outgrowth of America's historically dominant evangelical tradition, his predilections against the movement reveal themselves in various places. In describing the formative role of World War I, for instance, Cole lists fundamentalists alongside the Ku Klux Klan and "one hundred percent Americanism" as reactionary groups stoked by wartime passions.

> When hostilities ceased in Europe the abnormal emotional set of American minds was not easily curbed. Especially was this true with illiterate people. Exploiters of the masses soon set themselves to sublimate war hates into organized bursts of social unrest, class passion and religious prejudice.[3]

---

1. As mentioned above, this short definition of social activism comes from David Bebbington, *Evangelicalism in Modern Britain: A History from the 1730s to the 1980s* (Grand Rapids: Baker Book House, 1992), 12.

2. Ernest R. Sandeen, *The Roots of Fundamentalism: British and American Millenarianism, 1800–1930* (Grand Rapids: Baker Book House, 1978), 285.

3. Stewart G. Cole, *The History of Fundamentalism* (Westport, CT: Greenwood Press, 1931), 25.

Cole further describes Bible conference teachers, somewhat cynically, as men who "assumed the role of God's favored interpreters."[4] Sandeen concludes that despite the strengths of Cole's study, he "made no effort to disguise his own personal antipathy to the movement."[5] Interestingly, Cole points to the publication of *The Fundamentals* not just as a key catalyst in fundamentalist development but as the launch of the movement itself.[6]

A brief but full history of dispensationalism was later published in 1958: C. Norman Kraus's *Dispensationalism in America*. Kraus interacts in the book with fundamentalists such as A. C. Gaebelein and C. I. Scofield, but only as theologians. He doesn't discuss the social and denominational debates that forged fundamentalism, nor does he even mention fundamentalism itself. Still, his study contributed to a better understanding of the movement, as most fundamentalist leaders were either committed dispensationalists or highly influenced by it. Kraus traces dispensationalism's development from John Nelson Darby and the Plymouth Brethren through prophecy and Bible conferences, and he devotes the second, larger half of his book to the connection between premillennialism within dispensationalism. Though a careful work, the book includes Kraus's critiques of dispensationalism in its conclusion, specifically that the theological system's hermeneutic betrays "an inadequate concept of the nature of language and its use" and that dispensationalism sidelines much of Scripture as applicable only to Israel rather than the church.[7]

The next major study of fundamentalism itself was Norman Furniss's *The Fundamentalist Controversy*, published in 1963. Sandeen mentions that Furniss's book had become more widely cited than Cole's at the time of writing his own history.[8] Furniss's work is deeply researched, filled with details about people and events, and accurately portrays the fundamentalist-modernist conflict as having occurred both within churches and in broader

---

4. Cole, *History of Fundamentalism*, 31.

5. Sandeen, *Roots of Fundamentalism*, 285.

6. Cole, *History of Fundamentalism*, 53.

7. C. Norman Kraus, *Dispensationalism in America* (Richmond, VA: John Knox Press, 1958), 131–34.

8. Sandeen, *Roots of Fundamentalism*, 285.

society.[9] Furniss also identifies the Scopes Trial as a key turning point in fundamentalist history and a public relations defeat for the anti-evolutionist lawyer William Jennings Bryan, a perspective echoed in many more recent fundamentalist histories.

> The scene [meaning the trial] was a part, actually the climax, of the fundamentalist controversy, that acrimonious dispute over evolution in science and modernism in theology which had arisen after the first World War. ... When the court adjourned it was [defense attorney Clarence] Darrow who was surrounded by men and women eager to congratulate the victor; Bryan walked away alone.[10]

Despite the positives of Furniss's work, Sandeen criticizes it heavily for factual errors, a lack of consistent sourcing, and for including no working definition of fundamentalism.[11] Sandeen further accuses Furniss of drawing glib conclusions about the movement. "Even more disconcerting is [Furniss's] practice of allowing rhetorical momentum to override evidence, giving rise to false impressions."[12]

The last significant book-length study of fundamentalism released before Sandeen's *Roots of Fundamentalism* was Louis Gasper's *The Fundamentalist Movement*, published in 1963. Gasper's work complements Sandeen's chronologically, as his survey begins in 1930, the last year under investigation in Sandeen's book. His approach is similarly fair-minded; Gasper writes in a preface that his goal in the book is to "present an objective and definitive account of the developments within the organized fundamentalist movement."[13] Yet Gasper groups fundamentalists and neo-evangelicals together and focuses on two organizations, the American Council of Christian Churches (ACCC) and the National Association of Evangelicals (NAE), that are more historically relevant for how they differ than how they align. Gasper recognizes the gap between those who populated both

---

9. Furniss's section of the book devoted to social conflict between fundamentalists and modernists is entitled "Secular Aspects of the Controversy." See Norman F. Furniss, *The Fundamentalist Controversy, 1918-1931* (Hamden, CT: Archon Books, 1963), ix.

10. Furniss, *Fundamentalist Controversy*, 3, 9.

11. Sandeen, *Roots of Fundamentalism*, 285.

12. Sandeen, *Roots of Fundamentalism*, 285.

13. Louis Gasper, *The Fundamentalist Movement* (Paris: Mouton, 1963), v.

organizations, referring to the ACCC's constituency as "the heirs of the older or original fundamentalists ... aggressive and often vituperative in their militancy," while the NAE's constituency was "conciliatory toward other theological groups within Protestantism ... [and eager] to achieve their social goals through suasion."[14] Still, he declines to refer to neo-evangelicals by their preferred name and keeps them within the fundamentalist camp. Sandeen treats Gasper's book as a source of information rather than of insights, referring to it as "a factual, almost pedantic account."[15]

Sandeen's book, published in 1970, marked a turning point in the historiography of fundamentalism. Previous accounts had been written either by uncritical insiders or by scholars with little sympathy for the movement. Sandeen combined the tools of an academic historian with the understanding of someone who had grown up within fundamentalism and still claimed it as his own, resulting in a work of scholarship that sought to understand fundamentalists on their own terms and to better grasp what motivated and formed them. As he writes, "The book was published not only for an audience of historians but also for an audience of Fundamentalists, people from my own tradition."[16]

Sandeen categorizes fundamentalism primarily as a millenarian movement. His survey begins in 1800, before the emergence of John Nelson Darby's dispensational premillennialism, with a millennial revival in Britain. By his account, streams of dispensationalism, Princeton's biblical literalism, and the prophecy and Bible conference movement dovetailed with millennial interest throughout the nineteenth century, leading to the ascendance of millennial fundamentalism by the early twentieth century. "In the twenty years before World War I the millenarians reached the pinnacle of their national influence and were able to cooperate with other conservatives in the semblance of an alliance which apparently at least temporarily held Liberalism in check."[17] This position of power was not to last, however. Not only did key leaders die by the turn of the century but internal disputes among millenarians arose and the fundamentalist-modernist controversy erupted in full

---

14. Gasper, *Fundamentalist Movement*, v.

15. Sandeen, *Roots of Fundamentalism*, 28.

16. Sandeen, *Roots of Fundamentalism*, x.

17. Sandeen, *Roots of Fundamentalism*, 226.

following World War I.[18] By 1930, the date at which Sandeen's history ends, the movement was, in his words, "split and stricken."[19]

During the interwar period under investigation in this study, Sandeen notes the emergence of new leaders such as William Bell Riley and A. C. Gaebelein.[20] A pastor in Minneapolis for most of his ministry, Riley was a "rising star" of the movement and would lead the fundamentalist charge in social engagement against both evolution and alcohol. Gaebelein, also a pastor, provided theological leadership, publishing works that upheld and defended dispensational interpretations of Scripture. Together, these leaders represented well the social and theological sides of interwar fundamentalism—sides that could be seen as contradictory, given dispensationalism's lack of an explicit social agenda. The leaders themselves were not at odds, though. Sandeen argues that the antievolution campaign of interwar fundamentalists fit well with the morally focused legislative impulses of the era, yet he views such efforts as antithetical to dispensational precepts, calling them "the greatest anomaly of the Fundamentalist controversy."

> Antievolution and premillennialism appear to be the most characteristic beliefs of Fundamentalists during the twenties. And yet the philosophy of William Jennings Bryan and the antievolution crusade was incompatible with the assumptions on which millenarianism was built. The millenarian did not believe that legislative action could produce pure morals or right thinking.[21]

The apparent conflict between fundamentalist social action and dispensational theology will be studied in chapter 4 of this book.

Sandeen's study would pave the way for a new generation of fundamentalist scholarship, one that sought to uphold the standards of critical historiography while studying fundamentalists within their own intellectual and social worlds, rather than critiquing them from the perspectives of their opponents. A flood of quality academic histories of fundamentalism followed in the wake of *The Roots of Fundamentalism*, continuing to the present day.

---

18. For a helpful chart of the ages of millenarian leaders in 1875 and 1900, see Sandeen, *Roots of Fundamentalism*, 209.

19. Sandeen, *Roots of Fundamentalism*, 269.

20. Sandeen, *Roots of Fundamentalism*, 238–39.

21. Sandeen, *Roots of Fundamentalism*, 267.

The most significant in the years immediately afterward, and perhaps still the most widely cited and influential study of fundamentalism, was George Marsden's *Fundamentalism and American Culture.*

THE GEORGE MARSDEN STREAM OF
FUNDAMENTALIST INTERPRETATION

Originally published in 1980 by Oxford University Press, Marsden's book has become a standard account of the rise of fundamentalism around the turn of the twentieth century. Marsden charts the movement's emergence out of the splintering remains of America's previously dominant evangelical consensus, as differences between modernists and conservatives deepened and led, eventually, to a parting of ways that could not be resolved. The path toward this conclusion was bumpy, and Marsden traces the significant figures, denominational fracases, unexpected reversals, and key events involved. Together with Joel Carpenter's *Revive Us Again* and Marsden's subsequent work, *Reforming Fundamentalism: Fuller Seminary and the New Evangelicalism*, a full narrative of American evangelicalism from after the Civil War to the mid-twentieth century can be outlined, a story beginning with the fall from influence Marsden charts in *Fundamentalism and American Culture*, continuing through a period of retrenchment and institution-building covered in Carpenter's *Revive Us Again*, and culminating in the reemergence to public prominence of neo-evangelicals portrayed in Marsden's *Reforming Fundamentalism*.

Marsden wrote *Fundamentalism and American Culture* while a professor at Calvin College and during a sabbatical at Trinity Evangelical Divinity School, and he states in the preface that he approaches the movement as a member of a similar religious tradition; furthermore, the book is meant to represent "distinctly Christian scholarship."[22] While Marsden writes of his aim to be objective, similarly to Sandeen he does not apologize for adopting a sympathetic perspective. Marsden published *The Outrageous Idea of Christian Scholarship* in 1997, detailing his vision for Christian intellectual work, and this vision can be observed in the "insider" questions he asks and the

---

22. George M. Marsden, *Fundamentalism and American Culture: The Shaping of Twentieth-Century Evangelicalism: 1870–1925* (New York: Oxford University Press, 1980), v.

sensitivity to fundamentalist concerns that he brings to *Fundamentalism and American Culture*.[23]

Marsden defines fundamentalism as "militantly anti-modernism Protestant evangelicalism," and he identifies three formative characteristics of the movement: (1) fundamentalists' inclination to identify as outsiders of the American establishment; (2) fundamentalism's widely varied roots in revivalism, pietism, the holiness movement, Puritan Calvinism, and the ministry of D. L. Moody; and (3) fundamentalism's anti-intellectualism and commitment to a simple, "common sense" philosophy.[24]

Throughout the Civil War, evangelicalism had retained a substantial degree of cultural authority, though cracks began to appear, particularly in disagreements over slavery. Marsden begins his study in 1870, as the cracks widened, which he illustrates in part via the careers of pre–Civil War abolitionists Henry Ward Beecher and Jonathan Blanchard. The pair's theologies would be increasingly in conflict after the war.[25] Marsden concludes his study in 1925, a proximate turning point in Baptist and Presbyterian battles between modernists and fundamentalists, but, more pointedly, the year of the Scopes Monkey Trial in Dayton, Tennessee. Marsden frames this trial as the pivotal event that signaled the end of fundamentalists' early, more hopeful era, an era during which they could still legitimately hope to regain cultural influence. Afterward, in his view, the humiliation of the public spectacle of the trial forced fundamentalists into a period of decline. As he writes, "It would be difficult to overstate the impact of 'the Monkey Trial' at Dayton, Tennessee, in transforming fundamentalism." "[The movement] quickly lost its position as a nationally influential coalition."[26]

Some historians before Marsden had portrayed the effect of the Scopes Trial on fundamentalists in a more mixed manner. Willard B. Gatewood, for

---

23. Marsden describes the primary goal of *The Outrageous Idea of Christian Scholarship* as "provid[ing] some positive guidelines as to what I have in mind when I urge that Christian perspectives and the perspectives of other religious groups be accepted as legitimate in the mainstream academy." See George M. Marsden, *The Outrageous Idea of Christian Scholarship* (New York: Oxford University Press, 1997), 8. This approach of embracing a faith-based perspective, even while aiming for historical accuracy, marks Marsden's scholarship in *Fundamentalism and American Culture*.

24. Marsden, *Fundamentalism and American Culture*, 4.

25. Marsden, *Fundamentalism and American Culture*, 28–29.

26. Marsden, *Fundamentalism and American Culture*, 184, 6.

instance, acknowledges in his 1969 book, *Controversy in the Twenties*, that fundamentalists lost allies among other theological conservatives after the Scopes Trial due to their "growing penchant for sensationalism and vulgarity."[27] However, he also highlights a defense of fundamentalists arising from a secular but traditionalist literary group at Vanderbilt University,[28] as well as corollary successes to fundamentalists' antievolution efforts.

> Although the fundamentalists were able to secure the passage of anti-evolution laws in only five states, it would be erroneous to assume that their effort to make the school a guardian of traditional morality and piety was largely a failure. What they failed to achieve by statewide statute was often accomplished by local regulations and administration actions. Equally impressive was their success in using legislation to insure religious instruction or at least Bible reading in public schools.[29]

In the wake of Marsden, however, many historians have echoed his view that the Scopes Trial signaled the beginning of the end for fundamentalist public influence and cultural engagement. This "Marsden interpretation" can be observed in fundamentalist historiography soon after the publication of *Fundamentalism and American Culture* and continuing until the present time. Proceeding in chronological order, the following studies reflect what might be called the "fundamentalist defeat and decline" view of the Scopes Trial and its aftermath.[30]

Douglas W. Frank, in his 1986 book *Less Than Conquerors*, presents a historical analysis of evangelicalism between 1850 to 1920, a period during which, in his view, harmful theological currents arose and negatively redirected the movement. He describes the purpose of his book as one of unveiling "my own self-deceptions and those of the community of evangelicals to which I

---

27. Willard B. Gatewood, ed., *Controversy in the Twenties* (Nashville: Vanderbilt University Press, 1969), 40.

28. Marsden, *Fundamentalism and American Culture*, 335.

29. Marsden, *Fundamentalism and American Culture*, 224.

30. For a sociological study that predated and likely informed Marsden's view of a fundamentalist retreat in the 1920s, see David O. Moberg, *The Great Reversal: Reconciling Evangelism and Social Concern* (Nashville: Holman, 1977).

belong."[31] The harmful theological currents he identifies include dispensational premillennialism, Victorious Life theology, and evangelical revivalism, typified by the ministry of Billy Sunday.[32] In his preface Frank credited
Marsden with piquing his interest in nineteenth- and twentieth-century
evangelicals, and Marsden likewise endorsed Frank's book, calling it "an
important and prophetic theological critique of the foundational assump-
tions on which most of the distinctives of twentieth-century American
evangelicalism have been based."[33] Though Frank's analysis focuses on the
years before 1920, in an epilogue he writes that the subsequent interwar era
became one of decline for fundamentalists. Frank acknowledges the emergence of strong new leaders such as William Bell Riley, John Roach Straton,
and Frank Norris during the interwar period, yet he follows Marsden's interpretation by concluding that the tide turned on the movement during the
1920s, with the Scopes Trial being a turning point.[34]

> The initial euphoria generated by the formation of the fundamentalist
> coalition did not survive the decade of the 1920s. At Dayton, Tennessee,
> in 1925, fundamentalist forces won the battle against the teaching of
> evolution in the public schools, but they lost the war for the loyalties
> of the American people at large. ... By the end of the decade it seemed
> clear that evangelicals posed no serious threat to the advance of secu-
> larization and the loosening of moral standards in American culture.[35]

David O. Beale, a history professor at Bob Jones University, published in 1986
a fundamentalist history portraying the effect of the Scopes Trial in a similar
manner. Though Beale, as a fundamentalist insider, claims the movement
continued to thrive even after the emergence of neo-evangelicals—"rather
than dying, [fundamentalism] surged ahead as a vibrant religious force
in the world"[36]—he also views the trial as a major defeat that triggered a

---

31. Douglas W. Frank, *Less Than Conquerors: How Evangelicals Entered the Twentieth Century* (Grand Rapids: Eerdmans, 1986), ix.

32. Frank, *Less Than Conquerors*, 7–8.

33. Frank, *Less Than Conquerors*, back cover.

34. Frank, *Less Than Conquerors*, 273.

35. Frank, *Less Than Conquerors*, 273.

36. David O. Beale, *In Pursuit of Purity: American Fundamentalism Since 1850* (Greenville, SC: Unusual Publications, 1986), 341.

period of decline. He writes that the Scopes Trial "served to embarrass most Fundamentalists and to caricature their movement in the public eye for several generations" and that "the year 1925 was a grim one for American Fundamentalism ... when they found their movement struggling for mere existence."[37]

William Vance Trollinger Jr. disagrees in his 1991 book *God's Empire*, a study of William Bell Riley and fundamentalism in the Midwest, that fundamentalists struggled for existence after 1925, but he agrees they were defeated at a national level by 1930, including in their antievolution efforts.[38] Trollinger sees the movement restricted to regional battles instead in the years that followed.[39] Fundamentalists "had lost the fight" nationally in part because of the Scopes Trial, he writes, which "cemented ... in the popular consciousness" a picture of them as "uneducated, intolerant rustics."[40]

Lyle Dorsett's 1991 study of Billy Sunday, the well-known revivalist whose influence began to wane during the interwar era, credits Sunday's support of World War I, Prohibition, and the Republican party for his diminishing popularity,[41] and concludes that the Scopes Trial harmed Sunday as well. Sunday sought to distance himself from the trial, even though he was opposed to evolution, but the trial nevertheless had the broad effect of bringing "ill repute to the cause of conservative biblical Christianity."[42]

Marsden repeated his conclusions about the Scopes Trial in his 1991 book *Understanding Fundamentalism and Evangelicalism*, casting it as "an event that both thrust fundamentalism into worldwide attention and brought about its decline as an effective national force."[43] Due to press caricatures of the movement during the trial, Marsden concludes that "after 1925 fundamentalists had difficulty gaining national attention except when some of their

37. Beale, *In Pursuit of Purity*, 219, 228.

38. William Vance Trollinger Jr., *God's Empire: William Bell Riley and Midwestern Fundamentalism* (Madison: University of Wisconsin Press, 1991), 33.

39. Trollinger, *God's Empire*, 4.

40. Trollinger, *God's Empire*, 5.

41. Lyle W. Dorsett, *Billy Sunday and the Redemption of Urban America* (Grand Rapids: Eerdmans, 1991), 149.

42. Dorsett, *Billy Sunday*, 148–49.

43. George M. Marsden, *Understanding Fundamentalism and Evangelicalism* (Grand Rapids: Eerdmans, 1991), 60.

movement were involved in extreme or bizarre efforts."[44] A correlation between public humiliation and a loss of influence, coupled with retreat from cultural engagement, is often included as part of the "fundamentalist defeat and decline" view of the Scopes Trial.

In his 1997 book *Revive Us Again*, Joel A. Carpenter picks up the history of fundamentalism where Marsden's *Fundamentalism and American Culture* leaves it, tracing the movement through the 1930s and early 1940s, up to the emergence of neo-evangelicals such as Billy Graham and Harold Ockenga. Carpenter portrays fundamentalism as being down but not out during this late interwar period, retreating from public defeat to retrench within the safety of its own churches and organizations until it could reengage society successfully again. "Indeed, the movement was in retreat," he writes. "Forced by their failed antimodernist crusades to rely on their own institutional network, fundamentalists spent these years developing a distinct religious movement."[45] Carpenter interprets Scopes as a turning point that ushered in fundamentalism's decline, counting the years between the trial and Billy Graham's nationally covered crusades as fundamentalism's fallow period. Yet a harvest of revitalized public influence would follow this period. "The recovery of fundamentalism ... was fairly rapid. It was only twenty-five years from the Scopes trial to the rise of Billy Graham."[46]

Edward J. Larson's *Summer for the Gods*, a focused and thorough history of the Scopes Trial itself, was also published in 1997. Larson's perspective on the trial's effect on fundamentalism is more difficult to untangle, as he initially writes that Scopes was not the cause of fundamentalist withdrawal from politics in the 1930s.[47] Yet he later asserts that "fundamentalism became a byword in American culture as a result of the Scopes trial, and fundamentalists responded by withdrawing. They did not abandon their faith, however, but set about constructing a separate subculture with independent religious, educational, and social institutions."[48]

---

44. Marsden, *Understanding Fundamentalism and Evangelicalism*, 60.

45. Joel A. Carpenter, *Revive Us Again* (New York: Oxford University Press, 1997), 3, 13.

46. Carpenter, *Revive Us Again*, 239.

47. See Edward J. Larson, *Summer for the Gods: The Scopes Trial and America's Continuing Debate over Science and Religion* (New York: Basic Books, 1997), 229.

48. Larson, *Summer for the Gods*, 233.

Roger Olson's 1999 history of Christian thought, *The Story of Christian Theology*, though a textbook with a much broader focus than the fundamentalist era, lands in a similar place when Olson turns his attention to the Scopes Trial. Olson writes that "[defense attorney] Darrow and [newspaper columnist] Mencken together made Bryan and the forces of fundamentalism arrayed against evolution look like obscurantist fools."[49] While fundamentalism had been "a cultural and theological force to be reckoned with" before the trial, afterward—and following the departure of anti-modernist New Testament scholar J. Gresham Machen from Princeton in 1929—"fundamentalism went into a lengthy period of retreat."[50]

D. G. Hart's 2002 book *That Old-Time Religion in Modern America*, more akin to Larson's *Summer for the Gods*, paints a nuanced picture of the Scopes Trial's effect on fundamentalism. Hart acknowledges that antievolutionary efforts continued after the trial, noting the founding of the fundamentalist-led Religion and Science Association in 1935 and the work of Harry Rimmer and George McCready Price in developing the concept of "scientific creationism."[51] However, he also affirms Marsden's interpretation that Scopes "turned into a trial of evangelical Protestantism," organized by "secular elites" to "expose the backwardness of evangelicals' literal interpretations of the Bible."[52] A downturn in public influence began after the trial, in Hart's view, and fundamentalists came to be derided by the scholarly community—a downturn that would only be reversed around 1950 with Billy Graham and a new era of evangelicalism.[53] In the years between the Scopes Trial and Graham, interwar fundamentalism was a defeated foe in the public square. "At the beginning of the 1930s the idea of evangelicalism as a spent force in American life was one that occurred naturally to those who had witnessed the religious controversies of the 1920s."[54]

---

49. Roger E. Olson, *The Story of Christian Theology: Twenty Centuries of Tradition and Reform* (Downers Grove, IL: IVP Academic, 1999), 564.

50. Olson, *The Story of Christian Theology*, 564.

51. D. G. Hart, *That Old-Time Religion in Modern America: Evangelical Protestantism in the Twentieth Century* (Chicago: Ivan R. Dee, 2002), 43–44.

52. Hart, *That Old-Time Religion*, 25–26.

53. Hart, *That Old-Time Religion*, 82, 142.

54. Hart, *That Old-Time Religion*, 56.

One of the clearest summaries of the scholarly narrative that sees a fundamentalist decline continuing after Scopes until the emergence of neo-evangelicalism can be found in Markku Ruotsila's 2008 book *The Origins of Christian Anti-Internationalism*. A study of conservative evangelicals' resistance to the League of Nations, Ruotsila's book describes the interwar era in a manner similar to Marsden, Carpenter, and Hart, including no footnotes or supporting argumentation alongside his summary—an indication, perhaps, of the settled nature of the perspective. Ruotsila's description is worth citing in full, for it highlights the main points of the "fundamentalist defeat and decline" narrative succinctly.

> Technically, the fundamentalists and their allies won the Scopes trial and the teaching of evolution continued to be banned in most states. But popular opinion turned against them, and further political victories proved impossible. The incipient politicization of conservative evangelicalism was arrested, and for the next twenty-plus years the fundamentalists lived in their alternative parachurch communities, largely separated from the rest of society, engaged in countercultural and increasingly conspiracist discourse, unable to influence American politics and international relations. This started changing only in the late 1940s when a group of thus-far-separatist fundamentalists, now calling themselves the "New Evangelicals," emerged from their isolation and reengaged in the political conversation of their time.[55]

It is noteworthy that Ruotsila sees neo-evangelicals reengaging in politics in the late 1940s, implying that interwar fundamentalists were not only defeated after the Scopes Trial but gave up on even attempting to wield political influence in its wake.

Daniel K. Williams's 2010 history of the religious right, *God's Own Party*, focuses on developments after the neo-evangelical emergence, but as part of the background to his study, mentions the impact of the Scopes Trial on earlier fundamentalism. He describes the following as "a narrative that eventually became traditional wisdom":

---

55. Markku Ruotsila, *The Origins of Christian Anti-Internationalism: Conservative Evangelicals and the League of Nations* (Washington, DC: Georgetown University Press, 2008), 172–73.

Protestants had made a brief bid for political influence with their
antievolution campaign, but the Scopes trial had put an end to that. ...
After that, they retreated to their churches, and did not emerge again
as a political force until liberal Supreme Court decisions on school
prayer, pornography, and abortion induced them to reenter the public
square in the 1970s.[56]

Williams contests this narrative somewhat, arguing that fundamentalists
never stopped caring about politics as a tool to reform the nation's morals and
that they continued to support Prohibition into the 1930s. However, he ends
in much the same place, concluding fundamentalists "began to feel alienated
from the nation's political institutions" and "turned to prophetic speculation
[instead], viewing the political developments of the 1930s as portents of an
imminent divine judgment."[57]

Darren Dochuk presents a similarly mixed view of the Scopes Trial in his
2011 book *From Bible Belt to Sunbelt*, while ultimately concluding it was a disaster for the fundamentalist movement. He portrays fundamentalists "storming
courthouses, legislatures, and Southern Baptist and Methodist institutions,
demanding militancy on behalf of their truths" after the trial, yet he also
writes that Scopes was a "cataclysmic court decision," which spurred fundamentalists away from public education and into starting their own independent Bible schools.[58] No political agitation or support was needed, after
all, to keep the curriculum of independent schools theologically orthodox.

Kenneth Collins observes in his 2012 book *Power, Politics, and the
Fragmentation of Evangelicalism* that media portrayals of fundamentalist
ignorance and defeat at the Scopes Trial was largely "myth making" by cultural elites.[59] Yet this myth-making was successful in his view, and, with the

56. Daniel K. Williams, *God's Own Party: The Making of the Christian Right* (New York: Oxford University Press, 2010), 1-2.

57. Williams, *God's Own Party*, 3.

58. Darren Dochuk, *From Bible Belt to Sunbelt: Plain-Folk Religion, Grassroots Politics, and the Rise of Evangelical Conservatism* (New York: W. W. Norton, 2011), 15, 53. Dochuk's description of the Scopes Trial's decision as "cataclysmic" is somewhat puzzling, as the verdict upheld antievolution laws. Many historians of fundamentalism refer to the trial instead as a kind of Pyrrhic victory, wherein antievolutionists won the battle in the Dayton, Tennessee, courthouse but lost the larger war in the court of public opinion.

59. Kenneth J. Collins, *Power, Politics, and the Fragmentation of Evangelicalism: From the Scopes Trial to the Obama Administration* (Downers Grove, IL: IVP Academic, 2012), 44.

marginalizing effect of debates over modernism, combined to leave fundamentalists in a difficult cultural position by the 1930s. "Stripped of their dominance in American culture, and having lost any leadership role in the mainline denominations, fundamentalists retreated into an enclave of institutions such as Bible colleges, separatist churches, and mission boards."[60]

In their 2014 book, *The New Evangelical Social Engagement*, a study of changing political views among current-day evangelicals, editors Brian Steensland and Philip Goff sketch a brief history of evangelical cultural engagement in which the Scopes Trial likewise proves a key pivot point, separating progressive Christians who will continue to see the value in publicly tackling social problems from theologically conservative Christians who will not.

> The public battles among Protestants in the 1920s, epitomized by the
> Scopes trial in 1925, forced Christians who sought both conversion
> and social reform to choose sides. By the 1930s, liberal Protestantism
> was pitted against fundamentalism, with little talk of social activ
> ism among the latter. ... The result was not simply silence but active
> avoidance of anything beyond very local, often congregational, social
> action among evangelicals throughout the mid-twentieth century.[61]

Steensland and Goff's account focuses on political action meant to address social ills rather than to uphold theological beliefs, yet it implies that fundamentalists withdrew from both aims following the era of the Scopes Trial. Marsden's influence is arguably evident in this implication, as it is in the book's front matter as well, where the editors dedicate the volume to him and sociologist Robert Wuthnow.[62]

One final major work is worth mentioning in this section: Timothy E. W. Gloege's 2015 book *Guaranteed Pure*. As a history of the Moody Bible Institute, the book devotes little space to the Scopes Trial. Yet when Gloege does cover the trial, he treats it like Marsden, portraying it as a misstep for fundamentalists, a misstep that editors of the *Moody Bible Institute Monthly* recognized. Gloege reports that the magazine's coverage of the antievolution cause "dropped precipitously" once the trial began and that it afterward

60. Collins, *Power, Politics, and the Fragmentation of Evangelicalism*, 52.

61. Brian Steensland and Philip Goff, eds., *The New Evangelical Social Engagement* (New York: Oxford University Press, 2014), 7.

62. Steensland and Goff, *New Evangelical Social Engagement*, v.

questioned the antievolutionists' strategy in provoking the trial, claiming it had predicted the victory would turn to defeat.[63]

A couple of journal articles also reflect the "fundamentalist defeat and decline" view of the Scopes Trial. Brad Harper, in a 2006 essay for *Cultural Encounters*, writes that the trial "serv[ed] as the final popular straw in Christian fundamentalism's rejection of culture" and that "it would be difficult to overstate the impact of 'the Monkey Trial' at Dayton, Tennessee, in transforming fundamentalism."[64] Harper further contends newspaper coverage of the trial was biased against fundamentalists, painting them as either dumb or ill-motivated, a contention this study will investigate further.[65] Ruotsila echoes Harper's wording about fundamentalists' "rejection of culture" in a 2012 article on Carl McIntire, in which he refers to the years after the Scopes Trial as a "separatist interlude" for fundamentalists.[66]

Even though no historians of fundamentalism interpret Scopes identically, a few recurring points mark the perspective of those influenced by Marsden. First, fundamentalists lost the battle for public opinion at the trial and were widely shamed. Second, fundamentalists at some point came to recognize their defeat and the resulting ineffectiveness of their social activity. Third, they responded by retreating behind their own walls and spending the next fifteen to twenty years building up their independent institutions. Fourth, neo-evangelicalism would later emerge from behind fundamentalism's moated castles to reengage in the public square.

AN ALTERNATIVE INTERPRETATION OF
THE SCOPES TRIAL'S EFFECT ON FUNDAMENTALISTS

Marsden's interpretation of the Scopes Trial is not the only option, however. Hints of an alternative, if less fully formed, view of the trial can also be found in fundamentalist historiography. This view accepts that fundamentalists were depicted as ignorant and unenlightened by some, and that hostile

---

63. Timothy E. W. Gloege, *Guaranteed Pure: The Moody Bible Institute, Business, and the Making of Modern Evangelicalism* (Chapel Hill, NC: University of North Carolina Press, 2015), 224.

64. Brad Harper, "The Scopes Trial, Fundamentalism, and the Creation of an Anti-Culture Culture: Can Evangelical Christians Transcend Their History in the Culture Wars?" *Cultural Encounters* 3, no. 1 (2006): 7, 10.

65. Harper, "Scopes Trial, Fundamentalism," 12.

66. Markku Ruotsila, "Carl McIntire and the Fundamentalist Origins of the Christian Right," *Church History* 81, no. 2 (June 2012): 381.

cultural observers came to paint the trial as a defeat for theological conservatives, but it raises questions about an ensuing fundamentalist retreat. Some
of the nuances identified by Larson, Williams, and Dochuk, in other words,
take a more prominent role in this vein of interpretation.

Louis Gasper's pre-Marsden 1963 book *The Fundamentalist Movement*, surveyed above, portrays fundamentalists as losing their will for cultural battles
by 1930 but not because of the trial or its aftermath. Gasper instead appears
to wonder why the trial didn't give fundamentalists more of a positive bump:
"[The Scopes Trial] attracted the attention of the nation and other parts of the
world, but it did not seem to have helped the fundamentalists to any great
extent, even though Scopes was found guilty."[67]

Another pre-Marsden history of fundamentalism, George W. Dollar's
1973 *History of Fundamentalism in America*, written as an uncritical defense
of the movement by a self-identified fundamentalist, highlights the 1920s
as a "high-water mark" in the modernist-fundamentalist debate and an era
notable for strong fundamentalist leaders.[68] Dollar acknowledges William
Bell Riley's focus on combatting evolution during the decade,[69] despite key
challenges to fundamentalism arising, but does not mention the Scopes Trial.
This inattention is significant if Marsden's interpretation of the trial is accu-
rate, as it suggests the trial may not have been seen as a turning point by all
fundamentalists.

Roger A. Bruns's 1992 biography of Billy Sunday, *Preacher*, published six
years after Marsden's *Fundamentalism and American Culture*, does mention the
Scopes Trial directly, but Bruns interprets it oppositely to Marsden. Bruns
writes, "Billy and other fundamentalist leaders did not retire from the bat-
tlefield" after the trial and William Jennings Bryan's death, but rather these
events "fueled their determination to carry on, and the rhetoric and bit-
terness of Billy and his allies intensified."[70] Bruns provides examples of such
efforts: Sunday debating a Unitarian evolutionist in the pages of *Collier's* magazine in 1926; Gerald Winrod founding the antievolution and antimodernism

---

67. Gasper, *Fundamentalist Movement*, 14.

68. George W. Dollar, *A History of Fundamentalism in America* (1973; repr., Orlando: Daniels,
1983), 85.

69. See Dollar, *History of Fundamentalism in America*, 114, 162.

70. Roger A. Bruns, *Preacher: Billy Sunday and Big-Time American Evangelism* (Urbana, IL:
University of Illinois Press, 1992), 282.

Defenders of the Christian Faith that same year, an organization before which Sunday would speak in 1930; and the proposal of antievolution bills in more than twenty states throughout the 1920s.[71]

Michael Lienesch's 2007 study of the Scopes Trial, *In the Beginning*, portrays its effect on fundamentalism in much the same manner. Lienesch recounts fundamentalist pastor John Roach Straton predicting a wave of legislative victories following the trial.[72] Though such a wave never arose as Straton expected, his confidence displayed a different kind of attitude than that which the "fundamentalist defeat and decline" narrative normally highlights. Lienesch writes further that the trial was widely considered to be a public success rather than a loss by Bryan himself and other fundamentalists: "With Bryan taking the lead, antievolutionists proclaimed the outcome of the trial as a significant triumph, as well as a turning point for their cause. ... [Fundamentalists] went away convinced that they had won and that their victory would secure the success of their movement."[73]

Matthew Avery Sutton's 2007 biography, *Aimee Semple McPherson and the Resurrection of Christian America*, lists several social causes that the Pentecostal preacher engaged in throughout the interwar period.[74] Though evolution was not McPherson's primary target, she did speak against it, as well as against dance halls and political corruption.[75] Support for Prohibition and opposition to alcohol may have been the public stance McPherson identified with most strongly, and she continued to do so after both the Scopes Trial and the repeal of Prohibition itself.[76] As late as 1937, McPherson hosted a dramatized sermon at the Shrine Auditorium in Los Angeles that denounced

---

71. Bruns, *Preacher: Billy Sunday*, 273, 275, 282, 283.

72. Michael Lienesch, *In the Beginning: Fundamentalism, the Scopes Trial, and the Making of the Antievolution Movement* (Chapel Hill: The University of North Carolina Press, 2007), 165.

73. Lienesch, *In the Beginning*, 166, 170.

74. For a careful argument in favor of viewing Aimee Semple McPherson, a Pentecostal, as a member of the larger interwar fundamentalist/evangelical movement, see Matthew Avery Sutton, "'Between the Refrigerator and the Wildfire': Aimee Semple McPherson, Pentecostalism, and the Fundamentalist-Modernist Controversy," *Church History* 72, no. 1 (March 2003), 158–88.

75. Matthew Avery Sutton, *Aimee Semple McPherson and the Resurrection of Christian America* (Cambridge: Harvard University Press, 2007), 81.

76. Examples of McPherson's ongoing activities against alcohol can be found at Sutton, *Aimee Semple McPherson*, 157, 217.

Lenin, Mussolini, Hitler, the removal of the Bible from public schools, the end of Prohibition, and evolution.[77]

Barry Hankins's 2010 book *Jesus and Gin* picks up the theme of fundamentalist opposition to alcohol in the 1920s and studies it in-depth, finding in it a precursor to later evangelical political involvement at the end of the twentieth century. Hankins's aim is to display continuity between the social action of theological conservatives during the interwar era and during the current era; thus, he views the Scopes Trial as an important event in interwar fundamentalist social engagement—opposition to evolution and alcohol being the key social causes adopted by fundamentalists in the 1920s—and he does not see the trial as an end to such efforts. Hankins devotes a couple of pages in his chapter on the Scopes Trial to the "legend" surrounding it, highlighting the aspect of Larson's earlier interpretation that suggests the trial came to be viewed as a defeat after the publication of Frederick Lewis Allen's *Only Yesterday* in 1931 and the release of the film *Inherit the Wind* in 1960.[78] Hankins recounts throughout the book examples of fundamentalist social efforts against alcohol, and he notes that Aimee Semple McPherson became "a major force behind a referendum to pass an anti-evolution law in California ... in the wake of the Scopes Trial."[79]

A 2010 study of the Prohibition by Daniel Okrent, *Last Call*, surveys the political currents, events, and influential figures that both brought about Prohibition and then undermined it. Okrent's lens is wide, with fundamentalists playing only a supporting role in the narrative he recounts, but Okrent echoes Hankins in portraying conservative Christians as active opponents of alcohol even in the years following the Scopes Trial.[80] "No one had a stronger moral interest in Prohibition than the Baptist and Methodist clergymen who were its tribunes."[81]

A final major work related to fundamentalism and the Scopes Trial, Matthew Avery Sutton's 2014 *American Apocalypse*, directly questions the

---

77. Sutton, *Aimee Semple McPherson*, 237–38.

78. See Barry Hankins, *Jesus and Gin: Evangelicalism, the Roaring Twenties, and Today's Culture Wars* (New York: Palgrave Macmillan, 2010), 102–4.

79. Hankins, *Jesus and Gin*, 115.

80. See, for instance, Daniel Okrent, *Last Call: The Rise and Fall of Prohibition* (New York: Scribner's Sons, 2010), 302.

81. Okrent, *Last Call*, 302.

arc of fundamentalist history outlined by Marsden and Carpenter. Sutton
states that historians have "exaggerated the significance" of the trial and that
campaigns such as fundamentalists' involvement in the 1928 presidential
election and opposition to Franklin Roosevelt's New Deal policies demonstrate their ongoing cultural engagement.[82]

> While the Marsden-Carpenter rise-fall-rebirth narrative has dom-
> inated the way historians tell fundamentalist history, my work
> emphasizes continuity more than discontinuity. Cultural engagement
> rather than sectarian isolation remained both a priority and a reality
> between the late nineteenth century and the present. ... Despite the
> claims of post-World War II evangelicals such as Carl Henry, funda-
> mentalists never expressed indifference to the world around them nor
> did they ever lack interest in influencing the broader culture. They
> never retreated.[83]

Sutton further concludes that Carl F. H. Henry misrepresented fundamentalists in his *Uneasy Conscience of Modern Fundamentalism*. Henry's portrayal
of a fundamentalist retreat was, in Sutton's view, purposefully blind to fundamentalist-evangelical continuities, because Henry sought to craft a clean
reset of evangelical cultural engagement.

> But Henry did bad history. He mischaracterized pre-World War II fun-
> damentalism in order to give his generation a fresh start and a clean
> slate in the postwar period. ... Although his anticommunist sensibil-
> ities, conservative politics, apocalyptic premillennialism, and vision
> for rebuilding the evangelical movement had much more in common
> with interwar fundamentalism than he ever acknowledged, he tried
> to disavow the past. He minimized fundamentalists' intense interwar
> political activism and sought to disown all of the failed prophecy, ugly
> racism, and embarrassing internal squabbles of the interwar years.[84]

Two recent books on related subjects and three journal articles are worth sur-
veying in conclusion, as they also raise questions about the "fundamentalist

82. Matthew Avery Sutton, *American Apocalypse: A History of Modern Evangelicalism*
(Cambridge: Harvard University Press, 2014), xiii.

83. Sutton, *American Apocalypse*, xiii.

84. Sutton, *American Apocalypse*, 294–95.

defeat and decline" narrative. The 2018 study *Doctrine and Race* by Mary Beth Swetnam Mathews contrasts African American evangelicals with white fundamentalists during the interwar period. Both groups upheld conservative doctrine; however, black evangelicals tended to pay more attention to social justice-related issues. Where some African American evangelicals and white fundamentalists found common ground was in supporting Herbert Hoover, the pro-Prohibition candidate, for president during the 1928 presidential election.[85] At least on the social issue of alcohol, a number of black and white conservative Christians found themselves voting in concert.

The push by interwar fundamentalists to start Bible colleges, studied carefully in Adam Laats's 2018 *Fundamentalism U*, reflected a social agenda as well, since combating evolution and accusations of being anti-intellectual motivated such efforts. Such colleges were not merely a retreat. William Jennings Bryan criticized the University of Wisconsin in 1921 for hosting speakers supportive of evolution; in the years following his death, fundamentalist leaders "resolved to make sure students had schools they could rely on."[86]

Similarly, an early 1967 piece in *Foundations* by Hillyer H. Straton depicts John Roach Straton denouncing evolution publicly both before and after the Scopes Trial, with the trial doing nothing to slow the New York City pastor. According to the article, Straton's post-Scopes activities included addresses at Dartmouth and Harvard, five California debates against Maynard Shipley, and a more cordial, two-night discussion with theistic evolutionist and geology professor Kirtley Mather, held at Straton's Calvary Baptist Church.[87]

Paul Waggoner's 1984 *Trinity Journal* article, "The Historiography of the Scopes Trial: A Critical Evaluation" takes perhaps the most direct aim at Marsden's interpretation of any existing study. Waggoner labels this interpretation "the orthodox one," but argues publications about the trial from 1925 to 1931 do not support it, with that perspective arising solely after the

---

85. See chapter 4 of Mary Beth Swetnam Mathews, *Doctrine and Race: African American Evangelicals and Fundamentalism Between the Wars* (Tuscaloosa, AL: University of Alabama Press, 2018), 98–125.

86. Adam Laats, *Fundamentalism U: Keeping the Faith in American Higher Education* (New York: Oxford University Press, 2018), 41.

87. See Hillyer H. Straton, "John Roach Straton: The Great Evolution Debate," *Foundations* 10, no. 2 (April 1967): 139, 144, 145–46.

publication of Allen's *Only Yesterday*.[88] Waggoner investigates books, journals, and magazines to substantiate his claim, and his study is the work to date most similar to this current study.

Lastly, a 2011 *Fides et Historia* article by Barry Hankins examines the cumulative effect of three events in harming fundamentalism's public reputation: the Scopes Trial, Aimee Semple McPherson's claimed kidnapping, and J. Frank Norris's trial for murder. The events did, together, paint a negative picture of the movement, Hankins claims, but the Scopes Trial itself was not a cause of a fundamentalist retreat: "The problem with arguing that the Scopes trial itself had anything to do with fundamentalist demise in the latter half of the Roaring Twenties is that thus far there is no evidence that anyone interpreted the trial as a fundamentalist defeat until at least the thirties."[89]

RESTATING THE DIVIDE

In sum, a survey of interwar fundamentalist historiography reveals two primary views of the Scopes Trial. The first perspective, represented best by Marsden, Carpenter, and Ruotsila, is part of a more fully formed overarching narrative and concludes that fundamentalists suffered a public relations defeat at the Scopes Trial, despite their legal victory, and that this defeat propelled them into a period of cultural retreat, which ended with the emergence of 1940's neo-evangelicalism. The second perspective appears often in hints and counterarguments and is not as integrated into a broader account of fundamentalist cultural engagement, but it is becoming more common in recent works. Scholars such as Hankins and Sutton have presented it most clearly. This view concludes that the Scopes Trial was not widely seen as a defeat for fundamentalists either by themselves or their cultural opponents in its immediate aftermath and that interwar fundamentalists continued in their cultural engagement efforts following the trial.

The following chapters in this book will uphold the second view and present new evidence for it. They will document more thoroughly than has been done previously the ongoing social action of interwar fundamentalists.

---

88. Paul M. Waggoner, "The Historiography of the Scopes Trial: A Critical Re-Evaluation," *Trinity Journal* 5, no. 5 (1984): 156.

89. Barry Hankins, "The (Worst) Year of the Evangelical: 1926 and the Demise of American Fundamentalism," *Fides et Historia* 43, no. 1 (2011): 5.

2

FUNDAMENTALISM, EVOLUTION, AND NEWSPAPER REPORTING (1920–1933)

THE SCOPES TRIAL AT A GLANCE

The roots of Tennessee's evolution trial are not found in Dayton. They can be traced, first, to a growing consensus among conservative Christians that Darwinian evolution was incompatible with the Genesis account of divine creation and, second, a movement among public education systems in the early twentieth century to include evolution in science curricula. American education had long been decentralized; many local communities in the 1920s determined their own school budgets and educational programs.[1] Yet as public education became more widespread, science textbooks supportive of evolution were increasingly adopted: "This meant evolution confronted an unprecedented number of people, usually as a matter of children being taught the idea in schools."[2]

Meanwhile, fundamentalist opposition to the concept of evolution had coalesced into a firm position by the 1920s. The modern theory of evolution was not novel in 1925, the year of the Scopes Trial. It had become accepted in educated and secular circles and was also adopted by theological liberals, which was part of fundamentalists' motivation in opposing it.[3] Evolution

---

1. Eugenie C. Scott, *Evolution vs. Creationism: An Introduction* (Westport, CT: Greenwood, 2004), 87.

2. Edward Caudill, *Intelligently Designed: How Creationists Built the Campaign against Evolution* (Urbana, IL: University of Illinois Press, 2013), 17.

3. C. Allyn Russell, "William Bell Riley: Architect of Fundamentalism," *Foundations* 18, no. 1 (January 1975): 38.

comprised one plank of a modernist platform that included biblical criticism, denial of the miraculous, and the social gospel.[4]

Scholars of religion and science sometimes note an openness to evolutionary ideas among fundamentalist forerunners such as Charles Hodge and B. B. Warfield, as well as the friendly space given to evolutionary processes in James Orr's articles for *The Fundamentals*.[5] However, Hodge compared Darwinian forms of evolution to atheism.[6] Later fundamentalists followed in his wake, denouncing the evolution taught in public schools as tantamount to godlessness. Within the public sphere, fundamentalists supported anti-evolution legislation in the years surrounding the Scopes Trial, advocating for passage in thirty-seven states that introduced such laws and celebrating victory in four.[7] Within the church, they criticized preachers who hedged on the authority and scope of Scripture in order to accommodate evolution. In a *Fundamentals* article entitled "Evolution in the Pulpit," for instance, an anonymous layperson had charged even those pastors who held to "milder forms" of evolution, meaning forms in which God directed the process of natural selection, with a betrayal of the Bible: "This view, quite as much as the naturalistic, necessitates the giving up of the account in Genesis."[8]

Behind the Dayton trial, therefore, were two opposed and growing forces: one of educational support for evolution and another of fundamentalist opposition. The specific circumstances of the trial were contrived: Following Tennessee's passage of a law banning the teaching of evolution, the American Civil Liberties Union released a statement inviting a teacher to test the legislation in court, with assurances the trial would be an amiable one that would not cost the teacher their job.[9] Leaders in Dayton such as Fred E. Robinson, chair of the county school board, and Walter White, school superintendent, saw in the offer an opportunity to bring media attention to their city and

---

4. Russell, "William Bell Riley," 17.

5. Larson, *Summer for the Gods*, 20–21.

6. See Charles Hodge, *What Is Atheism?* (New York: Scribner, Armstrong, and Company, 1874), and Mark Noll and David N. Livingstone, eds., *B.B. Warfield: Evolution Science and Scripture, Selected Writings* (Grand Rapids: Baker, 2000).

7. Caudill, *Intelligently Designed*, 17.

8. Anonymous, "Evolution in the Pulpit," in *The Fundamentals*, 27–36, vol. 8 (Chicago: Testimony Publishing Company, 1910), 31–32.

9. Larson, *Summer for the Gods*, 83.

enlisted a local group to initiate proceedings.[10] White, for his part, "liked the antievolution law but loved publicity for his town even more."[11] When the organizing group approached twenty-four-year-old John Scopes to serve as defendant, he could not remember if he had ever taught evolution, since he had only ever served as a substitute in a higher-level biology class.[12] The textbook for the class did, however, include a section on evolution, which the organizing group deemed sufficient.[13]

The level of attention generated by evolution debates in the early twentieth century is illustrated by the prominence of the lawyers who agreed to argue the case, William Jennings Bryan and Clarence Darrow. The men had political similarities, both being Democrats and, largely, proponents of progressive causes.[14] Each had "sought to improve the lot of laborers, farmers, and others on the lower ends of the economy."[15] Neither was a dedicated fundamentalist, though Bryan was often labeled one, and Bryan's objections to evolution were not solely religious. He also feared the social engineering implications of Darwinism, including the intellectual rationale it could provide for aggressive capitalism, war, and eugenics.[16] Yet Bryan was a populist and Darrow an elitist; Bryan a Christian, Darrow an agnostic. Though Darrow shared Bryan's political concern for the common person and had made his reputation as a labor lawyer, he embraced the trial in part to undermine orthodox Christianity.[17] He viewed evolution as a bellwether issue separating enlightenment from ignorance, and in Dayton he perceived an opportunity to combat what he saw as anti-intellectual bigotry.[18]

The two men's rhetoric became personally charged throughout the trial. While on the stand, Bryan accused Darrow of insulting everyday people and calling them "yokels"; further, he claimed Darrow's motivation for taking on the trial was underhanded: "They [the defense team, led by Darrow] did not

---

10. Larson, *Summer for the Gods*, 89.

11. Larson, *Summer for the Gods*, 89.

12. Michael Lienesch, *In the Beginning*, 139.

13. Mano Singham, *God vs. Darwin: The War between Evolution and Creationism in the Classroom* (Lanham, MD: Rowman & Littlefield, 2009), 27.

14. Caudill, *Intelligently Designed*, 30.

15. Caudill, *Intelligently Designed*, 30.

16. Singham, *God vs. Darwin*, 14–15.

17. Lienesch, *In the Beginning*, 144.

18. Lienesch, *In the Beginning*, 144.

come here to try this case. They came here to try revealed religion."[19] Darrow replied, "You insult every man of science and learning in the world because he does not believe your fool religion."[20] Despite such interpersonal contention, the trial's verdict was largely expected and its resolution uneventful, until Bryan died unexpectedly five days after its conclusion.

Several secondary sources attest to a continued fundamentalist campaign against evolution following the trial. For instance, in 1926 William Bell Riley preached against evolution for ten consecutive Sundays from his pulpit in Minneapolis.[21] He also rented the Kenwood Armory to address 5,500 attendees on the threat of evolutionary theory as an atheistic, state-sponsored religion and traveled to nearby states to debate scientists, the result of the debates normally determined by audience vote and usually ending in his favor.[22] The Anti-Evolution League of Minnesota, which Riley led, further opposed the teaching of evolution at higher levels, targeting the University of Minnesota.[23]

Two of Riley's main arguments against the theory of evolution were not religious, or at least not wholly religious, but rather scientific and social: first, that it was based on a hypothesis without evidence, and second, that it undermined public morality by jettisoning the biblical doctrine of sin.[24] He further argued that Darwinism turned human beings into "developed monkey[s]," was incompatible with the biblical flood, that its underlying philosophy was false, that mathematics disproved it, and that society tended toward atheism and anarchy when under its influence.[25]

---

19. Clarence Darrow and William Jennings Bryan, *The World's Most Famous Court Trial: A Complete Stenographic Report of the Famous Court Test of the Tennessee Anti-Evolution Act, at Dayton, July 10 to 21, 1925, Including Speeches and Arguments of Attorneys* (Cincinnati: National Book Company, 1925), 288.

20. Darrow and Bryan, *World's Most Famous Court Trial*, 288.

21. Russell, "William Bell Riley," 39.

22. Russell, "William Bell Riley," 39. Russell notes that while Riley was an adept debater, he also freely admitted to packing the debates with "advocates and friends" to assist with positive outcomes. He only lost one of the public debates.

23. Russell, "William Bell Riley," 39. Riley also co-founded the Anti-Evolution League of America and gained national recognition for his efforts; see John Davies, "Science and the Sacred: The Evolution Controversy at Baylor, 1920–1929," *East Texas Historical Journal* 29, no. 2 (October 1991): 47.

24. Russell, "William Bell Riley," 38–39.

25. See, for instance, the writings included in William Bell Riley, *The Antievolution Pamphlets of William Bell Riley* (New York: Taylor & Francis, 1995).

Other fundamentalists employed a similar mix of biblical and secular critiques of evolution. John Roach Straton, pastor of Calvary Baptist Church in New York City and a one-time believer in theistic evolution, had come to see Darwinism as opposed to the Bible and hence preached against it and the materialistic philosophy it propagated, for undermining personal happiness and societal prosperity and peace.[26] For several years he carried on a campaign against the Hall of the Age of Man in the American Museum of Natural History, citing the lack of fossil evidence for evolution as a particular weakness.[27] In 1925, Straton also participated in a campus debate at Harvard University, during which the student newspaper reported that he accused evolution of taking the place of God, becoming a religion unto itself, reverting to a kind of "pagan pantheism," and promoting "degeneracy and crime," such as murder, divorce, and pornography.[28]

This chapter focuses on newspaper reporting before, during, and after the trial to explore its effect on fundamentalists' antievolution efforts. Overall, it will demonstrate that media coverage of fundamentalists was consistently mixed throughout, never uniformly negative, and that no observable decline in public engagement with the issue of evolution by fundamentalists can be demonstrated following the trial.

NEWSPAPER COVERAGE OF FUNDAMENTALISTS PRE-TRIAL (1920-1924)

Between the years 1920 and 1924, newspapers in New York, Pennsylvania, Illinois, and Ohio printed at least twenty-two articles containing the words "fundamentalism" and "evolution." Of these, six were positive toward fundamentalists, eight were negative, and eight were neutral. Newspapers throughout the decade often printed articles featuring quotes from a noteworthy individual on a debatable topic, without granting the other side an equal hearing. For the purposes of this study, such articles will generally be considered positive or negative toward fundamentalism, depending on the viewpoint of the figure being quoted. Articles using slanted language

---

26. Straton, "John Roach Straton," 137.

27. Straton, "John Roach Straton," 138, 141–43.

28. "John Roach Straton Condemns Evolution as Degenerate Cult: Defends His Creed as 'Christianity Founded upon Faith,' Approves Ban on Evolution in Schools," *The Harvard Crimson*, October 16, 1925.

or featuring depictions that clearly privilege one side or the other will also be considered positive or negative, respectively; all remaining articles will be deemed neutral.

The most notable feature of the reporting between 1920 and 1924 is its paltriness, with newspapers printing far fewer articles on fundamentalism and evolution before the Scopes Trial than during or after it. A likely reason for such limited coverage will be suggested ahead.

The positive articles bear little resemblance to each other. One, a religion column entitled "Sermonograms," playfully suggested a spiritual lesson about people's inhumanity toward one other using evolution as a foil: "Man may not be an evolution from the beast, but there are times when it looks very much as though he might have been."[29] Another reported one-sidedly, without critique, on a gathering of nine presidents of "orthodox colleges" to formulate plans against modernism in general and evolution in particular.[30] Convened by James Gray, president of Moody Bible Institute, the group included the presidents of Goshen College and Asbury College and discussed "satisfactory textbooks," "post-graduate institutions which may be safely patronized," and the need for a conservative scholarly journal.[31]

A few newspapers reported on debates and addresses featuring John Roach Straton, the well-known pastor of Calvary Baptist Church in New York City throughout the 1920s. One article in a Kittanning, Pennsylvania, newspaper reported Straton had defeated modernist pastor Charles Francis Potter in a debate by arguing evolutionary scientists' pronouncements contradicted each other and belief in evolution led to immorality.[32] This same debate was also covered by the *Sandusky Star Journal* in Ohio, which ran a similar piece. Local newspapers in the 1920s relied heavily on newswire services, which often resulted in attention-grabbing articles being printed in multiple papers on or near the same day in identical or near-identical form. The *Sandusky Star Journal* noted that Straton and Potter had a series of five

---

29. "Sermonograms," *Olean Evening Herald*, February 16, 1924. Note that many articles during this era do not include an author byline.

30. "Fundamentalists Meet to Plan for Campaign: To Attack Modernist Views, Especially Theory of Evolution," *Freeport Journal Standard*, November 10, 1924.

31. "Fundamentalists Meet to Plan for Campaign," *Freeport Journal Standard*.

32. "Fundamentalist Wins Second in a Series of Debates with Modernist," *Simpson's Daily Leader Times*, January 29, 1924.

debates planned, with Potter winning the first but Straton the second.[33] The topic of the second debate being: "Did the Earth and Man Come by Evolution or from a Living God?"[34] A year earlier, the bigger-city *Philadelphia Inquirer* spotlighted Bryan denouncing Darwinian evolution, not on that occasion as part of a debate, but rather at a Lord's Day Alliance gathering.[35]

One final positive article publicized a lesser-known pastor, the Rev. Roy H. Kleiser of Scott Street Methodist Church in Cincinnati, Ohio. The *Cincinnati Commercial Tribune* printed selections of a thoughtful antievolution sermon he had delivered without editorial comment. In the sermon, Kleiser emphasized that evolution should not be regarded as benign and positive, for it could just as easily be a force for evil as for good.

> Many of the doctrinaires of evolution have frequently carried us to conclusions wholly unwarranted by the facts. They paint glowing pictures of progress. ... They seem to forget that evolution may be downward as well as upward; that if savages may become civilized, civilization may also become savage; that to use a popular expression, if monkeys may become men, men may also degenerate into monkeys, or worse.[36]

The negative articles between 1920 and 1924 display more similarities, each one featuring learned observers or experts denouncing antievolutionary thought. In an April 1924 article in the local newspaper of Oak Park, Illinois, a suburb of Chicago, a Dr. Barton reviewed the city's pastoral leadership during the previous quarter century, concluding that it included "no radicals or revolutionaries."[37] Evolution and critical scholarship had been accepted, but not made divisive, and the gospel was preached: "Certainly there was none of the intolerance of modern fundamentalism."[38]

Along the same lines, in the town of Murphysboro, Illinois, the remarks of a British scholar at Aberdeen University, J. Arthur Thomson, comparing

33. "Straton Won Second," *Sandusky Star Journal*, January 29, 1924.

34. "Straton Won Second," *Sandusky Star Journal*.

35. "Bryan Advises Pledge Signing for President," *Philadelphia Inquirer*, May 21, 1923.

36. "Distinction Between Progress and Evolution Drawn by Methodist Minister," *Cincinnati Commercial Tribune*, June 11, 1923.

37. Dr. Barton, "Pulpits Then and Now," *Oak Park Oak Leaves*, April 19, 1924.

38. Dr. Barton, "Pulpits Then and Now," *Oak Park Oak Leaves*.

antievolutionary fundamentalism to the Ku Klux Klan as fanatical post-war movements were quoted at length. "It is always in some measure good that people should have strong convictions in regard to any serious question, but 'Fundamentalism' seems ill-informed and intolerant."[39] The *Coshocton Tribune* in Ohio printed a similar article about Thomson's remarks a week later. It is possible the article was derived from another address delivered by Thomson, but more likely the Coshocton newspaper simply held onto a newswire story until it had column inches to fill. The article included a long passage conflating the concerns of fundamentalists and the Ku Klux Klan.

> Cognate with "Fundamentalism" in the detached outsider's eyes, is another post-war phenomenon—the Ku Klux Klan movement. Both had their analogues after the Civil War. Both are expressions of the self-preservative instinct. For the operations of the Ku Klux Klan express a somewhat scare-driven determination to save America for the Americans, just as the Fundamentalists seek to secure their souls by becoming Defenders of the Faith.[40]

Two newspapers in Ohio printed a story about a British newspaper editor, Sidney J. Wicks of the *Manchester Guardian*, delivering observations about England and America while on a trip to the state. Fundamentalism and evolution emerged only briefly in his remarks, but when mentioned, fundamentalism was slighted as a backward American viewpoint, without any balancing opinion being offered. "In England the social issues about which America is quarreling today—fundamentalism and modernism—have been settled for 30 years. The Church of England has accepted evolution."[41]

Another expert opinion piece slanted against fundamentalists appeared in a newspaper in New Castle, Pennsylvania, on December 30, 1924. The article recounted Ohio State University zoologist Edward L. Rice's denunciation of William Jennings Bryan as "dangerous alike to religion, teaching, and the freedom of investigation": "Is there not at least a moral obligation that a man

---

39. David M. Church, "Briton Amazed at U.S. Ku Klux and Orthodoxy: Fundamentalism and Klan Are Discordant Notes, Says British Professor—Is Post-War Reaction," *Murphysboro Daily Independent*, May 14, 1924.

40. "Briton Amazed at U.S. Ku Klux and Orthodoxy," *Coshocton Tribune*, May 21, 1924.

41. "Macdonald Is Britain's Hope, Thinks Editor," *East Liverpool Evening Review*, April 23, 1924. See also the identically titled article in the *Xenia Evening Gazette*, May 19, 1924.

professing authoritative leadership on evolution should first familiarize himself with the subject?"[42] Nearly a year earlier, the *Cincinnati Commercial Tribune* had printed an article summing up the opinion of scientists generally to Bryan's objection to evolution, with Bryan painted again as ill-informed and obscurantist. "There are states in this country where it is impossible for a man of science to teach what all scientists believe. ... The cheek of it is stupendous, that a man like Mr. Bryan ... should be able to bully men who have given their lives to careful experiment, searching proof and constant thought."[43]

One final negative article appeared in the *Cincinnati Commercial Tribune* in May 1923. An opinion piece representing forty unnamed "distinguished American citizens, leaders in religion, academia, and science," the article argued that religion and science were not contradictory and criticized Bryan.[44] Most of the leaders were, according to the newspaper, conservatives. Still, they agreed with modernists in accepting scientific discoveries.

> The vast majority of the learned and unlearned are content to take revelation as it comes, in material and spiritual revealment, to the mind and to the heart, and let their lives react to the highest and best interpretation thereof. Still, there is no disposition to deprive William Jennings Bryan of his long-established right in freedom of speech without the formality of freedom in thought.[45]

The articles neutral toward fundamentalism between 1920 and 1924 reveal fault lines even while treating debated issues more even-handedly. They include an *Oak Park Oak Leaves* report in January 1924 that mentioned points both in support and in critique of antievolutionists and a *Bradford Era* article in May 1923 that described a series of sermons throughout Indianapolis pulpits arguing for and against modernism, Prohibition, Sunday laws, popular entertainment, the virgin birth, and evolution. Bryan was the most famous speaker participating in the multi-sermon event, which featured "advocates of modernism and liberalism in religion, and the exponents of

---

42. "Evolutionist at Washington Makes Attack on Bryan," *New Castle News*, December 30, 1924.

43. "Battle of Humanity with Tiny Enemies: Scientists-Bryanists," *Cincinnati Commercial Tribune*, January 2, 1924.

44. "Antagonism over Religion and Science," *Cincinnati Commercial Tribune*, May 29, 1923.

45. "Antagonism over Religion and Science," *Cincinnati Commercial Tribune*.

fundamentalism, air[ing] their conflicting views in a score of the city's pulpits."[46] Notably, the constellation of issues associated with antievolution in the *Bradford Era* article incorporated both spiritual and social concerns. A newspaper in Lock Haven, Pennsylvania, also reported in December 1923 on the upcoming debates between John Roach Straton and Charles Francis Potter, one of which a Kittanning newspaper would later report Straton had won.[47]

Even-handedly reported articles still sometimes sought to capture the drama of the debate over evolution. An Ohio newspaper reported in advance of the Presbyterian church's 135th general assembly meeting in Indianapolis that "ultra-conservatives" in the denomination and Bryan would "have their innings tomorrow."[48] He was expected to "loose broadsides on the progressives": "Bryan's battle line will be arrayed against evolution. ... Fear of discord in the church will not deter him from pressing the fight, he has affirmed."[49] The *Cincinnati Commercial Tribune* reported in the same vein a day later on sermons being delivered around Indianapolis in conjunction with the Presbyterian assembly. During an evening sermon at a Westminster Church, the article described Bryan "deliver[ing] an attack on the believers in the Darwinian theory of evolution and on the liberals, who question the virgin birth of Christ and other doctrines."[50] The *Findlay Morning Republican* reported on the same sermons, capturing some of Bryan's sense of humor in its article:

> "I don't think there is a busier man in this country," [Bryan] whimsically observed. "Just think of my lines. I've got to keep the Democratic Party straight. Then I've got to get Prohibition enforced and that's no small task, and I've got to defend religion, and that takes all my powers. I can promise you this though—there will be nothing done in this assembly that'll hurt Christianity."[51]

---

46. "Bryan Battles for Prohibition: For Saturday Night and Sunday Observance," *Bradford Era*, May 21, 1923.

47. "Modernists and Fundamentalists Soon Will Battle: Rev. C. F. Potter, Unitarian, and Dr. Straton, Baptist Leader, to Debate," *Lock Haven Express*, December 6, 1923.

48. "Bryan Takes Up Evolution Club," *Canton Sunday News*, May 20, 1923.

49. "Bryan Takes Up Evolution Club," *Canton Sunday News*.

50. "Presbyterians Indorse [sic] Resolution Presented by Bryan and Calling for Pledge of Total Abstinence," *Cincinnati Commercial Tribune*, May 21, 1923.

51. "Presbyterians Endorse W. J. Bryan Resolution," *Findlay Morning Republican*, May 21, 1923.

Interestingly, in the *Findlay Morning Republican* quote, Bryan linked the defense of Prohibition to the defense of religion, which included opposing evolution. The next chapter in this study will investigate interwar fundamentalists' social action on behalf of Prohibition; for now, it is enough to mention that their concern for both occasionally appeared together in newspaper accounts.

One final neutral article appeared in the *New Philadelphia Daily Times* in December 1923. In a roundup of sessions to be covered during the upcoming Federal Council of Churches ecumenical meeting, in which twenty-nine denominations and fifty million Americans were said to be represented, the topic of evolution was highlighted for its absence from the agenda. "Discussion of doctrinal controversies over evolution and fundamentalism were avoided at the opening session today. Leaders said any attempt to present the issues would be crushed back."[52] The decision to avoid evolution is noteworthy considering the topics that were covered in the sessions, such as the Ku Klux Klan and the following: "Mob violence. Co-operative evangelism. Prohibition. The 12-hour day in the steel industry. Law enforcement. Inter-racial co-operation. Rehabilitation of Protestant churches of Europe. Preservation of holy places in Palestine."[53] The meeting's organizers evidently saw more potential for rancor in discussions about evolution than in discussions about mob violence, Prohibition, and labor and race issues.

A few observations about the articles on fundamentalism and evolution between 1920 and 1924, whether positive, negative, or neutral, may be noted. First, William Jennings Bryan was associated with antievolutionary efforts more often than any other leader. Sufficiently well-known not to require an introduction, none of the newspapers mentioned his biography or past political achievements, and several used his nickname, "the Commoner," without explanation.[54] Such treatment highlights Bryan's national celebrity and the familiarity of his antievolutionary stance to readers. His interest in serving as prosecutor in the Dayton trial, as well as his selection for the post despite not having regular courtroom experience, make greater sense when viewed through the lens of his public leadership

---

52. "29 Denominations Attend Sessions," *New Philadelphia Daily Times*, December 12, 1923.

53. "29 Denominations Attend Sessions," *New Philadelphia Daily Times*.

54. See, for instance, "Evolutionist at Washington Makes Attack on Bryan," *New Castle News*, December 30, 1924.

on evolution in the preceding years. The trial would have appeared ready-made for his efforts.

Second, as mentioned above, very few articles on fundamentalism and evolution were published during these years. The most likely explanation is a lack of what reporters and editors considered newsworthy events. In every article surveyed, the battle lines between evolutionists and antievolutionists were consistent and largely assumed, so editors appear to have trusted in readers' awareness of the debate. Coverage would multiply during the Scopes Trial and in the years thereafter, indicating a willingness to devote space to fundamentalism and evolution when the occasion merited. The scarcity of articles may thus indicate a simmering debate with few boiling-over points between 1920 and 1924.

Third, the coverage of fundamentalists was fairly evenly split between positive, negative, and neutral articles. Though expert opinions pointed against antievolutionists, as displayed in every negative report of the period, newspapers would also occasionally publish articles friendly to fundamentalists. Church life and church debates sometimes appeared on front pages during these years, and fundamentalists were generally portrayed as a central piece of America's religious fabric. They could be fanatical in the eyes of newspaper reporters, but their sincerity tended to be believed and their efforts expected.

NEWSPAPER COVERAGE OF FUNDAMENTALISTS DURING THE SCOPES TRIAL (1925)

In 1925, newspapers in New York, Pennsylvania, Illinois, and Ohio printed at least 248 articles containing the words "fundamentalism" and "Scopes" or related terms such as "evolution" and "Bryan," which is more than a tenfold increase over the number of articles covering the antievolution movement in the previous half decade. Many of the articles appeared in July, the month of the trial, though a few reported in advance of it or summed up its impact months later. A large number also chronicled Bryan's sudden death. In total, 9 of the articles were positive toward fundamentalists, 26 negative, and 213 neutral.

The positive articles generally presented an unchallenged criticism of evolution. On July 20, the second-to-last day of the trial, a newspaper in New Castle, Pennsylvania, summarized a sermon by Presbyterian pastor Walter

E. McClure in which McClure stated evolution was not a new concept and that it required faith to believe it.[55] He blamed the controversies surrounding it on sophomoric troublemakers, "a certain kind of teacher who has a little smattering of knowledge, and then tries to spread out over the fields of philosophy and theology, shocking the minds of boys and girls and bringing down on the school the wrath of Christian parents."[56] The day after the trial, an Illinois newspaper reported on a Camden, New Jersey pastor seeking to ban the textbook at the heart of the Scopes Trial in his city: "Man did not evolve from a monkey or any form of lower life, and I am opposed to teaching our children that he did."[57]

An unusual news analysis piece also appeared in the *Canton Daily News* in the middle of the trial. It argued that the people of Tennessee were not backward, despite how some opinion writers had portrayed them, and accused news articles of contributing to the misconception: "Straight news reports have done little to dispel this."[58] The piece further argued that the law in Tennessee was not ill-conceived.

> The state of Tennessee stands above the average in intellectual attainments of its citizens. Its people are industrious as well as cultured. ... Tennesseans always have guarded carefully the courses in their public schools especially against insidious teaching which might destroy traditional faith. So they passed the law against evolution instruction in the public schools. It is not a fool law.[59]

Few articles can be found in this era, particularly articles that are not opinion pieces or quotes from fundamentalist leaders, which defend the antievolution stance so clearly as this.

In the days and months following the trial, a few articles continued the fight against evolution. The first was part of a newspaper's coverage of Bryan's burial on July 31. A short piece, it featured an excerpt from the closing speech Bryan had wanted to deliver at the Scopes Trial before the judge

55. "Immense Crowd Hears Rev. McClure Discuss Evolution on Sunday," *New Castle News*, July 20, 1925.

56. "Immense Crowd Hears Rev. McClure," *New Castle News*.

57. "Anti-evolution Move for Camden Schools," *Chester Times*, July 22, 1925.

58. "In Tennessee," *Canton Daily News*, July 16, 1925.

59. "In Tennessee," *Canton Daily News*.

abruptly ended the proceedings. In it, Bryan most likely refers to the Leopold and Loeb murder case, in which Clarence Darrow had served as a defense attorney, to connect evolution to criminality: "Evolution is a damnable philosophy. And, when the students become stupefied by it and commit murder neither they nor the universities are to blame."[60] In August, a United Press report recounted a challenge from John Roach Straton to Darrow to debate evolution in major cities across the nation. Straton's critique of Darrow echoes Bryan's: "Clarence Darrow is doing more to justify lawlessness and loose living among men than any other force in America today."[61]

A final positive article in 1925 stemmed from plans for a new fundamentalist school in Dayton, founded in memory of Bryan, which a Titusville, Pennsylvania, newspaper covered by noting Bryan's widow's support for the initiative. She expressed her wish that the new university would teach the "facts of science … in their true light," echoing a common argument made by fundamentalists that evolution misconstrues genuine scientific knowledge.[62]

Negative articles in 1925 featured a range of related critiques, including pastoral defenses of evolution, disparagement of Tennessee legislators, concerns about the fundamentalist-driven trial revealing a decline in religion, arguments that fundamentalists' antievolution aims undermine the separation of church and state and suppress educational freedom, and suppositions about antievolutionism being undergirded by a psychology of fear.[63] Most negative articles were printed before or after the trial rather than during it, when a preponderance of reporting was neutral.

Before the trial, the newspaper in Titusville that printed Bryan's widow's critique of evolution also published the opinions of a Dayton Methodist minister who claimed to be neither a fundamentalist nor a modernist, but who stressed that doing good was more important than humanity's origins or eschatological future. The minister upheld the Bible's inspiration, he said, but he mocked traditional views of its writing and transmission, which he characterized as believing

---

60. "Evolution as Assassin," *East Liverpool Review Tribune*, July 31, 1925.

61. "Fundamentalist Straton Assails Clarence Darrow," *The Freeport Journal-Standard*, August 18, 1925.

62. "Bryan's Widow and Son Approve School: Put O.K. on Fundamentalist Institution for Boys as Memorial to Commoner," *Titusville Herald*, August 25, 1925.

63. See, for instance, articles in the August 3 edition of the *Olean Times*, the June 9 *Indiana Evening Gazette*, and the December 27 and September 20 *Syracuse Herald*.

it to be "written in heaven, printed on India paper, sewed with silk, bound with calfskin, and tossed out the window."[64] An article in the *Xenia Evening Gazette* featured remarks from another religious leader, Mason Noble Pierce of the First Congregational Church of Washington, DC, who "declared that William J. Bryan had 'utterly misrepresented' the attitude of many religious thinkers and that Scopes' trial would be welcomed by many members of the clergy as a means of wiping out misrepresentations made by Bryan and others."[65] Pierce, who had served as a "spiritual adviser" to former president Calvin Coolidge, called evolution the "best hypothesis of how God works."[66]

Three opinion pieces critical of fundamentalists appeared in Ohio newspapers in the month before the trial. In the *Xenia Evening Gazette*, an article stated bluntly that the central question of the trial was: "Can a state of this Union establish an official religion? Tennessee has made an effort to do this."[67] Another article acknowledged that Scopes would likely be convicted under Tennessee's law but argued the more important issue was whether legislators ought to have democratic, majority-determined control over education. The piece's writer expressed the hope that the "defense takes occasion to show itself alive to the opportunity to assert the doctrine of educational independence."[68] The nation's founders would have upheld freedom of thought over legislative limits on education, the writer asserted. A third piece quoted George Bernard Shaw saying that what Bryan called fundamentalism was actually "infantilism."[69] The article's author concluded in acidic fashion:

> That will annoy Bryan, firmly convinced that when he leaves Miami his next stop will be Heaven, with a place in the front row, and a good, delightful view of Professor Scopes, of Tennessee, George Bernard Shaw, Darwin and Voltaire, all burning up together, in a place where the "worm dieth not."[70]

---

64. "Says Purpose in Life Is Important Thing: Minister Who Brought about Evolution Trial Gives Views to Press," *Titusville Herald*, July 3, 1925.

65. "Scopes Trial Will Help Country Says Coolidge's Pastor," *Xenia Evening Gazette*, June 10, 1925.

66. "Scopes Trial Will Help Country," *Xenia Evening Gazette*.

67. "Egotism of Ignorance," *Xenia Evening Gazette*, June 23, 1925.

68. "Menace in Bryan's Stand," *Canton Daily News*, June 19, 1925.

69. Arthur Brisbane, "Today," *Sandusky Register*, June 14 ,1925.

70. Brisbane, "Today."

As the trial began, a newspaper in Altoona, Pennsylvania, printed a glowing account of a speech by Darrow. It quoted key portions of his words, such as his accusation that the charges against Scopes were "a brazen attempt to destroy liberty," and reported "the courtroom sat amazed, some of the spectators awed by Darrow's daring ... others carried away by the eloquence of the speaker."[71] Another article claimed the prosecuting team had broken a gentleman's agreement and the trial had "aroused the prejudices of [Dayton's] simple mountain folk."[72]

The *Cincinnati Commercial Tribune* featured four front-page articles the day the trial started, two of which were slanted against fundamentalists. One included more Shaw quotes under the headline, "G. B. Shaw Calls Evolution Foes Moron-Makers."[73] That same day in the *East Liverpool Review Tribune*, an ostensibly straight news article reported that educational liberty and the constitutionality of Tennessee's law were ultimately to be decided upon, not whether Scopes had broken the law.[74] About a week later, the *Cincinnati Catholic Telegraph* ran a piece made up of quotes from Michael Williams, editor of *The Commonweal*, who objected that laws designed to bar "irreligion or any 'religious form' not to [fundamentalists'] liking" effectively made Protestant fundamentalism "a state-protected religion" even if Bryan denied it.[75]

By far the most critical article came from journalist H. L. Mencken, whose opinion piece entitled "Fundamentalism, Divine and Secular" ran in the *Syracuse Herald*'s editorial section a couple of months after the trial. Contemptuous in tone, Mencken's article described fundamentalists as "Homo boobiens," too unintelligent to understand evolution: "Its veriest elements were as far beyond their comprehension as the music of Bach or the theory of least squares. ... Half educated themselves, [fundamentalists] have sought to crowd an impossible education upon their victims."[76]

---

71. "Darrow's Great Speech Wins Dayton's Respect," *Altoona Mirror*, July 14, 1925.

72. William K. Hutchinson, "Tense Feeling Is Manifested in Scopes' Case," *New Castle News*, July 13, 1925.

73. "G. B. Shaw Calls Evolution Foes Moron-Makers," *Cincinnati Commercial Tribune*, July 10, 1925.

74. "Scopes Trial Issues Listed," *East Liverpool Review Tribune*, July 10, 1925.

75. "Catholic Editor Assails Bryan's Utterances," *Cincinnati Catholic Telegraph*, July 16, 1925.

76. H. L. Mencken, "Fundamentalism, Divine and Secular," *Syracuse Herald*, September 20, 1925.

Another article by Mencken in the *Canton Daily News* praised a recent recovery of interest in Friedrich Nietzsche. The column had little to do with fundamentalists, except Mencken took the opportunity to mock them in a short aside: "For out in the sticks, where fundamentalism rages, the official view of [Nietzsche], denounced in 1917, is still cherished, and so his name remains poisonous. ... The late W. J. Bryan dragged him into the trial of the infidel Scopes, and made the hinds of Dayton shiver."[77]

A final negative article in the *Cincinnati Commercial Tribune* quoted Scopes's defense attorney Dudley Field Malone at length, making the familiar argument that opposition to evolution unduly married church and state. Malone went a step further in suggesting that fundamentalism's efforts were an attempt to "write its scheme of salvation into law."[78] The motivation behind these efforts was fear, he said, and the results for the nation could be catastrophic. "[The] psychology of fear which crucified Jesus, banished Galileo, murdered Bruno and burned Jean d'Arc—the fear of political theology to test its power by the truth—today again animates a movement which is a menace to the internal peace of our country."[79]

The intensity of some negative articles notwithstanding, neutral articles throughout 1925 comprised the bulk of fundamentalist and Scopes-related reporting. Many narrated the basic events of the trial and of Bryan's death and funeral, yet a few investigated news angles beyond the courtroom proceedings.

Before the trial, a newspaper in St. Anne, Illinois, reported that the event was "deliberately arranged" by Scopes and his associates, with the American Civil Liberties Union behind it.[80] Three newspapers also noted the emergence of a fundamentalist antievolution campaign that stretched beyond Dayton, a precursor to many similar reports in the years after the trial. "[A] tremendous wave of fundamentalism is sweeping the country," one of these articles summarized. "Legislatures, school boards, college faculties, prominent attorneys, free-thought leagues—all these have been brought into the

---

77. H. L. Mencken, "Nietzsche Has Come Back. Proves War Over, Says Critic," *Canton Daily News*, August 23, 1925.

78. "Malone, Rebutting Bryan's Final Plea, Calls Evolution Fight Grave Threat for Combination of Church and State," *Cincinnati Commercial Tribune*, September 20, 1925.

79. "Malone, Rebutting Bryan's Final Plea," *Cincinnati Commercial Tribune*.

80. Edward W. Pickard, "News Review of Current Events," *The St. Anne Record*, June 4, 1925.

controversy, with the anti-evolutionists crying 'God or gorilla'?"[81] A version of the same article in a Sandusky, Ohio, newspaper listed fourteen states marked by antievolutionist efforts, including Tennessee, North Carolina, Florida, Texas, Oklahoma, Arizona, Kentucky, Illinois, Minnesota, Oregon, Arkansas, Iowa, West Virginia, and North Dakota.[82] This article printed a slogan on the opposing side as well: "There's no monkey in the evolutionists [sic] family tree."[83]

The *East Liverpool Review Tribune* in Ohio published an article that surveyed Tennessee legislators on their reasons for supporting the state law banning the teaching of evolution. Although mildly negative toward fundamentalists in outlook, the article gave space to legislators on both sides, including an extended quote for a fundamentalist lawmaker. A W. Mack Fuqua of Nashville said he had not voted for or against the bill but believed those who supported it did so out of fear of rural voters.[84] Meanwhile, Roy C. Wallace of Lenoir City defended the bill strongly.

> I voted for the law because I thought it a good one. Every intellectual person believes in evolution in many forms so long as it does not conflict with the Holy Bible. I notice that Dr. Nicholas Murray Butler of Columbus University, has stated that enactment of this law was a show of ignorance. ... I suppose he thinks it was a bunch of ignoramuses who led in volunteering in all our wars. I suppose he thinks it was a bunch of ignoramuses who helped break the Hindenburg line. The time has come when Tennessee will protect her young from the influence of such educated fools.[85]

One piece before the trial reported on a series of evolution debates held on the West Coast between Maynard Shipley, head of the Science League of America, and William Bell Riley. The Minnesota fundamentalist leader had won four of five publicly decided debates and one of two judge-decided

81. "'God or Gorilla' Cry of Antis: Those Opposed to Teaching of Evolution Threaten War on Scientists," *Chester Times*, June 5, 1925; see also, "'Down with Darwinism' Movement Gains Ground," *The Altoona Mirror*, June 2, 1925.

82. "Fourteen States Aroused to War on Evolutionists," *Sandusky Star Journal*, June 1, 1925.

83. "Fourteen States Aroused to War," *Sandusky Star Journal*.

84. "Tennessee Legislators Declare They Passed Famous Evolution Law Because They Believe Theory 'Interferes with Holy Bible,' " *East Liverpool Review Tribune*, June 9, 1925.

85. "Tennessee Legislators," *East Liverpool Review Tribune*.

debates, according to the article, though Shipley accused Riley's team of offering attendees "lunch and cash" and seeking to stock audiences with fellow fundamentalists.[86] Another newspaper prepared its readers for the upcoming trial with a humorous article that gently poked fun at Bryan: "Bryan has stated that after the Scopes Trial he will quit public speaking for good. This has led everybody to demand that the trial be held sooner than July 10."[87]

A more serious piece written by a United Press correspondent just two days before the trial began highlighted points made by both the defense and the prosecution. It noted, further, that the trial was a first step for fundamentalists, with "the distant goal of organized fundamentalism" being a national constitutional amendment banning the teaching of evolution from all American schools.[88]

Throughout the trial itself, which ran from July 10 to July 21, most newspaper articles were procedural, offering near-daily updates about lawyers' arguments, witnesses, and decisions made by the judge, John Raulston. A few captured the drama of the trial: One article reported Clarence Darrow had been fined $5,000 by the judge and ordered to appear at a separate hearing the following Tuesday for treating him with "contempt and insult."[89] In the same day's publication, another article recounted that former president Woodrow Wilson, under whom William Jennings Bryan had served as US Secretary of State, submitted a brief to the court in support of evolution.[90]

Similarly, several newspapers reported on a long, defense-submitted document of 65,000 words that compiled affidavits from eight scientists who attempted to prove evolution. One such article stated that some scientists claimed science could not be practiced apart from evolutionary theory.[91]

A few articles also captured reactions to the trial from Europeans. In one, a German professor marginally praised the United States for not being guided solely by economic concerns, since he perceived opposition to evolution as

---

86. "Science Group Head Loser in Darwin Debate," *Canton Daily News*, June 29, 1925.

87. "All Set and Ready for Hot Weather," *Cincinnati Commercial Tribune*, July 5, 1925.

88. "Constitutional Amendment Back of Scopes Case," *Sandusky Star Journal*, July 8, 1925.

89. "Scopes' Defense Chief Compelled to Furnish $5,000 Bond by Court," *East Liverpool Review Tribune*, July 20, 1925.

90. "Woodrow Wilson's Voice Lifted to O.K. Evolution," *East Liverpool Review Tribune*, July 20, 1925. See also "Wilson Brought In," *Marysville Evening Tribune*, July 20, 1925.

91. "Scientists in Lengthy Report," *Marysville Evening Tribune*, July 20, 1925. See also "Last Arguments by Lawyers End Trial of Scopes," *Defiance Crescent News*, July 20, 1925.

an ideological commitment, while he also portrayed fundamentalism as an outgrowth of the church's greater influence in America. "Fundamentalism is the natural consequence of this puritanism, just as the prohibition law. I even can foresee an anti-tobacco law but it is easier to ridicule such things than to appreciate the inherent value of them."[92] The connection the professor drew between fundamentalist denunciation of evolution and fundamentalist support for Prohibition is worth noticing again here.

Another article reported on a statement released by French scientists decrying the indictment of Scopes. Notable among the signatories of this statement was the physicist and chemist Marie Curie, who is quoted as saying, "Among the forms of oppression, those which tend to limitations of the rights of thought are the most horrible and also useless. No political or religious organization has the right to impose such limitation and we protest with indignation against the Dayton lawsuit."[93]

In the immediate aftermath of the trial, newspaper articles tended to focus on what was next for the antievolution cause and the trial's participants. No evidence of a fundamentalist retreat can be detected in these pieces. For instance, Walter White, the superintendent of Rhea County Schools and also a Scopes prosecutor, stated that US Representative W. D. Upshaw of Georgia would be introducing a bill to the US Congress to withhold federal money from colleges and schools that taught evolution.[94] An opinion writer in the *Xenia Evening Gazette* suggested along the same lines that the Scopes Trial was part of a larger fundamentalist plan for the nation, and the writer granted that the trial may have granted fundamentalists "the temporary limelight."[95] A Canton, Ohio, newspaper speculated more specifically about Bryan's next steps.

> The political observer finds it generally taken for granted that Mr. Bryan will endeavor to write fundamentalism into the next platform of the Democratic party and if he is successful in such a fight there is no reason why he should not expect further consideration, for

---

92. "German Professor Holds Scopes Trial Proves America Not Dollar-Chaser," *Defiance Crescent News*, July 20, 1925.

93. "Scientists Rap Trial of Scopes," *Canton Daily News*, July 21, 1925.

94. "Scopes Prosecutor Names Upshaw to Push Federal Evolution Bill," *Cincinnati Commercial Tribune*, July 22, 1925.

95. "Mr. Bryan's Gigantic Conspiracy," *Xenia Evening Gazette*, July 25, 1925.

in Democratic National Conventions, the presidential candidate is named after the platform is adopted. In such a contingency Mr. Bryan would expect to attract independent and Republican fundamentalists to the Democratic banner of the new crusade.[96]

Bryan would die the very day this article was published, but the grand nature of the venture assumed for him suggests that some believed fundamentalists had emerged from the trial with political momentum.

A few articles published later in 1925 stand out as well. A Huntingdon, Pennsylvania, newspaper followed up after the trial to report on Scopes' replacement by the Dayton-area school board with a new, fundamentalist teacher.[97] Another piece quoted Scopes's defense attorney Dudley Field Malone, saying that he attended a fundamentalist church himself but didn't view evolution as antifundamentalist.[98] Finally, a report on an address by Abram Simon, president of the Central Conference of American Rabbis at an annual meeting in Cincinnati, cited Simon upholding fundamentalism as having a legitimate right to hold its beliefs, but decrying efforts to enshrine those beliefs in Tennessee law.[99] Simon believed the issue was ongoing: "The Scopes Trial is not an isolated phenomenon."[100]

In sum, the relative impartiality of most newspaper articles on the Scopes Trial in 1925 belie conclusions of a public relations defeat for fundamentalists. In the minority of articles that did display bias, more were negative toward fundamentalists than positive, but fundamentalists received support in newspapers as well, and several articles pointed to longer-term, national goals of fundamentalists.

A few smaller observations are also worth noting. First, even in neutral articles, Darrow's framing of fundamentalism as anti-intellectual and Bryan's claims about Scripture's truthfulness came through clearly. The lawyers' talking points consistently found their way into papers around the country. Second, otherwise objective articles sometimes portrayed the residents of

96. "Speculation on Plans of Bryan," *Canton Daily News*, July 26, 1925.

97. "Dayton Refuses to Retain Scopes: School Board Picks Reporter for Teaching Post after Fundamental Test," *Huntingdon Daily News*, August 19, 1925.

98. "Faith and Law," *Sandusky Star Journal*, October 3, 1925.

99. "Rabbis Score Fundamentalism as State Law, Teaching of Religion in Schools as Nation-Church Union," *Cincinnati Commercial Tribune*, October 21, 1925.

100. "Rabbis Score Fundamentalism as State Law," *Cincinnati Commercial Tribune*.

Dayton as simple and as "mountain folk," thereby associating fundamental-ism with a rural outlook. Third, certain slanted articles were supportive of evolution, but not critical of antievolutionists, a distinction with a difference when evaluating the impact of the trial on fundamentalism.

NEWSPAPER COVERAGE OF FUNDAMENTALISTS POST-TRIAL (1926–1933)

If interpretations of fundamentalist history that view the Scopes Trial as a turning point in public influence and engagement are correct, it might be expected that newspapers would have reported either less frequently or more negatively on fundamentalism in the trial's aftermath. The number of articles mentioning "fundamentalism" and "evolution" between 1926 and 1933 did decrease following the intense coverage of the trial in 1925, but they still greatly surpassed the number of articles between 1920 and 1924. Additionally, coverage was neither mostly negative nor even more negative than in 1925. In total, newspapers in New York, Pennsylvania, Illinois, and Ohio printed at least 117 articles on fundamentalism and evolution from 1926 to 1933; seven were positive toward fundamentalists, eighteen negative, and ninety-two neutral.

A couple of the positive articles cover fundamentalists starting new post-Scopes campaigns against evolution. A newspaper in Indiana, Pennsylvania, reported in April 1926 that a wealthy businessperson named George Washburn had arisen as a "standard-bearer" for the cause after Bryan's death. Washburn, based in Boston and Clearwater, Florida, had held a three-thou-sand-person rally and "dedicated his life and fortune to war on the teaching of evolution."[101] His aim was to "save the orthodox Bible from the onslaughts of modernism."[102] A newspaper in Freeport, Illinois, reported similarly in January 1929 on a new antievolutionary organization being launched by the Chicago fundamentalist leader Paul Rader. Called Defenders of the Christian Faith, the organization offered a thousand dollar reward to anyone who could disprove via science a single fact of the Bible.[103] Rader stated the organization was populated not by "bigots," but by people exercising simple "horse sense."

---

101. "His Wealth to Carry on for Bryan," *Indiana Evening Gazette*, April 8, 1926.

102. "His Wealth to Carry on for Bryan," *Indiana Evening Gazette*.

103. "Organization of Fundamentalists Is Established: And First Thing It Does Is to Issue Challenge to Evolutionists," *Freeport Journal Standard*, January 26, 1929.

In his words: "Evolution is a pernicious doctrine because it is unproven. It is destructive of faith and morality and tends to debase every decent instinct. We cannot permit it to trample underfoot the Bible, which never yet has been found misleading or in error."[104]

Rader garnered further positive coverage in an Ohio newspaper a couple months later, when it reported on an address he gave in advance of a large, weeklong Defenders of the Christian Faith conference to be held in East Liverpool. The piece labeled Rader "the happiest Christian" and printed without editorializing his summary of a nationwide survey that had concluded "fundamentalists in the U.S. outnumber evolutionists a thousand to one."[105] Rader went on to read a statement he'd received from A. H. Clark of the Smithsonian Institute that strongly and specifically attacked the theory of evolution, and the article quoted this at length.

> Regarding man, structurally and anatomically he is very close to the man-like anthropoid ape. This is beyond dispute, but it is also beyond dispute that there is a sharp, clear-cut and very marked difference between man and the ape. Every bone of the body of man is at once distinguishable from the corresponding bone in the body of the ape. ... The difference between man and the ape seems to be too great ever to have been bridged by intermediates, and of all the fossils that have been found, not one represents indubitably a "missing link."[106]

Another positive article spotlighted the opening of Bryan University in 1930, the university about which plans had previously been reported shortly after Bryan's death. Published by the local newspaper of Hanover, Pennsylvania, the article quoted George Guille, a Bible teacher and the first president of the university, explaining the school's purpose as follows:

> William Jennings Bryan University believes in the wisdom of God and repudiates the wisdom of men where contradictory to divine revelation. The issue at the Scopes trial was not the validity of the Tennessee evolution law. It was between darkness and light, between error and

---

104. "Organization of Fundamentalists Is Established," *Freeport Journal Standard*.

105. "Fight Evolution in Ohio Meeting," *Defiance Crescent News*, March 26, 1929.

106. "Fight Evolution in Ohio Meeting," *Defiance Crescent News*.

truth, between men's silly theory of evolution and the revelation of the creative acts of God.[107]

A final positive article featured John Roach Straton's son, Hillyer Hawthorne Straton. The article labeled him "New York's youngest exponent of Bryanesque fundamentalism," explaining that his views were similar to his father's, although somewhat tempered.[108] The younger Straton was against evolution and wanted the Old Testament to be taught in public schools as literature, though he would allow students to accept or reject various parts of the Bible in an educational setting. He also didn't see the world in quite as negative a light as his father, according to the piece: "The youth is not convinced that some of the world's sins cannot be corrected."[109] Although established fundamentalist leaders like the elder Straton campaigned hard against the teaching of evolution, this article's writer had evidently sensed a limit to what they believed could be accomplished, perhaps a reflection of their largely dispensational theology. Chapter 4 of this book will investigate the theological underpinnings of interwar fundamentalists' social action more closely.

Articles negative toward fundamentalism ranged from reprints of measured critiques to reports of alarm at antievolutionist activities. A Poughkeepsie, New York, newspaper devoted a full page (markedly long for an article of that era) to a speech by Wake Forest College president William J. Poteat, in which he reassured listeners of fundamentalists' ultimate failure. After citing legislative and school board victories for antievolutionists, Poteat concluded that when resisted fundamentalists could be overcome: "Remember, this ado has been worked up. ... The average man does not know what evolution is and does not care to know."[110]

A July 1927 article in Kittanning, Pennsylvania, reported on a decision by Winthrop College's board of trustees not to reappoint an evolution-supporting sociology professor. Framing it as a case of intellectual freedom, the article called the professor "one of the best-known educators in the South"

---

107. "Bryan University Opens at Dayton: Institution at Place in Which Scopes Trial Took Place Is Dedicated to Beliefs of Commoner Who Died There," *The Evening Sun*, September 19, 1930.

108. "Minister's Son Turns Blast on Modernists," *Canton Daily News*, July 18, 1926.

109. "Minister's Son Turns Blast on Modernists," *Canton Daily News*.

110. "Fundamentalism Is Analyzed: Poteat Advocates Freedom of Belief, Declares Liberty without Restraint Is Not Liberty," *Poughkeepsie Miscellany News*, March 9, 1927.

and his firing a "fresh outbreak of the ancient struggle between the old ideas and the new."[111] Similarly, an article in Bradford, Pennsylvania, spotlighted William Bell Riley's World Christian Fundamentalist Association as an organization beginning to agitate against evolution in the north: "Citizens of northern states who have laughed at southern states for legislating against evolution might well stop laughing and attend to their own approaching problems."[112] An Ohio newspaper carried the same report and connected antievolution efforts to a measure to mandate Bible reading in schools that had been vetoed by the state's governor two years earlier. "Ohio boasts more colleges than any other state in the country, and yet it is likely to be the scene of just as silly a warfare as that represented by the Dayton, Tenn., trial."[113]

The president of Millikin University urged students in a June 1926 graduation speech reprinted by the *Decatur Review* (Illinois) to read the Bible in "the light of biology and evolution and it will be of definitely greater value to you than you dream. Modern science will give you a Bible fraught with value and meaning."[114] A couple of years later, the editor of a Salem, Ohio, newspaper acknowledged in an opinion piece that God existed but argued that a God of growth—i.e., the God of evolution—was more likely than the static God of fundamentalism.[115]

The same kind of academically minded criticism can be detected in a *Cincinnati Commercial Tribune* book review that surveyed four biographies of Charles Darwin released after the Scopes Trial. The review levied a much sharper rebuke to fundamentalists, however: "The evolution fracas in Tennessee was almost universally decried as a vulgar exhibition of unbelievable provinciality which made the United States the laughing stock of the world."[116]

Readers could also decry fundamentalism, as displayed in a December 1928 letter to the editor of the *Sandusky Register* by an Otto B. Schott. Responding

111. W. Y. Ferrol, "Scopes Case Recalled by the Dismissal of Professor Burgin from S. C. College," *Simpson's Daily Leader Times*, July 1, 1927.

112. "Militant Fundamentalism," *Bradford Era*, August 12, 1927.

113. "Militant Fundamentalism," *Evening Independent*, August 12, 1927.

114. "Penney Points out Five Qualities of Educated Man: Millikin University President Addresses Graduating Class at Commencement," *Decatur Review*, June 15, 1926.

115. D. H. Rummel, "Cosmological Study," *Salem News*, August 18, 1928.

116. "Ripples from Tennessee Keep Growing," *Cincinnati Commercial Tribune*, January 1, 1928.

to a news article about Arkansas becoming the second state to ban the teaching of evolution, Schott asserted that fundamentalists were seeking to weed out qualified teachers with their laws and to breed ignorance in students.[117] "Then our boys and girls will finish school with the same ideas they had when they started."[118]

Near the end of the years being studied, in late 1932 and 1933, a couple of Pennsylvania newspapers printed three articles critical of fundamentalists and of anyone opposing evolution. A columnist at the *Somerset Daily Herald*, A. E. Truxal, wrote two of them. In the first, he accused fundamentalists of failing to be Christlike toward opponents and identified their reverence for the Bible as the root of their errors.

> Science always wins and the principle of fundamentalism loses. It has been so from the days of Copernicus and Galileo on. … Science wins because it seeks facts on which to base its reasoning. Fundamentalism assumes too many things. Its fundamental mistake is the assumption that everything in the Bible must necessarily be true. That position has produced more false theology and instigated greater evils than anything else.[119]

In the second piece, Truxal argued that growth and evolution were the very nature of history itself. What is the cause of fundamentalists' misunderstanding of history? "1. Belief in the verbal inspiration of the Scriptures. 2. The spirit of fundamentalism."[120] Despite the causticity of his pieces, it's interesting to notice that Truxal correctly identified the accuracy and authority of the Bible as a key, guiding commitment of fundamentalists and the root of his intellectual disagreement with them.

A final negative article reported on a modernist leader, Albert Dieffenbach, taking a new position at a publication called the *Transcript* after previously serving as editor of *The Christian Register*. Dieffenbach was one of the most vocal religious proponents of modernism in the early 1930s, as will be seen

---

117. Otto B. Schott, "Evolution," *Sandusky Register*, December 7, 1928.
118. Schott, "Evolution."
119. A. E. Truxal, "Our Saturday Column: The Blessings of Science," *Somerset Daily Herald*, September 3, 1932.
120. A. E. Truxal, "Our Saturday Column: What Is History?" *Somerset Daily Herald*, November 12, 1932.

in some of the neutral articles ahead, and the notification about his new position was slanted in appreciation of him, presuming his critiques of fundamentalists were wise and helpful.[121]

Among the articles neutral toward fundamentalists between 1926 and 1933, a couple of outliers reported a diminishment in conflicts over evolution.[122] However, most chronicled ongoing tensions in a balanced manner. A DuBois, Pennsylvania, article lauded these tensions for the revival they had spawned in the art of public debate.[123] In Alton, Illinois, a newspaper reported in April 1926 of a fundamentalist candidate for mayor of Clarence, Missouri, losing to a modernist candidate. The fundamentalist, a retired farmer, characterized his beliefs as "exactly like that expressed by William Jennings Bryan at the Dayton evolution trial."[124] The Alton newspaper covered denominational fights over evolution in Baptist and Methodist denominations a few years later,[125] and a newspaper in Bolivar, New York, took the occasion of the purchase of a Gutenberg Bible for $106,000 to laud the Bible as a unifying book: "Seemingly we may have our battles over evolution and fundamentalism ... but when the smoke of religious difference has cleared away, the Book of Books still stands as a rock in the hearts of the people."[126]

Several articles tracked evolution conflicts in states and denominations. In Mississippi, legislators decided against passing a law to oppose evolution, even though the state's population was considered largely fundamentalist, because of the explosiveness of the issue.[127] Meanwhile, an organization founded in Wilmore, Kentucky, where Asbury College was located, announced it would seek to pass such a bill in its own state, with an eye toward eventually achieving the aim nationwide.[128] An editorial piece upheld Mississippi's decision because the alternative, it said, would be a patchwork

---

121. "Manchester Native on Transcript Staff," *Hanover Evening Sun*, August 18, 1933.

122. See, for instance, "Distant Mutterings, *Alton Evening Telegraph*, May 13, 1929, and William J. Losh, "Evolution Issue about Forgotten," *Altoona Mirror*, January 8, 1926.

123. "Debates," *DuBois Courier*, February 7, 1928.

124. "Modernist New Mayor of Clarence, Mo.," *Alton Evening Telegraph*, April 7, 1926. See also "Liberals Win City Election," *Marysville Evening Tribune*, April 7, 1926.

125. "Complications," *Alton Evening Telegraph*, June 14, 1929.

126. "A Priceless Book," *Bolivar Breeze*, February 25, 1926.

127. "Mississippi Assembly Fights Trend," *Cincinnati Commercial Tribune*, January 8, 1926.

128. "Kentucky Fundamentalists Organize to Ban Darwin Teaching in Schools," *Cincinnati Commercial Tribune*, January 8, 1926.

nation where some states disallowed publicly funded schools from teaching evolution and others didn't, which could lead to oppression in either direction.[129] The article speculated about a "revival of the bigotry and intolerance of the seventeenth century" if states each went their own way.

At least two newspapers in Ohio reported on an incident in New Jersey where a young student's father complained to his Kiwanis club about an evolution-friendly passage in a world history textbook. The father, a Lutheran minister, was not reported to have been a fundamentalist, but the passage in the book was shocking to his and others' sensibilities nonetheless, and the school superintendent was understanding of their concern.[130] The newspapers included the following quote from the textbook:

> The first people had hair growing, not just on their heads, but all over their bodies, just like some shaggy dogs. They simply lay down on the ground when night came. They were bloodthirsty. They liked to drink the warm blood of animals they had killed, as you would a glass of milk. They talked to each other with some sort of grunts—umfa, umfa—glug, glug. ... A cave man got his wife by stealing a girl away from her own cave home, knocking her senseless and dragging her off by her hair, if necessary.[131]

Fundamentalists and modernists clashed during a 1926 meeting of Northern Baptists in Washington, DC, with disagreement over evolution playing a part in the conflict.[132] Evolution remained a live issue in many denominations six years later, when a newspaper reported on United Methodists remaining firm against the doctrine: "In an age of modernism, with the doctrines of fundamentalism and evolution clashing at high pitch, the Methodist church, least of all Protestant sects, has refused to be swayed one iota by the beating assaults of science against the age-old religion that binds the church securely."[133] Adventists took the unique position of denouncing both funda-

---

129. "In Troubled Waters," *Xenia Evening Gazette*, February 17, 1926.

130. See "'Umfa, Umfa—Glug, Glug' School Girl Greeted Her Parent and Now Text Book Is in Question in N. J.," *Sandusky Star Journal*, February 6, 1931, and "Girl Cause of Revision of School Books," *Athens Sunday Messenger*, February 8, 1931.

131. "Umfa, Umfa—Glug, Glug," *Sandusky Star Journal*.

132. "Baptists Scrap over Evolution," *Marysville Evening Tribune*, May 25, 1926.

133. "Unchanging Methodism," *Newark Advocate*, May 12, 1932.

mentalists and evolution, with an Adventist speaker arguing that evolution was only a theory and therefore not worthy of inclusion in college curricula.[134]

Key figures for and against evolution also emerged prominently in neutral news reports. On the fundamentalist side, a couple of articles featured the businessperson George Washburn, described in one as an "enormously rich descendant of the Mayflower Puritans."[135] Washburn had donated one million dollars to an organization called the Society of Bible Crusaders and Defenders of the Faith, probably the organization he led himself.[136] He is quoted as saying, "I hereby dedicate myself ... to the task of stamping out the theory of evolution and the teaching of anything disrespectful to the Holy Bible."[137]

One of the articles about Washburn featured him side by side with a marginal figure named E. Y. Clarke, a former Ku Klux Klan organizer who had founded a new organization called the Supreme Kingdom. This organization sponsored an exhibit of a live monkey inside a large Atlanta street-front window with a sign nearby that proclaimed: "He May Be Your Grandfather— But Not Ours!"[138]

A short piece about William Bell Riley's World Christian Fundamentals Association reported that the organization planned to begin their fight against the theory of evolution in Georgia and then go to neighboring states, the rest of the nation, and finally overseas to "France, England, China, South America and Australia."[139] The piece acknowledged that some people would disagree with the association's views but complimented their conviction: "These southern fundamentalists may be right or they may be wrong, but they are intensely earnest about it and that merits some respect when a large portion of mankind is notably indifferent about its beliefs if it happens to have any."[140] The Midwestern Riley was not a Southern fundamentalist, of

134. "World Apostasy Adventist Theme," *Indiana Evening Gazette*, July 21, 1931.

135. "Enlisting Monkeys and Millions in the Battle for and against the Bible," *Hamilton Evening Journal*, March 27, 1926.

136. The article "W. J. Bryan's Evolution Fight Has New Leader," *Lima News*, April 11, 1926 appears to say that Washburn led the organization, though it gives it a slightly different name, the Bible Crusaders of America.

137. "W. J. Bryan's Evolution Fight Has New Leader," *Lima News*.

138. "Enlisting Monkeys and Millions," *Hamilton Evening Journal*.

139. "War on Evolution," *Portsmouth Daily Times*, May 10, 1927.

140. "War on Evolution," *Portsmouth Daily Times*.

course, so the article's association of him with Southern fundamentalism may indicate either that much of his national support came from the South or that such a perception existed, whether true or not.

By far the most covered fundamentalist leader was John Roach Straton, who appeared in multiple news reports during these years. A 1927 profile article mentioned his views and effectiveness and questioned whether he would take up Bryan's political mantle.[141] Several months later, a newspaper printed his rebuttal of a forthcoming book by fundamentalist opponent Albert Dieffenbach. Straton's remarks displayed both his familiarity with the relevant literature and his ability to craft intellectual arguments.

> The all sufficient answer to Dr. Dieffenbach's book on religious liberty is Dr. Ernest Gordon's book, "The Leaven of the Sadducees." In his book Dr. Gordon has exposed with complete and unanswerable historical facts not only the deceit and subtle, insidious duplicity of the modernists, but their actual and definite dishonesty. ... Modernism is a religious hybrid, sired by Satan and mothered by Intellectual Vanity. It has neither heart, conscience nor real brains.[142]

The following year a newspaper reported on Straton swapping pulpits with the pastor of First Baptist Church of San Jose, California. Straton announced he would "attack evolution, the present trend of public school education and modern religious tendencies" while guest speaking at the church.[143] His presence in San Jose stirred up opposition, with Maynard Shipley, president of the Scientist League of America, deciding to deliver a lecture in the area, and a Dr. Gilchrist, a Stanford University medical faculty member, agreeing to join Straton in a public debate.[144] Straton had become arguably the nation's most

---

141. "Dr. John Roach Straton, Fighting Fundamentalist, Carries on Bryan Policies," *Portsmouth Daily Times*, June 25, 1927. This article also reported that five deacons at Straton's New York church had resigned over him "toying with 'pentecostalism.' " The accusation is interesting because Pentecostal leaders like Aimee Semple McPherson regularly called themselves fundamentalists, and in the following chapter, her efforts and those of more mainstream fundamentalist leaders overlap in supporting Prohibition.

142. "Blistering Attack on Fundamentalism Receives Counter Blow by Dr. Stratton [sic]; Same Old Rotten Dishonesty, He Says," *Washington C. H. Herald*, October 20, 1927.

143. "Straton Begins Duties in California Pulpit," *Cincinnati Commercial Tribune*, February 6, 1928.

144. "Hearing about Evolution," *Findlay Morning Republican*, March 8, 1928.

visible fundamentalist leader at this point: "Since Bryan's death Dr. Straton has been declared the ablest defender of Fundamentalism in America."[145]

Yet he died the following year. On October 30, 1929, a notice in the *Sandusky Register* stated Straton had suffered a fatal heart attack at age fifty-four while recovering at a sanitarium in Clifton Springs, New York; the newspaper also reported he'd had a nervous breakdown a month earlier.[146] An obituary in another newspaper suggested Straton's zealousness may have led to his early death, though it upheld his motivation as admirable: "A person might disagree violently with Dr. Straton, might question his judgment, might be amazed at some of his methods and beliefs; but the man always challenged respect, and nobody could question his sincerity or desire to do his duty in the world."[147]

Among the opponents to fundamentalism featured in newspaper articles during these years, Albert Dieffenbach was covered most often. A 1927 piece reported he was "gathering modernistic forces to combat the alleged onslaught of the fundamentalists."[148] Dieffenbach mentioned William Bell Riley and his World Christian Fundamentalist Association specifically in the article, accusing them of seeking to ban the teaching of evolution and to instill fundamentalism in every state of the country; he further claimed that antievolution activities were already underway in twenty-two states, predicting that the turmoil caused by them would surpass the turmoil caused by the Anti-Saloon League's passage of the Eighteenth Amendment.[149] It is notable that Dieffenbach did not believe fundamentalists had been defeated by the Scopes Trial and that he associated opposition to evolution with support for Prohibition, even if indirectly.

Another article reviewed Dieffenbach's book, entitled *Religious Liberty, the Great American Illusion*, released later the same year. Dieffenbach had been the main religious opponent of fundamentalism since 1922, according to the piece, and in his book he asserted that other modernist leaders had failed in the cause, naming Harry Emerson Fosdick, Henry Sloane Coffin,

145. "Hearing about Evolution," *Findlay Morning Republican*.
146. "Rev. Straton, Darwinism's Foe, Is Dead," *Sandusky Register*, October 30, 1929.
147. "John Roach Straton, Crusader," *Xenia Evening Gazette*, November 4, 1929.
148. "Genesis or Jail Campaign Seen," *Cincinnati Commercial Tribune*, August 1, 1927.
149. "Genesis or Jail Campaign Seen," *Cincinnati Commercial Tribune*.

and the deans of Harvard and Yale divinity schools among the vanquished.[150] In somewhat alarmist language, Dieffenbach also foresaw a possible fundamentalist state church in the country's future and portrayed fundamentalist efforts as overturning religious liberty.[151] In an address to the First Unitarian Congregationalist Church of Cincinnati, he summed up his concern about fundamentalism succinctly: "Americans cannot be monarchists in religion and democrats in politics. If the doctrine of authority commands the mind in religion, the doctrine of freedom cannot guide the mind in politics."[152]

Other opponents of fundamentalism who appeared in newspaper articles during these years include D. J. Slosser, Philip de Ternant, and the Scopes Trial lawyer Clarence Darrow. Slosser, in an address to the Defiance College YMCA, said the fundamentalist-modernist debate needed to be dropped so that religion could regain its place in society. There was no doubt who he believed should concede their position in order to end the debate: "Time was when for a man to admit that he was an evolutionist was to admit that he was an agnostic. Today, to say he is a real Christian, a man must understand and believe in evolution."[153] Philip de Ternant, a Catholic priest, looked to church history and the ideas of Origen and other early church fathers to gently argue for evolution as a natural, secondary cause by which God created the universe.[154] Darrow, meanwhile, though he had largely avoided the evolution debate post-Scopes, made news in 1931 for appearing in a United Motion Pictures documentary film called *The Mystery of Life* that sought to disarm fundamentalist objections to evolution.[155]

In sum, the newspaper articles on fundamentalism and evolution published between 1926 and 1933 leaned slightly against fundamentalists, when biased, but not more so than during the Scopes Trial, with some articles still printed in support. The total number of articles nearly quintupled the modest number printed between 1920 and 1924, revealing heightened public

---

150. "Spirited Religious Controversy Looms as Dr. Albert Dieffenbach Prepares to Launch Attack on Fundamentalists," *Washington C. H. Herald*, October 19, 1927.

151. "Spirited Religious Controversy Looms," *Washington C. H. Herald*.

152. "Monarchism in Religion in America Is Menace to Democracy of Country, Says Boston Editor; Cites Evolution Ban," *Cincinnati Commercial Tribune*, February 9, 1928.

153. "Holds Evolution Is Aid to Religion," *Defiance Crescent News*, January 17, 1927.

154. "The Church and Evolution," *Cincinnati Catholic Telegraph*, June 28, 1928.

155. "Darrow Completes Evolution Film," *Edwardsville Intelligencer*, April 15, 1931. See also "Darrow's Film Is Near Completion," *Dixon Evening Telegraph*, April 16, 1931.

interest in the antievolution controversy following the Scopes Trial. Most significant during these years, reported in positive, negative, and neutral articles alike, were the new fundamentalist organizations launching against evolutionism and existing fundamentalist organizations increasing their efforts against it. Straton, Riley, Rader, and Washburn emerged as leaders in the antievolutionist movement, as did organizations such as the World Christian Fundamentalist Association, Defenders of the Christian Faith, and William Jennings Bryan University. Fundamentalists also continued their fight against evolution within existing denominations, not focusing solely on the public square and new institutions. Newspapers reported struggles over evolution in state legislatures, school districts, and denominational schools and meetings.

CONCLUSION

Newspaper coverage, both in the number of articles printed and in the portrayals contained in those articles, reveal scant evidence of a public relations disaster for fundamentalists or of a denominational or cultural retreat. Instead, articles between 1920 and 1933 suggest an opposite reaction: that a fundamentalist movement which had been relatively less engaged on evolution before the Scopes Trial became mobilized to greater efforts thereafter. Stated as clearly as possible, histories of fundamentalism that tie its decline to Dayton cannot be substantiated by news reports of the time period.

The reporting on evolution and fundamentalists throughout the 1920s and early 1930s displays instead a movement that continued in its public aims post-Scopes. Through the lens of hindsight we know antievolution efforts in the United States would ultimately prove to be fruitless, at least in outlawing public teaching of the theory. Yet a creationist movement would emerge in the decades following this early interwar period, confirming that theologically conservative Christians never accepted defeat on evolution. The next chapter explores newspaper reporting on another public issue fundamentalists engaged during these years, Prohibition, to see if any decline in their activity can be detected in the wake of the Scopes Trial.

3
___

FUNDAMENTALISM, ALCOHOL, AND NEWSPAPER REPORTING (1920–1933)

OPPOSITION TO ALCOHOL
AND THE PROHIBITION COALITION

The United States' path to Prohibition began early, even before the nation's founding. Sermons during the Great Awakening decried drunkenness, viewing it as widespread and ineffectively restrained by civil authorities.[1] By the middle of the following century, this attitude had coalesced into the seeds of a movement, and many pastors could assume their congregations viewed alcohol as a social evil. The Reverend Albert Barnes on February 1, 1852, delivered a sermon at First Presbyterian in Philadelphia entitled "Throne of Iniquity, or, Sustaining Alcohol by Law," in which he argued politically and biblically for the government's right to restrain the liquor traffic. As he framed the debate, laws prohibiting alcohol did not need a defense so much as laws allowing for the sale of alcohol. "A law which assumes that a thing is wrong, and yet tolerates it; which attempts only to check and regulate it, without utterly prohibiting it ... is one of those things in human affairs with which the throne of God can have no fellowship."[2] After citing a Supreme Court case upholding states' rights to prohibit alcohol, Barnes referred to 1 Timothy 1:9 as

---

1. See the description of George Whitefield's sermon, "The Heinous Sin of Drunkenness," a 4,600-word address based on Ephesians 5:18, in Christopher C. H. Cook, *Alcohol, Addiction and Christian Ethics* (Cambridge: Cambridge University Press, 2006), 70.

2. Albert Barnes, *Throne of Iniquity, Or, Sustaining Evil by Law* (Philadelphia: T. B. Peterson, 1852), 4.

a biblical basis for civic laws against wrongdoing.[3] He concluded his sermon by extolling the righteousness of the cause in God's eyes.[4]

Prohibition proceeded on a state-by-state basis throughout the late 1800s. In 1884, a letter to the *Andover Review* traced the progress of prohibitory legislation in Kansas, the first state to enact a full ban on the sale of alcohol, detailing the election of key public figures along the way. The tenor of the letter was not celebratory but exhortative. "The war is not over. A few battles have been fought and won. Victory seems certain to the prohibition forces; but if they throw away every advantage ... the war will be a long one."[5] By the time Prohibition became a constitutional amendment in 1919, a consensus had emerged, particularly among Christians, that legal action against alcohol was appropriate; this conviction was especially strongly held by fundamentalist and fundamentalist-leaning believers.[6]

Yet the coalition that promoted and upheld Prohibition was never solely conservative. Some theological liberals defended it just as zealously. Charles Clayton Morrison, editor in the 1920s of the leading mainline periodical *The Christian Century*, combined a passion for pacifism with an antipathy toward alcohol.[7] Both beliefs were based on his theological commitment to the social gospel, which he viewed as the "religion of Jesus," a religion "that welcomed the stranger, loved its enemies, and helped to bring about the commonwealth of God."[8] Morrison upheld Prohibition as an example of kingdom values because it improved individual morality and mitigated the social ravages of alcohol.[9]

Prohibition could also have a unifying effect on theological conservatives and theological liberals. Fundamentalist and moderate factions within the Southern Baptist Convention argued over evolution in the 1920s, for example,

---

3. Barnes, *Throne of Iniquity, Or, Sustaining Evil by Law*, 14.

4. Barnes, *Throne of Iniquity, Or, Sustaining Evil by Law*, 31.

5. James Dougherty, "Prohibition in Kansas," *Andover Review* 1, no. 5 (May 1884): 516.

6. See Daniel Okrent, *Last Call: The Rise and Fall of Prohibition* (New York: Scribner's Sons, 2010), 36–37, for a discussion of the Anti-Saloon League's vast and effective grassroots network among "the nation's literalist Protestant churches and their congregations."

7. Gary Dorrien, "America's Mainline: Gary Dorrien Tells the History of Charles Clayton Morrison and the *Christian Century*," *First Things* (November 1, 2013): 29.

8. Dorrien, "America's Mainline," 29.

9. Dorrien, "America's Mainline," 29.

but found common ground supporting Prohibition.[10] The career of Edgar Young Mullins at Southern Baptist Theological Seminary illustrates this tension and resolution. A graduate of the seminary, Mullins had pastored northern churches in Baltimore and Newton Centre, Massachusetts, before being appointed as the school's president in 1899.[11] He was a complex figure who held "mild social-gospel views," cooperated with certain progressive political groups, and in 1923 sought to pave the way as president of the convention for a qualified acceptance of evolution; yet he also contributed an article to the theologically conservative manifesto, *The Fundamentals*.[12] As the 1920s progressed, Mullins moved to the right both theologically and politically, fearing the gospel-undermining unorthodoxy of full-blown religious liberalism.[13] Perhaps also wearied by his conflict with fundamentalists over evolution, in 1927 Mullins allowed a pro-Prohibition tract he had written to be reprinted, and in 1928 he joined the campaign against the election of anti-Prohibition presidential candidate, Alfred E. Smith; as a result, "his fundamentalist Baptist brethren ... now resumed friendly relations with him after years of bickering over the evolution issue."[14]

Still, theological conservatives were arguably the most consistent opponents of alcohol and the strongest core of support for Prohibition. Fundamentalist leaders who led antievolution efforts could also be found defending Prohibition. John Roach Straton, pastor of Calvary Baptist Church in New York, politicked against the presidential candidate Al Smith, a Democrat like himself, in part because of Smith's "wet" stance.[15] The Texas-based fundamentalist J. Frank Norris hosted Straton at his Fort Worth church for an anti-Smith address, and after the Prohibition candidate Herbert Hoover defeated Smith in the 1928 election, Straton likewise invited Paul Rader from Chicago to speak to his congregation, where Rader hailed Hoover's election as a moral victory for the nation.[16]

---

10. William E. Ellis, "Edgar Young Mullins and the Crisis of Moderate Southern Baptist Leadership," *Foundations* 19, no. 2 (April 1, 1976): 183.

11. Ellis, "Edgar Young Mullins and the Crisis," 171–72.

12. Ellis, "Edgar Young Mullins and the Crisis," 174, 177.

13. Ellis, "Edgar Young Mullins and the Crisis," 178.

14. Ellis, "Edgar Young Mullins and the Crisis," 183.

15. Hankins, *Jesus and Gin*, 209.

16. Hankins, *Jesus and Gin*, 215.

Two of the interwar period's fundamentalist celebrities, Billy Sunday and Aimee Semple McPherson, [17] made alcohol a focus of their public ministries. Sunday was for many years the most well-known evangelist in the United States. A former professional baseball player who converted to Christianity at the age of twenty-three while a member of the Chicago White Stockings, he became a traveling assistant to the evangelist J. Wilbur Chapman in 1894. [18] Taking over for Chapman several years later, after the older man's return to the pastorate, Sunday gained renown for his flamboyant style and conservative theological views. [19] He mocked evolutionism and non-Christian ideologies, preached against immorality, and delivered his messages with rare athleticism and energy; he would kick and shout, skip across the stage, shadowbox, and pretend to throw boulders into the crowd. [20]

By 1909 to 1911 Sunday was speaking to crowds in mid-sized towns that could number as many as five thousand people. [21] The height of his ministry may have come in 1917 when he embarked on a New York City campaign. He employed twenty-six staff members at the time and spoke to hundreds of thousands during the ten weeks of meetings; more than ninety-eight thousand attendees were recorded as making decisions for Christ. [22] Sunday's influence began to wane during the interwar period, with a speaking engagement in New York City in 1930 drawing only one thousand people. [23] Yet he maintained a public speaking ministry until his death in 1935, and several social issues galvanized his attention throughout, chief and most consistent among them the sale of alcohol.

Sunday effectively advocated for the Anti-Saloon League's positions beginning in the early 1900s, making him a political ally of otherwise unalike public figures, such as the feminist and founder of modern social work, Jane

---

17. For a careful argument in favor of viewing Aimee Semple McPherson, a Pentecostal, as a member of the larger interwar fundamentalist/evangelical movement, see Matthew Avery Sutton, "'Between the Refrigerator and the Wildfire': Aimee Semple McPherson, Pentecostalism, and the Fundamentalist-Modernist Controversy," *Church History* 72, no. 1 (March 2003): 158–88.

18. Dorsett, *Billy Sunday*, 27–28, 52.

19. Dorsett, *Billy Sunday*, 1.

20. Bruns, *Preacher*, 13–15.

21. Dorsett, *Billy Sunday*, 89.

22. Dorsett, *Billy Sunday*, 106–7.

23. Bruns, *Preacher*, 287.

Addams.[24] An Anti-Saloon League publication in 1913 stated that the "liquor interests" hated Sunday more than anyone else; another magazine the next year tabbed Sunday as the eighth-greatest man in America, so his popularity and frequent speaking—up to 250 messages a year—may have contributed to the dislike of the liquor companies.[25] Sunday was not merely prominent and partial to the temperance cause, however. He spoke often and strenuously against alcohol, employing colorful and down-to-earth language in his appeals. "I'm trying to make America so dry [alcohol-free] that a man must be primed before he can spit," Sunday's traveling colleague and music leader Homer Rodeheaver recorded him saying.[26] "When church members stop voting for the saloon, liquor will go to hell."[27]

Billy Sunday relished expounding in detail the social costs of alcohol. He listed these costs most thoroughly in his well-known "Booze Sermon," an address that he delivered in various forms during his ministry. At its longest, the sermon could be more than twelve thousand words, split into fifteen sections, and likely would have taken over an hour to deliver.[28] Of the fifteen sections in this long version, five focused on the harm done by alcohol to individuals and families, four criticized the business of alcohol, three outlined personal and societal consequences of alcohol abuse, two explicated the national-level economic drain, and two broached political implications. "I am a temperance Republican down to my toes," Sunday stated at one point in the sermon.[29]

In language that sounds insensitive today, he further blamed the majority of crime and social problems on alcohol:

> Listen! Seventy-five percent of our idiots come from intemperate parents; eighty percent of the paupers; eighty-two percent of the crime is committed by men under the influence of liquor; ninety percent of the adult criminals are whisky-made. The *Chicago Tribune* kept track

24. Okrent, *Last Call*, 41.

25. Okrent, *Last Call*, 97.

26. Homer Rodeheaver, *Twenty Years with Billy Sunday* (Nashville: Cokesbury Press, 1936), 68.

27. Rodeheaver, *Twenty Years with Billy Sunday*, 66.

28. This chapter's quotations from Sunday's "Booze Sermon" can be found in the following edition of his address: William A. Sunday, "The Famous 'Booze' Sermon," *Criswell Theological Review* 5, no. 2 (2008): 71–98.

29. Sunday, "Famous 'Booze' Sermon," 72.

for ten years and found that 53,556 murders were committed by men under the influence of liquor.[30]

One of the largest gatherings to celebrate the impending start of Prohibition on January 16, 1920, the day before the Eighteenth Amendment went into effect, was a revival meeting Sunday held in Norfolk, Virginia. About ten thousand people gathered in a tabernacle "to hear him announce the death of liquor and reveal the advent of an earthly paradise."[31] Even as Sunday's popularity declined, he remained in the public eye and continued to support Prohibition. As late as 1933, when state conventions began ratifying one at a time the Twenty-First Amendment's re-legalization of alcohol, Sunday criticized drinking in an autobiographical article series he wrote for the *Ladies Home Journal*. He included "whisky-soaked" in a list of attributes of the "modernistic world [that] is going to hell so fast she is breaking the speed limit."[32]

Twenty-eight years younger than Sunday, Aimee Semple McPherson's public platform began to hit its peak as his declined. McPherson was born in Ontario, Canada, in the small town of Ingersoll, and served as a missionary to China for a brief time until her first husband's death in 1910.[33] After remarrying and working as a traveling evangelist throughout the 1910s, she opened Angelus Temple as her ministry base in Los Angeles in 1923, which functioned as a five-thousand-seat church sanctuary and the center of social programs.[34] It is estimated the Temple served hundreds of thousands of meals to people in need throughout the Depression.[35]

McPherson preached theatrically, cultivated media attention, and launched a Christian radio program, making her "one of the most famous American personalities of the interwar years" and "the first religious celebrity of the mass media era."[36] She earned criticism for her attention-grabbing ways, her role as a woman preacher, and the self-proclaimed victimhood of a

---

30. Sunday, "Famous 'Booze' Sermon," 73.

31. Okrent, *Last Call*, 2.

32. William A. "Billy" Sunday, *The Sawdust Trail* (Iowa City: University of Iowa Press, 2005), 84–85.

33. Douglas Jacobsen, *Reader in Pentecostal Theology: Voices from the First Generation* (Bloomington: Indiana University Press, 2006), 185.

34. Jacobsen, *Reader in Pentecostal Theology*, 186.

35. Jacobsen, *Reader in Pentecostal Theology*, 186.

36. Matthew Avery Sutton, *Aimee Semple McPherson and the Resurrection of Christian America* (Cambridge: Harvard University Press, 2007), 3.

kidnapping, which may have been a cover for an illicit sexual affair. Yet she remained anchored in conservative theology and preached evangelistically throughout it all. McPherson combined her fervor for world evangelism with strong support for the social renewal of America. She spoke and organized against evolution, dance halls, and political corruption. Overall, she "brought conservative Protestantism back from the margins to the mainstream of American culture, by arguing that Christians had an obligation to fight for the issues they believed in and boldly proclaiming that patriotism and faith were inseparable."[37] Although it was never her sole concern, Prohibition was prominent among the social issues she supported.

McPherson's political activism would lead to questionable alliances, such as occasional partnership with the Ku Klux Klan on issues she saw as patriotic and good for society, including defense of Prohibition.[38] For groups committed to the fight against alcohol, McPherson's prominence made her a useful ally. In 1924, the Women's Christian Temperance Union enlisted her to announce its candidate for vice president of the United States, Marie Brehm. McPherson also used her radio program to not just preach messages of salvation but to extol and defend Prohibition.[39]

During the scandal surrounding McPherson's claimed kidnapping and the investigation and trial it spawned, her role in opposing alcohol came up more than once. McPherson claimed the scandal was a Satanic attack against her ministry because of her stance against evolution in public schools and being in favor of Prohibition. She vowed immediately after returning to ministry to continue to preach "good old-fashioned fundamentalism" and to defend Prohibition, with a supporter writing to the Los Angeles Times that McPherson's ministry was so effective it would make jails and Prohibition agents unnecessary if allowed to continue.[40]

In a short newsreel clip produced by Hearst Metrotone News in the early 1930s, filmed when McPherson was about to embark on a trip to the Holy Land, she told a humorous story in which a preacher denounced alcohol but then inadvertently called his listeners back to it. McPherson concluded, "And

37. Sutton, *Aimee Semple McPherson*, 84, 4.
38. Sutton, *Aimee Semple McPherson*, 32.
39. Sutton, *Aimee Semple McPherson*, 64, 81.
40. Sutton, *Aimee Semple McPherson*, 107, 113, 121.

that's the way perhaps with us over here in America: we teach [Prohibition], but so often those who profess to make the laws do not quite live up to them."[41]

McPherson's support of the "dry" cause continued throughout Prohibition and, indeed, past its repeal. She held a media-friendly debate in defense of Prohibition at Angelus Temple in the early 1930s; had two of her talks against alcohol turned into newsreels in 1932 and 1933; and in a New Year's Day play in 1937 denounced Lenin, Mussolini, Hitler, evolution, removal of the Bible from public schools, and the end of Prohibition.[42] As the nation's most famous religious figure for much of the interwar period, McPherson consistently sought to return America to its Christian heritage, and opposition to alcohol ranked among her key concerns for the country's social renewal.

NEWSPAPER COVERAGE OF FUNDAMENTALISTS AND PROHIBITION PRE-TRIAL (1920–1924)

Newspaper reporting on fundamentalist support for Prohibition has not been carefully examined, as far as this researcher is aware. Sermons, church events, radio addresses, and public talks demonstrate that such support existed, but how much of it was captured by reporters? Before investigating interwar newspapers directly, two observations may be helpful.

First, as in the previous chapter, the aim of this study is to determine whether fundamentalists withdrew their public opposition to alcohol following the Scopes Trial. If the thesis of fundamentalist disengagement following the trial is correct, a decline in the number of articles about fundamentalist support for Prohibition should be expected—and perhaps even reporting on fundamentalists' actual withdrawal from the cause.

Second, a more nuanced picture than was revealed about evolution may be anticipated, because fundamentalists were never alone in upholding Prohibition. A fairly broad Protestant coalition could be depended upon to oppose alcohol throughout the early interwar period; additionally, fundamentalists tended to be closely associated in news articles with their anti-evolution efforts. Unearthing their engagement on alcohol thus requires looking below the surface of some Prohibition-related articles and tracing

---

41. Aimee Semple McPherson, "Aimee McPherson Says Goodbye: California's Noted Preacher leaves for Holy Land with a Parting Word on Prohibition," Hearst Metrotone News, early 1930s.

42. Sutton, *Aimee Semple McPherson*, 157, 217, 238.

connections between Prohibition-supporting denominations and groups and their fundamentalist constituencies.

From 1920 to 1924, in the interwar years leading up to the Scopes Trial, newspapers in New York, Pennsylvania, Illinois, and Ohio printed only eleven articles clearly related to fundamentalism and Prohibition. Of these, two were positive toward fundamentalists, one was negative, and eight were neutral.

The positive articles both profiled a significant Prohibition supporter. The first, an opinion piece published in Ohio in 1923, celebrated William Jennings Bryan. According to the editorial, after previous defeats in the Presbyterian general assembly—including losing a vote for moderator, having a teetotaling resolution he sponsored dismissed, and seeing his resolution calling Presbyterians "back to fundamentalism" amended with weaker wording—Bryan had been revitalized with a new victory.[43] The general assembly had voted to accept his most recent alcohol abstinence resolution. Bryan was no longer dead within the denomination as his detractors had hoped, according to the article.

> But, low [sic] and behold, brethren, the corpse stirs, the corpse breathes again, the corpse awakens to life more vital and potent than ever before. Bryan dominates the general assembly, his teetotal resolution is unanimously adopted; with enthusiasm he carries Presbyterianism to a solemn and solid reiterant of its old and fundamental teachings. Here is another adjuration to remember: You can't keep a good man down.[44]

The second positive article profiled the Rev. Noah E. Yeiser, who had taken over leadership of the Anti-Saloon League in sixteen counties, including Clearfield County, Pennsylvania, the location of the newspaper that published the article. Yeiser was not identified as a fundamentalist in the article but as a former Lutheran missionary to India within the Evangelical Lutheran Church, which was conservative theologically. During a local address, Rev. Weiser showed the film *Lest We Forget*, which depicted "old time conditions before Prohibition, and those who saw it stated that they were glad there

---

43. "Always a Mistake," *Portsmouth Daily Times*, May 25, 1923.
44. "Always a Mistake," *Portsmouth Daily*.

was something to remind them of what had gone before."[45] Rev. Yeiser further called on "well-wishing people" to vote, stating that only 35 percent of women and 40 percent of men voted, while "bad people nearly always go and vote."[46] The article concluded on a firm note: "Rev. Weiser said the Eighteenth Amendment will be enforced only where the men or women in office are in sympathy with and patriotic enough to obey it themselves."[47]

The single negative article during this time period recounted an address given by a professor at Aberdeen University named J. Arthur Thomson. This article appeared in the previous chapter, too, as it recounted the remarks of the British professor on a host of conservative cultural and religious expressions he considered related. Thomson derided fundamentalists and the Ku Klux Klan together with antievolution and nativist views; those supportive of Prohibition were included also. "Like the prohibitionists, they [Ku Klux Klan members] are characteristically contradictory expressions of the great country where the flag of freedom flaps so furiously."[48] Thomson further called fundamentalism "a frightened rebound behind the bulwarks of an outworn orthodoxy which proclaims itself impregnable and hypnotizes the credulous into accepting an illusion. The most remarkable feature about 'Fundamentalism' is the insecurity of its foundations."[49]

Most reporting on fundamentalism and Prohibition during this period was neutral in tone and outlook, however, and the neutral articles bear little similarity to each other, apart from several covering denominational or political gatherings. One article that appeared in various versions in a few newspapers spotlighted William Jennings Bryan again, who had addressed the annual Southern Baptist convention. In his address, Bryan called for the president, his cabinet, members of Congress, and other public officials to publicly pledge total abstinence as a way of strengthening the country's legal will to enforce Prohibition.[50] One key problem confronting Prohibition, he said,

45. "Newly Appointed Head Anti-Saloon League Was Here," *Clearfield Progress*, May 20, 1924.

46. "Newly Appointed Head Anti-Saloon League Was Here," *Clearfield Progress*.

47. "Newly Appointed Head Anti-Saloon League Was Here," *Clearfield Progress*.

48. David M. Church, "Briton Amazed at U.S. Ku Klux and Orthodoxy," *Murphysboro Daily Independent*, May 14, 1924.

49. Church, "Briton Amazed at U.S. Ku Klux," *Murphysboro Daily Independent*.

50. "Bryan Advises Pledge Signing for President," *Philadelphia Inquirer*, May 21, 1923. In an aside, Bryan also mentioned to the convention that he had nearly won election as moderator of the Presbyterian church, being only twenty-six votes short in the Presbyterian general assembly,

was that its lack of enforcement was undemocratic, spurred by a minority of the population who opposed the law: "There was a time when I supposed that law enforcement would never be a problem in this country. I thought it was the ideal of our government that the minority should acquiesce to the will of the majority."[51]

In a longer article on the same address, Bryan also humorously blamed politicians who were drinkers themselves.

> The next thing is to get rid of the wets who are entrusted with enforcing Prohibition. It's absurd. It's unconstitutional to appoint a wet official to enforce a dry law. Doesn't the constitution say we shall not inflict any cruel and unusual form of punishment, and what can be more cruel and unusual than to require a wet official to cut off his own source of supply![52]

As a creative solution, Bryan proposed a new law that would increase an individual's income tax based on how much alcohol remained in their home, presumably left over from when selling alcohol was legal.[53]

Another article reported on a speech given by H. P. Faris of the Prohibition party. Faris called on Christians not to vote primarily for a Democrat or a Republican for president, but rather for a Prohibition candidate. The article did not label Faris a fundamentalist, but his views were conservative, and he enlisted the church overtly in his campaign. "The churches of America, through their voting membership can have anything they want of the national government, if only they will unitedly demand it."[54] Faris accused President Warren Harding of opting not to enforce Prohibition as he should. He also claimed, similarly to Bryan, that the majority of Americans supported the law. "Mr. Faris declared it was his 'candid opinion' that fully 75 percent of the citizenship is at heart against the continuance of the liquor traffic and want the Volstead act enforced. 'I am told there is more drinking now than

---

in which case he would have appeared before Southern Baptists as an official representative of another "great Christian assembly."

51. "Bryan Advises Pledge Signing for President," *Philadelphia Inquirer*.

52. "Presbyterians Indorse Resolution Presented by Bryan and Calling for Pledge of Total Abstinence," *Cincinnati Commercial Tribune*, May 21, 1923.

53. "Presbyterians Indorse Resolution Presented by Bryan," *Cincinnati Commercial Tribune*.

54. "Prohibition," *The Evening Independent*, June 5, 1924.

there ever was before prohibition. My view is that most persons are not drinking at all.' "[55]

One last neutral news article should be highlighted. A piece on the Augustana Lutheran Church's 65th annual convention in DeKalb, Illinois, explicitly linked fundamentalism and Prohibition. During the meeting, it was reported, the synod had affirmed both. "Without a dissenting vote resolutions were adopted reaffirming the unalterable stand of the Lutheran church on the bible as the absolute rule of faith, ... [which] placed them squarely on the side of the fundamentalists."[56] In addition, "unqualified endorsement was given to the eighteenth amendment in another set of resolutions in which the synod acknowledged the beneficent effects already accomplished by the prohibition law and declared itself 'unswervingly for its continued enforcement without modification.' "[57] This kind of dual, public approval of fundamentalism alongside Prohibition was rare in denominational life throughout the early interwar period, but it was not out of place. Christian morals, conservative theology, opposition to alcohol, and, occasionally, rural outlooks were often portrayed as fitting together comfortably.

A few observations may be made about newspaper articles related to fundamentalism and Prohibition between 1920 and 1924. First, as with reporting on fundamentalism and evolution during the same years, coverage was sparse. Most likely this was due to relatively little controversy surrounding Prohibition in its early years. Fundamentalists stood on the same side as the recently passed national law, and they were arguably part of a majority in America in doing so. A few of the articles that did feature fundamentalist and conservative Protestant support for Prohibition emphasized this point. Unlike antievolution laws, which were highly contested and passed in only a few states, Prohibition had decades of legislation and social activism behind it. There was scant reason for fundamentalist opposition to alcohol to draw special attention.

Second, though many articles covered Prohibition during these years, most did so in a procedural manner, reporting on officials, arrests, and the state of enforcement. Newspapers spotlighted Prohibition as an important

---

55. "Prohibition," *The Evening Independent*.
56. "Lutherans Argue War Resolution; Action Postponed," *Moline Daily Dispatch*, June 14, 1924.
57. "Lutherans Argue War Resolution," *Moline Daily Dispatch*.

domestic policy, similarly to how developments in foreign policy or elections were covered. The religious support for Prohibition, including fundamentalist support, didn't appear to have been viewed as particularly newsworthy. A significant election related to Prohibition, the presidential contest of 1928, would draw increased attention to fundamentalists' political involvement, but that was still several years away.

Third, William Jennings Bryan loomed large as a fundamentalist leader on Prohibition just as he did on evolution. It would be hard to overestimate his stature within the media, which covered him regularly and knew well the handful of issues he cared most about. He was a national figure, active in politics and religious affairs, and a personality—articles would sometimes mention his manner and characteristics alongside portrayals of his addresses and stances. When Bryan died suddenly following the Scopes Trial, fundamentalism lost perhaps its most widely recognized and mainstream national representative.

NEWSPAPER COVERAGE OF FUNDAMENTALISTS AND PROHIBITION (1925)

During the year of the Scopes Trial, newspaper reporting on fundamentalism and Prohibition increased, just as reporting on fundamentalism and evolution did, though not to the same degree. At least forty-six articles on the subject were published in New York, Pennsylvania, Illinois, and Ohio that year, two positive, five negative, and thirty-nine neutral.

One of the positive articles was an especially reverent obituary of William Jennings Bryan. Nearly every newspaper solemnized his death, but most articles tended toward a respectful yet even-handed coverage of his career. However, this piece compared him to Leo Tolstoy, spotlighted his sincerity, and quoted an admirer named Dr. Ikirt at length on his virtues as a Christian and a leader.

> He [Bryan] was a martyr to the cause of Christianity. In my opinion Bryan had no equal in the United States. By his oratory he could easily sway crowds into tears. He came from the common people and always had their cause at heart. He was a deep thinker and could see things in the future as no one else could. He was an advocate of woman suffrage and prohibition. People laughed at him. Today we have both.

In his death, the United States has lost one of its biggest men and a
man whose loss will be keenly felt.[58]

The other positive article was a kind of devotional. As an opinion piece based
on a Bible study of the book of James, it drew principles from the epistle
and applied them to readers' lives. Obedience was one of the principles, and
Prohibition was mentioned as an application. "Law observance is one of the
great underlying problems of our world. Clear-cut and ringing, and completely pertinent, is James' 'A man who has kept the law as a whole, but who
has failed to keep one command, has become guilty of violating all.' Evidently,
there is no room for a Christian amidst the scoffers who flout the prohibition
statutes."[59] The writer of the piece didn't mention his own religious convictions, but his high view of Scripture was friendly to fundamentalists, as was
his support for Prohibition. He concluded with a call to Scripture: "Let us get
back to this succinct and livable Letter of James. In a bewildered generation,
it will stabilize our thinking and clarify our conduct."[60]

The negative articles featured several well-known figures, the first
piece again related to William Jennings Bryan. Published by a newspaper
in Middletown, New York, several months before the Scopes Trial, the article speculated about Bryan's possible run for Senate from his new home
state of Florida. Its critical tone dismissed his previous work as "forgotten
political issues."[61] The piece also mocked Bryan, suggesting he would run as
a promoter of real estate and winter vacations in Florida rather than as a
Prohibition supporter or a fundamentalist.

> So if Bryan goes to the United State Senate from Florida next year, it
> will not be as a Democrat or as a dry, nor as a fundamentalist, but as a
> "boomer" of Florida real estate. His platform will not be construed of
> grapejuice bottles [another reference to Prohibition] and Eve's leaves
> encrusted with free silver, but will be a glorious thing of orange blos-
> soms, palmetto leaves, peanut shells and Palm Beach bathing beauties.[62]

---

58. "Tolstoi of America," *East Liverpool Review Tribune*, July 27, 1925.

59. William T. Ellis, "Tart Words by Jesus Brother Are Good Precepts to Follow," *Syracuse Herald*, August 1, 1925.

60. Ellis, "Tart Words by Jesus Brother," *Syracuse Herald*.

61. "Bryan and the Senate," *Middletown Orange County Times*, March 31, 1925.

62. "Bryan and the Senate," *Middletown Orange County Times*.

Another negative article summarized two criticisms, including one from the famous author George Bernard Shaw. Presented as a string of loosely interconnected observations, separated by dashes, the article first discredited Prohibition as being ineffective and then quoted Shaw in denouncing fundamentalism as bad for religion. About Prohibition, the anonymous author observed, "The saloons are closed and will stay closed, that is sure. But when whisky is made the national drink ... you realize that putting prohibition in the Constitution does not necessarily mean perfection."[63] About fundamentalism, the piece reported, "Bernard Shaw says workmen and others are made irreligious by the teachings of fundamentalism. If you teach intelligent men in the name of religion that which they know to be nonsense, you destroy their respect for all religion."[64] Arguments about the enforceability of Prohibition were somewhat common, appearing in newspapers throughout the duration of the Eighteenth Amendment, yet direct, back-to-back criticisms of both Prohibition and fundamentalism were rarer, even in articles that might denounce one or the other.

Perhaps unsurprisingly, the columnist H. L. Mencken disparaged both at the same time. A severe and consistent opponent of fundamentalism, Mencken suggested in a late September editorial that Prohibition and the rise of fundamentalism were fictions, as in both existed as ideas, but not in real-life practice. He connected Prohibition explicitly to fundamentalism and viewed them, mutually, as hypocritical fronts.

> Observing the uproar of fundamentalism they assume glibly that the whole country has taken suddenly to religious exercises. Marking the fact that prohibition is official, they proceed to discuss it as if it were actual. There is, I fear, serious error in both assumptions, and in all like them. The truth is that prohibition is no more effective in the rural areas than it is in the towns, which is to say, it is not effective at all. ... As official morality has gone up, actual morality has gone down. And so in every other department. Fundamentalism menaces us all as a hypocrisy, not as a fact.[65]

63. "Today," *East Liverpool Review Tribune*, August 9, 1925.

64. "Today," *East Liverpool Review Tribune*.

65. Henry L. Mencken, "The Decay of Idealism," *Syracuse Herald*, September 27, 1925. See also Henry L. Mencken, "Gay Cavortins Follow Harsh Law Says Critic," *Canton Daily News*, September 27, 1925.

Still, the vast majority of articles related to fundamentalism and Prohibition in 1925 were neutral in tone, even if their conclusions could be either favorable or unfavorable to the anti-alcohol cause. An opinion piece by Clinton W. Gilbert that ran several months before Mencken's editorial reviewed a Prohibition "catechism" created by Roy A. Haynes. Gilbert favored the aims of Prohibition, but doubted whether it had achieved its aims: "There are still such vast quantities of liquor sold and drunk that it is doubtful whether any of the above benefits are real."[66] The piece recounted the leader of a large business, "a wet," who despite his own approval of drinking had to report that drunkenness had gone up at his business since the passage of the Eighteenth Amendment; other business leaders attested to the same experience.[67] The piece included churches in the Prohibition coalition and quoted directly from Haynes's catechism: "Q. Who was responsible for the beginning of the Prohibition movement? A. W.C.T.U. [Women's Christian Temperance Union], churches, parents, business men."[68]

A news article that appeared in Chester, Pennsylvania, a couple of weeks later similarly questioned Prohibition's efficacy. Summarizing a view purportedly held by many Washington legislators, it reported that laws prohibiting and regulating activities were losing support, though no legislators were identified by name. These legislators "sense[d] a popular reaction setting in against the last few years' hysteria of regulating everybody's personal habits, conduct, morals, even thought, by statute."[69] The article appeared to reference fundamentalists when it mentioned "ultra-puritans": "Up to a certain point the average American, something of a puritan himself, might have stood it [regulations] indefinitely. But the ultra-puritans kept at it until they'd pass that point far and away."[70] One of the key factors pushing public sentiment away from regulations, according to the article, was "the prolonged failure of Prohibition to prohibit."[71]

---

66. Clinton W. Gilbert, "Business Men Appraise Results of Prohibition," *Syracuse Herald*, June 12, 1925.

67. Gilbert, "Business Men Appraise Results of Prohibition," *Syracuse Herald*.

68. Gilbert, "Business Men Appraise Results of Prohibition," *Syracuse Herald*.

69. Charles P. Stewart, "'Anti-ism' on Wane in U.S.," *Chester Times*, July 1, 1925.

70. Stewart, "'Anti-ism' on Wane in U.S.," *Chester Times*.

71. Stewart, "'Anti-ism' on Wane in U.S.," *Chester Times*.

An article introducing the Scopes Trial made a connection with Prohibition, too, in the person of Walter White, the school superintendent involved in the case on the fundamentalists' side. Interestingly, women's suffrage was mentioned among the issues White supported, demonstrating a similar political outlook to that of Bryan, perhaps. "The prosecutor [is] Walter White, superintendent of schools, author of the Tennessee Women's Suffrage amendment, leader in state prohibition, candidate for 13 counties for governor."[72] That antievolution leaders could also be Prohibition leaders would not have been surprising, though religious support for Prohibition made the news less often in 1925.

An article spotlighted Bryan himself a week later, in the middle of the trial, and included remarks by him that connected Tennessee with the evolution law and support for Prohibition; Bryan further associated New York with evolution support and anti-Prohibition efforts.[73] The piece quoted Bryan at length.

> My friends ... if the people of Tennessee were to go to the state of New York, the one from which this impulse comes to stop the enforcement of your law [the antievolution law in Tennessee], on a similar mission, don't you think it would be regarded as an impertinence? They [New Yorkers] passed a law repealing the enforcement of prohibition. Suppose the people of Tennessee had sent attorneys up to fight that law or to oppose it after it was passed, and experts to show how good a thing prohibition is for the nation, I wonder if there would have been any lack of determination of the papers in speaking out against the offensiveness of such testimony.[74]

This comparison by Bryan reinforced the stereotype that Southerners, who were also widely seen as more conservative religiously, aligned against evolution and alcohol, while Northeasterners were in favor of both. There appeared to be a hint of an accusation of media bias as well, as Bryan asserted that newspapers in New York would clearly oppose any Tennessean intervention in New York's lack of Prohibition enforcement.

72. "Sleepy Hamlet," *East Liverpool Review Tribune*, July 10, 1925.
73. "Evolution Theories Key to Testimony," *Cincinnati Commercial Tribune*, July 17, 1925.
74. "Evolution Theories Key to Testimony," *Cincinnati Commercial Tribune*.

An article that appeared in at least four newspapers quoted Hans Driesch, a former biologist and professor at Leipzig University, who also related fundamentalism to antievolution views and support for Prohibition. "The Tennessee trial does not surprise those who have been following up the development of fundamentalism in America in the last two years," Driesch said. "The broad masses of America are much more religious than ours. The church, socially and morally, is more powerful. Fundamentalism is the natural consequence of this Puritanism, just as the prohibition law was."[75] Although the United States' teetotaler coalition was broader than conservative Christians, Driesch saw fundamentalism underlying both the Scopes Trial and Prohibition.

Following Bryan's death on July 26, 1925, obituaries appeared in newspapers across the country. Many highlighted his fundamentalism and political efforts on behalf of Prohibition. The *Canton Daily News* printed a chronological list of the public stances Bryan had taken throughout his life. Alongside positions on monetary standards, railroads, and banks, the list included his support for Prohibition in 1911 and 1918: "His advocacy of Prohibition became one of his leading activities and in March, 1918 he became president of the National Dry Federation."[76] A short piece in an Illinois newspaper cited the bigger-city *New York Sun* in noting Bryan had also predicted, while fighting for Prohibition, that he would die on behalf of a great cause.[77] His death right after the Scopes Trial was seen as a confirmation of this intuition. The piece highlighted Prohibition and evolutionism as two of his main concerns during the final years of his life, and other pieces in the same paper that day reinforced his standing as one of the nation's leading fundamentalists. Bryan's quote, delivered years previously at a Prohibition address in Peoria, Illinois, had a heroic ring to it: "Some day I will be fighting for a cause like this and some interior weakness of which I have no knowledge may stop me. When history is written I want my children to know that I died fighting."[78]

A long obituary in another Ohio newspaper included more details about Bryan's teetotaler efforts. It revealed he had banned wine from diplomatic

---

75. "How Germany Sees Evolution Trial in U.S.," *New Castle News*, July 20, 1925.

76. "Bryan Stood For," *Canton Daily News*, July 27, 1925.

77. "Died at Career's Climax," *Centralia Evening Sentinel*, July 27, 1925.

78. "Died at Career's Climax," *Centralia Evening Sentinel*.

corps events as Secretary of State, serving grape juice instead.[79] His commitment to the cause was long-term and effective, according to the article. "Indeed, Mr. Bryan in his long advocacy of teetotalism was credited by many with having done more than any other American outside of the Prohibition party, to force the adoption of the Eighteenth Amendment to the constitution making the United States a 'dry' nation."[80] One of the great disappointments of his life had been his failure in 1920 to "have a dry plank included in the [Democratic party] platform," as his own party would not subscribe officially to what was to become the law of the land: "My heart is in the grave with our cause," he had said after the 1920 Democratic convention. "I must pause until it comes back to me."[81]

Two other obituaries are worth mentioning. In one, a photo caption of his wife, Mary Baird Bryan, described her with a short summary of his career: "Invalid wife of the former secretary of state, prohibition enthusiast, candidate for president three times and a shining light in the recent Scopes trial."[82] In the other, Bryan was labeled "the Greatest Democrat of His Generation," and Prohibition was listed among his life's achievements: "He lived to see four of his pet ideas become the law of the land. Prohibition, woman suffrage, direct election of United States senators and Direct Primaries."[83] Although Bryan could never be reduced solely to fundamentalist causes, since his decades-long political career had reached the presidential cabinet and spanned a number of issues, by the time of his death, the vision of a passionate fundamentalist leader fighting against alcohol and evolution had been cemented in public imagination. Multiple newspapers mentioned fundamentalism, Prohibition, and the Scopes Trial in their obituaries of Bryan, some including all three.

Newspapers surveyed the political landscape in the days following Bryan's death as well, drawing varying conclusions about what his passing would mean for the causes he upheld. A short article about an Anti-Saloon League statement unsurprisingly emphasized Bryan's devotion to Prohibition:

---

79. "Bryan Thrice Defeated for President," *Evening Independent*, July 27, 1925.

80. "Bryan Thrice Defeated for President," *Evening Independent*.

81. "Bryan Thrice Defeated for President," *Evening Independent*.

82. "Mrs. W. J. Bryan," *Moline Daily Dispatch*, July 27, 1925.

83. "Call Bryan Greatest Democrat of His Generation," *Sandusky Star Journal*, July 27, 1925.

For the past 10 years William Jennings Bryan has co-operated as a
factor of great force in the work of the Anti-Saloon League. In 1919 his
services helped bring about the ratification of the Eighteenth amendment. ... His death is greatly mourned by all those who realize the
permanent value of Prohibition."[84]

Although Prohibition would be overturned in 1933, no clear indication of
this reversal could yet be detected in most newspaper reporting.[85] The article stated further that Bryan had accepted an invitation to speak at an Anti-
Saloon League biennial convention shortly before his death, demonstrating
that the issue remained important to him to the end.[86]

A Pennsylvania newspaper analyzed the fallout from Bryan not being
present to influence the Democratic party and upcoming 1928 Democratic
convention, where it supposed he may have been a key leader. The piece
also echoed a view Bryan himself had mentioned about fundamentalism's
relative strength in the South: "Probably fundamentalism is strongest in
the south, where evangelical Protestantism predominates, largely in the
Baptist and Methodist churches."[87] Another article questioned the prospects
for antievolution legislation in states across the country without Bryan's
ongoing advocacy, quoting the governor of Wisconsin, John J. Blaine, in strong
opposition to such legislation. Blaine appeared to equate it with Prohibition:
"Zealousness in creating sin by legislation is evidence of decay and degeneracy. We can speak with complacency and pride only when substantive law
decrees against injury to another instead of punishing mere disobedience
under mandates of absolutism and prohibition."[88]

Although Bryan dominated the news related to fundamentalism in 1925, a
few relevant articles unattached to him appeared in the latter half of the year.
A report on Lincoln Clark Andrews, assistant secretary of the US Treasury

---

84. "Anti-Saloon League Mourns Bryan's Death," *Zanesville Times Recorder*, July 29, 1925.

85. As just one example, see "College Presidents Talk on Prohibition and Youth," *Chester
Times*, August 1, 1925. The article interviewed leaders of several US colleges and universities,
concluding throughout that Prohibition was effective in reducing crime and supported by most
people. Failures of enforcement often made headlines and some articles openly questioned
whether it was even possible to ban alcohol, but predictions of Prohibition's demise were rare.

86. "Anti-Saloon League Mourns Bryan's Death," *Zanesville Times Recorder*.

87. "Party Situation in 1928 Might Have Been Directed by Bryan," *DuBois Courier*, July 30, 1925.

88. "Anti-Evolution Measures Scarce," *Altoona Mirror*, July 30, 1925.

and a leading figure in Prohibition enforcement, highlighted the Methodist Episcopal Church's support of his efforts. As a couple of articles in the previous chapter demonstrated, Methodism at the time was understood to be generally resistant to modernism, and the denomination strongly advocated for Prohibition.[89] The church's statement on behalf of Andrews was openly political: "Every United States official, whether connected with the prohibition unit or the federal courts, every investigating officer, every prosecuting attorney, every United States commissioner, every United States marshal, should be a supporter of the American policy of liquor suppression."[90] The Board of Temperance, Prohibition, and Public Morals of the Methodist church further asserted that Andrews was a "friend of prohibition because he is the enemy of law breaking."[91]

Another article about a Methodist social outreach leader, Rev. Dr. William A. Ferguson, predicted somewhat over-optimistically that Christian rescue missions would pass away because of Prohibition since they were geared toward ministry to alcoholics. In Ferguson's view, Prohibition marked the pinnacle in a decades-long trend away from alcohol and drunkenness.

> The rapid decline in the amount of work done by the old type mission is one of the unmistakable signs of the worth of prohibition. ... The "down-and-outer" of today is of a different type and must be reached in a different way. This changing condition has been going on for more than fifty years with the gradual improvement in social conditions in respect to drunkenness. At that time there were four times as many saloons as existed immediately before the passage of the eighteenth amendment.[92]

One last article in 1925 is worth highlighting: a long political analysis piece. Focused on divisions in the Democratic party and whether they could be

---

89. See "Distinction Between Progress and Evolution Drawn by Methodist Minister," *Cincinnati Commercial Tribune*, June 11, 1923, and "Unchanging Methodism," *Newark Advocate*, May 12, 1932, which included the following quote: "In an age of modernism, with the doctrines of fundamentalism and evolution clashing at high pitch, the Methodist church, least of all Protestant sects, has refused to be swayed one iota by the beating assaults of science against the age-old religion that binds the church securely."

90. "Dry Defense Line along Border Is Andrews' Project," *Lock Haven Express*, July 29, 1925.

91. "Dry Defense Line along Border," *Lock Haven Express*.

92. "Old Type Mission Is Disappearing," *Chester Times*, August 22, 1925.

bridged, the article described Prohibition and fundamentalism as commitments of rural people rather than city people. About fundamentalism, the piece stated: "The religious controversy between Fundamentalism and Modernism was largely a contest between country and city. The states where Fundamentalist laws have either got on the statute books or have made most progress are chiefly states with a large rural population." Similarly, with Prohibition: "Prohibition is quite largely a controversy between country and city. The Anti-Saloon League is distinctly an institution of the farms and villages." Although the article did not assess the strength or lack of strength of the Prohibition movement, it tied fundamentalism and support for Prohibition to rural America and portrayed the political divide between those beliefs and opposing positions falling between rural concerns and city concerns.

Several observations may be made about newspaper coverage of fundamentalism and Prohibition in 1925. First, the Scopes Trial raised Bryan and fundamentalism's media profile, making both newsworthy, and as this happened, the number of articles related to fundamentalism and Prohibition also increased. Fundamentalist figures such as Bryan and Walter White were attached to both causes, just as fundamentalist critics like Mencken opposed both.

Second, fundamentalism and Prohibition were often associated with rural America and the South, both by a leader like Bryant and by outside observers. As seen in the previous chapter, opposition to evolution was viewed similarly. This constellation of concerns—fundamentalism, alcohol, and evolution— was not unique to the South, since northern leaders like John Roach Straton and Paul Rader also upheld them, but social support appeared to be strongest in the South and rural America. This demographic perception had political implications, as the article on the Democratic party's divisions illustrated.

Third, the Methodist church consistently led the way among denominations in promoting Prohibition. It had a standing board and leadership positions devoted to it, issued public statements, and was unafraid to venture into politics. Concerns about separation of church and state, though occasionally voiced by critics, were not part of Prohibition discussions in the same way they were part of the evolution debate, and the Methodist church was undeterred by them regardless. A largely conservative denomination that made space for fundamentalist sensibilities, Methodism was also devotedly teetotal.

Fourth, as mentioned in the previous section, Bryan's death was a blow for fundamentalism. No other leader quite matched his profile, political experience, and ability to attract media attention. As a national spokesperson for fundamentalist social causes, his reach was unmatched. Interwar newspapers would never again cover a single figure who so well typified fundamentalist support for Prohibition.

NEWSPAPER COVERAGE OF FUNDAMENTALISTS AND PROHIBITION POST-TRIAL (1926–1933)

From 1926 to 1933, in the interwar years following the Scopes Trial, newspapers in New York, Pennsylvania, Illinois, and Ohio printed at least ninety-nine articles related to fundamentalism and Prohibition. Of these, seven were positive toward fundamentalists, seventeen were negative, and seventy-five were neutral.

The positive articles were published evenly throughout these years and differed from each other, sharing no discernable themes. A 1926 piece in the *Syracuse Post Standard* profiled a Prohibition enforcement official named Lowell Smith, who mentioned both that he was proud to be the son of a Methodist minister and that his support for Prohibition was moral rather than political. "I am not in politics; wet politics, dry politics, or any other kind of politics. I believe in prohibition. I am proud of the fact that I can go to my father and say that never, even in the line of duty, have I taken a drink. I believe that prohibition can be enforced. That is why I want to stay in the department."[93] A couple of years later, a long opinion piece about cultural shifts in the West appeared to argue that some changes were incorporable within society while others were not. Prohibition was seen as a good change, along with women voting, but having children outside of marriage was portrayed negatively, and the article's writer decried such childbearing in a manner that also defended fundamentalism.[94] "Still, gratification of the maternal instinct beyond the pale of wedlock cannot be undertaken without violating the laws which have carried civilization through all its stages

---

93. "Lowell Smith, Bootleg Foe, Spurns Graft, Proud of It," *Syracuse Post Standard*, August 29, 1926.

94. "Current Comment," *Daily News Standard*, January 27, 1928.

down to the present. It violates the inhibitions of revealed religion. It relegates fundamentalism to the rear and brings modernism into the spotlight."[95]

Another long editorial argued explicitly for Prohibition, emphasizing its support among Christians and "the sound and sane majority of the American people."[96] Responding to a different newspaper's anti-Prohibition article, it stated, "To characterize millions of upstanding, God-loving and God-fearing men and women of the churches of the United States as fools and fanatics is a serious charge."[97] The editorial further pointed to the results of the previous presidential election as proof Americans sided with the "God-loving and God-fearing" espousal of Prohibition: "We would assume that the Hoover-Smith vote would be a fair wet and dry test. The returns show that Mr. Hoover received 21,392,190 to Governor Smith's 15,016,443. Is not that decisive enough?"[98] The conservative Christian backbone of support for Prohibition was clearly emphasized in this piece.

One final positive article related to fundamentalists and Prohibition appeared less than a year before alcohol was legalized in December 1933. An upstate New York newspaper printed a long feature story about a pastor, Dr. Christian F. Reisner of New York City's Broadway Temple Methodist Episcopal Church, who was able to keep crowds coming to his church throughout the Depression. Reisner hosted famous musicians such as Cab Calloway and guest speakers that even included Franklin D. Roosevelt, who had not yet assumed the presidency.[99] Reisner was a showman and attention-grabbing, but his theology was conservative, according to the article: "Although the doctor's methods are sensational, his religion is ultra-conservative. He preaches fundamentalism and prohibition."[100] The connection between fundamentalism and Prohibition, embodied in Reisner, highlights again the conservative streak within the deeply Prohibitionist Methodist Episcopal church.

Among the negative articles, a couple stand out, being reprinted multiple times in various newspapers. In one, an interview with Thomas Edison in Florida, the inventor disparaged fundamentalism while seeing a future for

95. "Current Comment," *Daily News Standard*.
96. "Wet Consistency," *Oil City Derrick*, January 21, 1930.
97. "Wet Consistency," *Oil City Derrick*.
98. "Wet Consistency," *Oil City Derrick*.
99. William Gaines, "About New York," *Canandaigua Daily Messenger*, February 10, 1933.
100. Gaines, "About New York," *Canandaigua Daily Messenger*.

Prohibition. William Jennings Bryan's fundamentalism was "obsolete long ago," Edison said, and "there is more truth to be found in nature than in the Bible, for nature never lies."[101] Yet Edison saw hope for Prohibition if it were well-enforced. "The first 20 years are the hardest. It's a good thing for the children of today."[102] The other much-reprinted negative article was a short analysis of social science studies related to Prohibition enforcement and fundamentalism. The general outlook of the piece was indifferent toward Prohibition, but negative toward theologically conservative religion. It reported that young people "do not differ greatly from adults in their attitude toward law," a mixed observation that would seem to indicate, contra Edison, no growing support for Prohibition enforcement among those who had grown up under it.[103] Fundamentalism, however, tended to be embraced by less intellectually accomplished students, according to the report. "Young people in schools who have radical ideas, or at least liberal ideas, in regard to religion, are brighter in their studies than those who have more conservative or orthodox ideas. A psychologist says the less advanced tend to orthodoxy."[104]

Several of the other negative articles were editorial columns. A piece in the *Chicago Sentinel* by Charles Joseph quoted the Col. Samuel Harden Church, president of the Carnegie Institute of Pittsburgh—likely a reference to the Carnegie Institute of Technology, a precursor to Carnegie Mellon University— approvingly in his denunciation of Prohibition as a Christian plot to undermine the United States' separation of church and state.

Some of the Protestant churches of our land, either by banding together or by working independently, but reciprocally, and all of them using prohibition as an entering wedge, are aiming by indirect methods to affect a union of church and state through the back door, when the Constitution of the United States prohibits them from accomplishing that purpose through the front door. The Methodist

101. "Edison," *Portsmouth Daily Times*, February 12, 1926. See also "Edison, 79, Says He Really Is about 120," *Salamanca Republican Press*, February 12, 1926; "Edison Is 120, He Says, on His 79th Birthday," *Cincinnati Commercial Tribune*, February 12, 1926; "Edison Gives Job to Ford and Burbank," *Hamilton Daily News*, February 12, 1926.

102. "Edison," *Portsmouth Daily Times*, February 12, 1926.

103. Grove Patterson, "The Way of the World," *Oil City Derrick*, January 21, 1930. See similarly titled articles on January 21, 22, 23, and 24 in the *Olean Evening Herald, Marion Star, New Castle News, Washington C. H. Herald*, and *Xenia Evening Gazette*.

104. Patterson, "The Way of the World," *Oil City Derrick*.

Church is out-Heroding Herod in its demand for religious control of our people. They are striving with the zeal of Torquemada for the ecclesiastical mastery of private conduct, not through Gospel, but through law.[105]

As stated above, the charge of seeking to institute a state religion appeared much more often in newspaper stories on evolution than on Prohibition, but it was not unheard of in either debate. Church's quote again confirmed the Methodist church's leading role in upholding Prohibition.

An opinion piece by Rupert Hughes compared America to Sweden on several issues, including murder rates, the achievements of women, Prohibition, and divorce laws. Hughes saw Sweden as superior to America on every front, largely because of its more liberal approach to moral regulation. Fundamentalists were at the heart of America's problem, according to Hughes:

Isn't it a strange coincidence that in those countries, and in our own states, where rigorous laws, the strictest moral and religious convictions, indifference or hostility to science and high education, and religious fundamentalism are in vogue, they coincide with the highest percentage of illiteracy and crime and the strictest adherence to the good old-fashioned idea of women as inferior beings whose chief duty is obedience and child-breeding.[106]

A few months later in the same Ohio newspaper, Mencken wrote an editorial on Bolshevism in which he backhandedly criticized fundamentalism and Prohibition. After suggesting that socialism was no longer a threat in the United States, Mencken lumped fundamentalists and support for Prohibition together as bad aspects of American capitalism that nonetheless did not discredit the system itself.

The more rational objections to capitalism almost always turn out, when they are examined, to be objections, not to the thing itself, but to individuals who misuse it. This or that capitalist oppresses his employees; another one throws his wealth on the side of prohibition,

---

105. Charles H. Joseph, "Random Thoughts," *Chicago Sentinel*, April 23, 1926.
106. Rupert Hughes, "Some Facts about the 'Big Swedes,'" *Canton Daily News*, June 26, 1926.

or fundamentalism, or service, or some other such folly; yet another, having attained to political power, employs it corruptly.[107]

The headline the newspaper editor wrote for Mencken's piece described him as a "caustic Baltimorean."[108]

In a different kind of opinion article, a book review of *America Comes of Age* by a French author named André Siegfried, the author was quoted relating fundamentalism and Prohibition to the Ku Klux Klan. "He [Siegfried] sees in Fundamentalism, Prohibition, and the Ku Klux Klan the worst aspects of our original heritage; all three tend to that narrow-mindedness which prevents the development of the individual in science, art, or politics. The conclusion forced upon one is that we are a young country with a child's weaknesses."[109] The association was unflattering but not altogether untrue; as mentioned in this chapter's first section, Aimee Semple McPherson did speak alongside the Ku Klux Klan on some issues, and the group would join fundamentalists in defending the Bible and conservative values. The newspaper reviewer concluded that Siegfried's book was "a mature and shrewd piece of analytical criticism," revealing the writer's own sympathies.[110]

One last negative article should be highlighted, a political analysis piece that charged the Republican party with selling out to fundamentalism in exchange for power. "Republican success purchased by a surrender to Bryanism, Cannonism, fundamentalism, ignorance and bigotry of backward districts would be worse than defeat."[111] The writer accused the Republican party of adopting Bryan's principles, Bryan being a lifelong Democrat, in order to gain voters. This "Bryanism" was reflected in Republican stances on foreign policy, economic regulations, and Prohibition, which Bryan and Hoover, the current Republican president, both supported.[112] The piece intertwined fundamentalism, Prohibition, and rural America, which was common, but it incorporated the Republican party as well, viewing fundamentalist influence as a political negative that drew the party away from its core values.

---

107. H. L. Mencken, "Red Peril Dead, Slain by Bolshevism, Asserts Caustic Baltimorean," *Canton Daily News*, October 3, 1926.

108. Mencken, "Red Peril Dead," *Canton Daily News*.

109. "Untitled," *Buffalo Bee*, March 16, 1928.

110. "Untitled," *Buffalo Bee*.

111. "Back to Republicanism," *Carbondale Daily Free Press*, November 12, 1930.

112. "Back to Republicanism," *Carbondale Daily Free Press*.

The neutral articles between 1926 and 1933 covered a broad range of events and figures. A brief notice in an Ohio newspaper revealed that Prohibition would be the subject of a local Methodist church's Sunday sermon: "Worship and preaching at 10:30 a.m., 'Prohibition The Standard of Our Nation.' Good singing."[113] An article about a Billy Sunday event at Cincinnati's music hall reported four thousand people in attendance and that the fundamentalist revivalist had vowed to run for president himself if neither party nominated a pro-Prohibition candidate.

> If both parties nominate candidates opposed to prohibition, I am going to run as an independent. I want your votes and if you think I can not get millions of votes, you have another guess coming. I am going to fight, fight, fight until my tongue hangs from my mouth and my last breath leaves my body. Remember prohibition is here to stay, and not bootleggers, grating politicians and traitors shall ever be able to remove it.[114]

Although Sunday was a religious leader, he sought to enlist political support for Prohibition; this support would be demonstrated by voting in the upcoming 1928 presidential election. As seen earlier, other fundamentalist leaders also campaigned for the eventual pro-Prohibition candidate in 1928, Herbert Hoover, contributing to his victory.

An opinion piece in a Quincy, Illinois, newspaper lamented Americans' lack of moderation and balance. The writer, Florence Smith Vincent, listed alcohol and religion as examples of issues about which Americans often held extreme views. "Take any subject under the sun—prohibition, the League of Nations, fundamentalism: Do many of us meet on middle ground in calm, unprejudiced discussion, admitting the good of this, granting the evil of that; blending opinion, acquiring perspective, developing constructive thought and action? Or are we recklessly, rabidly either 'for' or 'agin' it?"[115] Vincent's concern wasn't with the issues themselves but with the tenor of the conversation surrounding them; still, the issues she chose to highlight were all of

---

113. "Lindenwald M. E. Church," *Hamilton Daily News*, February 27, 1926.

114. "'Billy' Sunday Flays the Wets," *Marysville Evening Tribune*, April 7, 1926.

115. Florence Smith Vincent, "Living and Loving," *Quincy Morning Whig Journal*, April 15, 1926.

interest to many conservative believers, from fundamentalism to the League of Nations and Prohibition.

In April 1926, a number of newspapers printed versions of the same report on the vote for a new moderator of the Presbyterian church in the United States. Held during the denomination's 138th general assembly, the vote had resulted in Dr. William C. Thompson's election, Thompson being described as a fundamentalist who was willing to make space for liberals. "Dr. Thompson is known as a fundamentalist but his attitude toward the members of the church leaning towards a more liberal interpretation of the scripture had set him distinctly apart from the fundamentalism expressed by his defeated opponent, Dr. Lapsley McAfee."[116] The only pronouncement Dr. Thompson made to the full assembly after being elected was a defense of Prohibition, evidently considered a safe subject among the stricter fundamentalists who had voted for his opponent and the moderate fundamentalists and modernists who had voted for him. "As newly elected moderator, one of my first official acts will be to proclaim to the world sympathy with an approval of the Eighteenth amendment to the constitution and the Volstead act [a Prohibition-related measure] and its enforcement."[117]

An unusual article in the *Richwood Bulletin* quoted a pseudonymous writer at length on the subjects Americans most wanted to read about, which turned out to be fundamentalism and Prohibition.[118] Many publications were missing readers' interest in the topics they chose to cover, according to the writer.

> I have been traveling a good many thousand miles in the United States and Canada trying to find out what engages the people's mind more than anything else. ... I have talked with all sorts of people, and have had editors in various places help me through their staffs. I am almost afraid to tell you what the result is. But whether you like it or not, here

---

116. "Dr. W. O. Thompson New Moderator of General Assembly," *DuBois Courier*, May 28, 1926. See also "Dr. Thompson Is Mild Fundamentalist," *Zanesville Times Recorder*, May 28, 1926; "Fundamentalist Is Elected as Moderator," *Titusville Herald*, May 28, 1926; "W. O. Thompson Is New Head of Presbyterians," *Cincinnati Commercial Tribune*, May 28, 1926; "Dr. Thompson Is Moderator," *Bradford Era*, May 28, 1926; "Thompson Named as Presbyterian Assembly Chief," *Findlay Morning Republican*, May 28, 1926; "Presbyterians Name Thompson," *Defiance Crescent News*, May 29, 1926.

117. Dr. W. O. Thompson New Moderator of General Assembly," *DuBois Courier*, May 28, 1926.

118. "What People Think About," *Richwood Bulletin*, August 26, 1926.

goes: the two subjects uppermost in the minds of the plain people of the United States today is [sic] Fundamentalism and Prohibition.[119]

The writer did not investigate fundamentalists' ongoing support of Prohibition. However, the correlation between fundamentalism and Prohibition and the reported common-person interest in both topics demonstrates they could be viewed as concerns that went together.

An article about Puritanism drew a sideways connection between fundamentalism and Prohibition as well. Excerpted from a longer magazine piece in *Harper's Magazine*, the article defended the Puritans and sought to rehabilitate their reputation as normal people who drank, had sex—"their sexual life was abundant, productive"—and were not narrowly restrictive.[120] The article contrasted the Puritans with fundamentalism and Prohibition, not to argue against either but simply to use their reputation as a foil against which to compare the Puritans. "It is the fashion in our time to designate as 'puritanic' any encroachment on our individual liberties. Puritanism has been lately confounded with Prohibition and Fundamentalism. I find that most people know little about the Puritans, who they were, what they thought, what they did."[121] Like the previous article, this one, too, placed fundamentalism and Prohibition back to back as similar, related forces, suggesting that some saw fundamentalism underlying Prohibition. The criticism of being puritanical was sufficiently common the author could assume readers were familiar with it, but the article contained no hint that Prohibition was nearing reversal as a result.

In a humorous article about Aimee Semple McPherson, fundamentalism and Prohibition were again paired, though this time they were matched with bobbed hair, because McPherson had cut her hair short. The article reported that "half her congregation stampeded" at the bold move.[122] In an aside, the writer proclaimed, "If anyone asks me the three vital problems of the century, I would say prohibition, fundamentalism and bobbed hair. The human race has a peculiar partiality for walking over haystacks and stumbling over

---

119. "What People Think About," *Richwood Bulletin*.

120. "The Puritans Not So Bleak," *Circleville Daily Union Herald*, May 2, 1927.

121. "The Puritans Not So Bleak," *Circleville Daily Union Herald*.

122. Olive Roberts Barton, "Aimee Bobs Her Hair and Also Her Power," *Sterling Daily Gazette*, May 7, 1927. See also the similarly titled article printed the same day in the *Altoona Mirror*.

straws."[123] Though not immediately obvious to the current-day reader, perhaps, the joke appeared to imply that bobbed hair was not important enough
to bother with, and the author may have been insinuating that Prohibition
and fundamentalism were not as worthy of concern as the furor that sometimes surrounded them either.

On certain occasions, fundamentalism and Prohibition were linked in
opponents, as those who stood against both could be identified by such a
stance. In a short news report about an Episcopal priest who had become
involved in the Sacco-Vanzetti case, a murder trial involving two Italian
immigrants, the priest's standing as a liberal minister was summed up by
the formulation "a foe of fundamentalism and prohibition."[124] Theological
conservatives and liberals could work together on Prohibition, but the conservative connection between fundamentalism and Prohibition was often a
more certain proposition.

As the presidential election cycle of 1928 approached its conclusion, a few
articles featured fundamentalists' involvement. One recounted John Roach
Straton's efforts against Al Smith, the Catholic governor of New York and
Democratic nominee, who was an open opponent of Prohibition. Straton
had called Smith the "chief friend of liquor in America today."[125] The article,
which described Straton as a "champion of fundamentalism," reported that
he spent eight days touring the South and speaking at anti-Smith events.[126]
Straton's comments in the article came from an address he had given in his
own church in New York City, during which he accused Smith of having cast
"all his dice in one wild and reckless throw for liquor and all that goes with
it" and concluded the "worst forces of hell were behind Governor Smith."[127]

Another such article featured Southern Baptist Theological Seminary
professor A. T. Robertson, who spoke at the Central Baptist Church in New
York City on the spiritual damage of disobeying Prohibition.[128] Robertson

---

123. Barton, "Aimee Bobs Her Hair," *Sterling Daily Gazette*.

124. "Pastor Resigns Over Sacco-Vanzetti Dispute," *Hanover Evening Sun*, November 22, 1927.

125. "Dr. Straton Renews Attack on Smith," *Hanover Evening Sun*, September 8, 1928.

126. "Dr. Straton Renews Attack on Smith," *Hanover Evening Sun*.

127. "Dr. Straton Renews Attack on Smith," *Hanover Evening Sun*.

128. Though Robertson is not identified as a fundamentalist in the article, he can be viewed
as one. See, for instance, James B. Williams and Randolph Shayler, eds., *God's Word in Our Hands*
(Greenville, SC: Emerald House Group, 2003), 1–38.

contended Prohibition violation was due to "common human desire to do wrong because of the spice attached to a little evil" and said the wealthy were most likely to yield to the temptation.[129] However, doing so would only lead to "punishment that follows inevitably" and "the harvest of corruption."[130] The sermon had political implications, delivered in a big-city pulpit during an election season, yet Robertson chose to emphasize the spiritual consequences of disobedience to the civil law banning liquor consumption.

An opinion piece framed as a fictional letter to the editor captured well the depth of conservative believers' moral commitment to Prohibition. Written by an imagined brother of a Methodist minister, the writer explained that ministers' support for Prohibition was not adequately understood.

> You voted "dry" every time the issue was presented, when you had an opportunity, and you favored prohibition when it came in. Your "dryness," however, is not at all the "dryness" of the typical Methodist preacher. ... For him, prohibition is a moral conviction, exactly like his conviction upon any other point in morals. It it [sic] a belief, not merely of the intellect, but of the emotions. He positively, and sincerely feels—notice that I say "feels," not "thinks"—that taking a drink is an immoral act. ... Prohibition is a thing that he labored for, and looked forward to, with all the power of this emotional conviction that it was necessary for the well-being of the human race. Now, when he sees this holy thing threatened, or thinks he sees it threatened, which is the same thing, by one of the candidates for President, he could no more help feeling an intense, emotional opposition to that candidate than he could help feeling abhorrence of blasphemy—and for the same reason.[131]

That conservative believers were in view was suggested both by the denomination chosen for the minister and by his offense at blasphemy, which was not a leading concern of modernists. Though fictional, the letter captured the conservative Christian's passion and long-term support for Prohibition.

---

129. "Holds Spice of Evil Causes Drinking," *Hanover Evening Sun*, September 8, 1928.

130. "Holds Spice of Evil Causes Drinking," *Hanover Evening Sun*.

131. S. A. Tucker, "As I View the Thing," *Decatur Evening Herald*, October 18, 1928.

Small-town churches devoted service time to Prohibition during the election season as well. A newspaper in Titusville, Pennsylvania, printed an announcement for a local Methodist church that had tackled fundamentalism and modernism—likely indicating support for fundamentalism, since the subject was avoided at Methodist denominational gatherings wishing to sidestep controversy—and Prohibition on the same Sunday. The Prohibition discussion was directed at choosing a presidential candidate.

> The services at the Methodist church on Sunday were interesting and well attended. The pastor, Rev. C. A. Hoover, preached in the morning on "Modernism and Fundamentalism." At the meeting of the young people in the evening prohibition was discussed in connection with the candidates for the Presidency of the United States. Mrs. C. C. Hopkins led the meeting and interesting talks were given by Prof. Smith, Prof. Baumgardner, and Miss Bertha Kruger.[132]

Opponents also captured headlines in the days before the election. On November 1, just five days before the vote, an Ohio newspaper reported on a Democratic rally for Smith at which Scopes Trial defense attorney Clarence Darrow had spoken. Darrow was described as a "famous attorney and opponent of fundamentalism and prohibition."[133] Just as he had fought with fundamentalists over evolution, Darrow also confronted them over Prohibition.

Following the election of the Republican, pro-Prohibition candidate Herbert Hoover, fundamentalists' hopes for stricter enforcement appeared to be fulfilled, at least initially. Hoover instituted an enforcement commission, which would oversee Prohibition-related laws, and he sought feedback from both sides.[134] One wet and one dry representative were mentioned in an Ohio newspaper article, with Bishop James Cannon Jr., the chairman of the Methodist Board of Temperance, filling the dry slot. His role was policy-oriented and not merely that of a religiously conservative figurehead, as he "gave President Hoover advice on the appointment and scope of the impending law enforcement commission."[135]

---

132. "Church Announcements," *Titusville Herald*, October 31, 1928.

133. "Big Rally for Dems in Ohio," *Steubenville Herald Star*, November 1, 1928.

134. Raymond Clapper, "Say Hoover Commission Named Soon," *Sandusky Star Journal*, May 13, 1929.

135. Clapper, "Say Hoover Commission Named Soon," *Sandusky Star Journal*.

Yet newspaper coverage related to fundamentalists and Prohibition declined as Hoover's term continued, perhaps indicating a lack of success in enforcement efforts. In October 1930 fundamentalists suffered a setback when John Roach Straton died at age fifty-four of a heart attack. An obituary in the *Cincinnati Commercial Tribune* listed several issues and controversies he had engaged in, including, near the end of his life, opposing the Democratic presidential candidate Smith.[136] Straton had called Smith "the deadliest foe in America of the forces of moral progress and true political wisdom."[137] Both charges were likely Prohibition-related, and in Straton's death, fundamentalists lost another capable spokesperson who could reliably generate headlines. A couple of months earlier, a newspaper had published a retrospective on Bryan that highlighted his conservativism late in life, as he became "a crusader for prohibition, peace, and fundamentalism."[138] The national influence of leaders such as Straton and Bryan could not easily be replaced.

Only a handful of articles on fundamentalism and Prohibition appeared in the final years of the Eighteenth Amendment. In a fictional story published in an Illinois newspaper, the main character recalled chain letters being mailed widely to generate prayer for spiritual and social concerns.[139] Nearly all the concerns the character listed were fundamentalist in outlook, including Prohibition, evidence perhaps of a real-life practice of fundamentalists sending chain letters in support thereof.[140] A Pennsylvania news article in 1930 reported on a Prohibition debate between Clarence Darrow and Clarence True Wilson of the Methodist Board of Temperance, Prohibition, and Public Morals.[141] The debate was to be held at the Metropolitan Opera House, which could indicate a sizable expected crowd. A few weeks later, a humorous piece associated fundamentalism and Prohibition with early rising. "I still don't

---

136. "Dr. J. R. Straton Evolutionists' Arch Foe, Dies," *Cincinnati Commercial Tribune*, October 30, 1929.

137. Dr. J. R. Straton Evolutionists' Arch Foe, Dies," *Cincinnati Commercial Tribune*.

138. "Forty Years Ago," *Moline Daily Dispatch*, August 12, 1929.

139. Ethel Hueston, "Ginger Ella," *Carbondale Free Press*, August 26, 1929.

140. Hueston, "Ginger Ella," *Carbondale Free Press*. The concerns in the chain letters encompassed "prayers for almost everything, for the sick, for foreign missions, for prohibition, for fundamentalism, for the second coming of the Lord, for the release of anarchistic prisoners condemned to death."

141. "Characters Contrast in Prohibition Debate," *Philadelphia Daily Pennsylvanian*, March 17, 1930.

know why the farmer gets up at 4 o'clock in the morning. It is not only bad for him, but it hurts the rest of us as well. Populism, fundamentalism and prohibition can all be traced to this early rising."[142]

Even as newspaper coverage dwindled, no evidence emerged of a fundamentalist reversal on Prohibition. A Syracuse, New York, article reported on a 1930 leadership meeting of the Methodist Episcopal Church at which increased giving and continued support of Prohibition were discussed. D. Stewart Patterson of the church's Board of Temperance, Prohibition, and Public Morals "urged the church to continue to support reform movements and to fight non-Christian opponents of prohibition, who are using the issue to attack the church."[143]

One final article in 1933, published months before Prohibition's repeal, again described a liberal activist by what he stood against and included both fundamentalism and Prohibition in the list. Arthur Garfield Hays, a cofounder of the American Civil Liberties Union, although the article didn't mention it, was described as opposing "censorship, the Ku Klux Klan, the Bible in the public schools, the death penalty, the power trust, prohibition, labor injunctions, Wall Street, war, fundamentalism, and the deportation of the Countess Cathcart."[144] As the early interwar era and the Eighteenth Amendment itself came to an end, fundamentalism and Prohibition could still be seen as part of a conservative collection of interrelated issues.

A few observations about newspaper coverage of fundamentalism and Prohibition between 1926 and 1933 may be made. First, the Methodist church was not alone in defending Prohibition, as the Presbyterian church's 1926 general assembly demonstrated, but it continued to lead the way among denominations in generating headlines for its support. This advocacy never wavered, continuing into the early 1930s. Second, familiar foes of fundamentalism from the evolution debate also appeared in newspaper articles as opponents of Prohibition. Clarence Darrow and H. L. Mencken were among the most prominent foes, with Darrow's approach centered on arguments and debates while Mencken's centered on ridicule. Third, Herbert Hoover's 1928 election to the presidency was sought by fundamentalists as a buttress for Prohibition,

142. "Comment from the Side Lines," *Norwalk Reflector Herald*, April 10, 1930.

143. "Church Opens Drive to Spur Quota Funds," *Syracuse Herald*, August 29, 1930.

144. Lemuel F. Parton, "Who's Who in News of Today," *Altoona Mirror*, September 28, 1933.

and their efforts appeared at first to be successful, yet Hoover's term ultimately achieved little. Although his early enforcement efforts included consulting a Methodist leader, Prohibition was weaker when he left office four years later than when he began. It would be overturned within a year of Franklin Delano Roosevelt's inauguration.

CONCLUSION

The central conclusion revealed by this survey of newspaper coverage of Prohibition between 1920 and 1933 is that no decline in fundamentalist support as a result of the Scopes Trial can be detected. In the first few years after the trial, the number of articles related to fundamentalism and Prohibition reached a peak, and Methodist, Presbyterian, and national elections all spotlighted the issue. The overall tenor of articles remained steady following the trial; most were neutral throughout the full years under investigation with few overtly positive or negative portrayals. Coverage did diminish in the early 1930s, but not likely due to a fundamentalist retreat; no articles in this study revealed any kind of retrenchment. Instead, religious support for Prohibition overall appeared to become less newsworthy. Viewed through the lens of newspaper articles, Prohibition died with a whimper rather than a bang, despite continued support by conservative Christians.

As mentioned at the beginning of this chapter, fundamentalists were not as closely or solely associated with anti-alcohol legislation as they were with antievolution legislation. More attention was therefore paid in this survey of newspaper reporting to discerning fundamentalist support amid a broader movement. A clear association between rural America, the South, conservative religious views, and Prohibition emerged, observable both in newspaper reporting and in opinion pieces. This association misrepresented some fundamentalists—neither John Roach Straton nor Aimee Semple McPherson could be considered rural, for instance—but the portrayal nevertheless revealed a common impression that fundamentalists were part of the Prohibition coalition. Key fundamentalist leaders spoke publicly in support of Prohibition and in opposition to those who would undermine it. As with evolution, fundamentalist support did not lead to lasting success in banning alcohol, yet the effort was there. The deaths of key leaders like Bryan and Straton may have stalled fundamentalism's public momentum on both issues.

In the next chapter, the theological commitments of interwar-era fundamentalists will be evaluated for their relevance to social action, and an underlying or functional theology of fundamentalist cultural engagement will be suggested. Most fundamentalists were either dispensational or deeply influenced by dispensationalism. Thus, the question of whether dispensational theology spurred or hindered public action, and whether it was consistent or inconsistent with fundamentalist social action, will be considered.

4

FUNDAMENTALIST SOCIAL ACTION AND DISPENSATIONAL THEOLOGY

One of the common criticisms levied against fundamentalists was that their commitment to dispensational premillennialism and its pessimistic view of history led to social inaction and to overlooking world problems the church ought to have addressed. Carl F. H. Henry presented a version of this argument as a sympathetic insider in his *Uneasy Conscience of Modern Fundamentalism*, calling fundamentalists to reengage their Christian responsibility of cultivating public righteousness and opposing social ills.[1]

The previous two chapters have revealed that this criticism was overstated; fundamentalists never retreated entirely from social action. They continued to oppose evolution and support Prohibition throughout the early interwar period. Suggestions as to why Henry may have advanced the critique nonetheless will be mentioned in the following chapter. For now, another question will be investigated: If fundamentalists were not always world-denying, were their efforts to redeem society inconsistent with their theology? More specifically, should adherence to pre-Tribulation premillennialism have discouraged them from seeking to align the culture with biblical values? Should dispensationalism have granted them an understanding of the church's life and mission that excluded social action?

The influence of dispensationalism on interwar fundamentalism was pervasive. Key figures who appeared in previous chapters, such as William Bell Riley, John Roach Straton, Paul Rader, and Frank Norris, were whole-hearted dispensationalists, and Aimee Semple McPherson and Billy Sunday were

---

1. Carl Henry wrote numerous articles urging fundamentalists, and later neo-evangelicals, toward cultural engagement, but his best-known work on the subject is his early book *The Uneasy Conscience of Modern Fundamentalism* (Grand Rapids: Eerdmans, 1947).

shaped by it.[2] It is thus fair to ask whether the social action of such leaders matched their dispensational theology. This chapter will seek to answer the question by examining what early dispensational theologians such as Harry A. Ironside, Arno C. Gaebelein, C. I. Scofield, and especially Lewis Sperry Chafer, wrote about the Bible, sin, salvation, anthropology, the church, and eschatology, the doctrinal loci most relevant to cultural engagement.

Chafer was the great early systematician among dispensational theologians. From his position as president of Dallas Theological Seminary, he began writing theological articles for *Bibliotheca Sacra* throughout the 1930s, culminating in the publication of an eight-volume systematic theology in 1948.[3] The following sections draw largely from his work, but also from publications by his theological contemporaries, Ironside and Gaebelein, and by his theological predecessor Scofield. Each section summarizes dispensational doctrine around a theological locus, rather than attempting to survey the entirety of dispensational writing on the subject, with attention paid primarily to the aspects most germane to social action.

Overall, these summaries will demonstrate that certain tenets of dispensational theology accorded well with fundamentalist social action, while others did not. Dispensational priorities clearly motivated fundamentalists in their social endeavors, yet dispensationalism also imagined limits on what cultural aims could achieve—limits fundamentalist social leaders largely ignored. Fundamentalists who were active in the public square thus operated from a kind of inconsistent dispensationalism, which did not impede their efforts but may have hampered their effectiveness.

---

2. For mention of these fundamentalist leaders' dispensational leanings, see William Vance Trollinger, *God's Empire: William Bell Riley and Midwestern Fundamentalism* (Madison: University of Wisconsin Press, 1990), 27–28; Markku Ruotsila, *The Origins of Christian Anti-Internationalism: Conservative Evangelicals and the League of Nations* (Washington, DC: Georgetown University Press, 2008), 27–52; Gail Ann Sindell, "Gerald B. Winrod and the Defender" (PhD diss., University of Michigan, 1973), 124; Gerald T. Sheppard, "Pentecostals and the Hermeneutics of Dispensationalism: The Anatomy of an Uneasy Relationship," *Pneuma* 6, no. 1 (Fall 1984): 5–33; and David Weston Baker, ed., *Looking into the Future: Evangelical Studies in Eschatology* (Grand Rapids: Baker Academic, 2001), 359.

3. This work can be obtained today in an updated, four-volume set: Lewis Sperry Chafer, *Systematic Theology* (Grand Rapids: Kregel, 1993).

THE BIBLE

Foundational to the identity of early fundamentalism, especially in contrast to theological modernism, was a commitment to the veracity of Scripture. While modernists employed various methods of biblical criticism, dispensational fundamentalists not only disagreed with the validity of such methods but dismissed them as rabbit trails. Chafer slighted biblical criticism as "extratheological," falling outside the bounds of true systematic theology.[4] Progress in the science of theology could only be made if one was a biblicist: "For the student who in spite of the claims of the Bible to be the Word of God is yet groping for added light on that aspect of truth cannot even begin the study of systematic theology."[5]

A high view of Scripture afforded the doctrine of bibliology a central place in dispensational theology. Dispensationalists upheld Scripture as supernatural in origin, without resorting to mechanical or dictation theories. Rather, "God so directed the human authors that, without destroying their individuality, literary style, or personal interest, His complete and connected thought toward man was recorded."[6] Amid Chafer's many articles for *Bibliotheca Sacra*, he wrote a two-part series on this aspect of bibliology alone, so significant did he consider the Bible's teaching on inspiration.

Chafer defined biblical inspiration as "a reference to that controlling influence which God exerted over the human authors by whom the Old and New Testament were written," this influence including the author's "reception of the divine message and the accuracy with which it is transcribed."[7] Though Chafer stopped short of dismissing human participation, he did not allow for any kind of dynamic or partial inspiration in which elements of solely human origin could be found within Scripture. The full Bible was verbally inspired by God. This divine quality "constitute[d] the very warp and woof of the Bible doctrine of Inspiration" and did not appeal to unbelievers

---

4. Lewis Sperry Chafer, "Introduction to Bibliology," *Bibliotheca Sacra* 94, no. 374 (1937): 132.

5. Chafer, "Introduction to Bibliology," 132.

6. Lewis Sperry Chafer, *Major Bible Themes: Presenting Forty-Nine Vital Doctrines of the Scriptures, Abbreviated and Simplified for Popular Use, Including Suggestive Questions on Each Chapter, with Topical and Textual Indices* (Chicago: Moody Bible Institute, 1926), Google e-book edition, 15.

7. Lewis Sperry Chafer, "Bibliology No. 2.1 Inspiration," *Bibliotheca Sacra* 94, no. 376 (1937): 389.

but rather "repel[led] the spiritually darkened mind of the unregenerate man—a darkness which is in no way relieved by human learning."[8]

For the believer, the Bible's inspiration, alongside its authority and revelation, constituted a "grand actuality."[9] Chafer grounded inerrancy partly in inspiration and addressed various objections, such as claims that Jesus sought to turn the disciples away from the Jewish tradition of inerrancy, or conversely, that the apostles accommodated Jewish beliefs about inerrancy despite knowing them to be impossible. He also addressed the contention that the apostles introduced errors of ignorance into the New Testament and the appearance of alleged contradictions in their writings.[10] Chafer dismissed all such claims on the basis of archaeological evidence, the Bible's surpassing excellence, and the apostles' trustworthiness, even if they were not divinely inspired.[11]

Chafer further grounded inspiration in biblical exegesis. He devoted the largest part of his second journal article on inspiration to the study of 2 Timothy 3:16 and 2 Peter 1:21. In response to scholarly interrogation of the Greek word θεοπνευστος, "God-breathed," which appears only once in the New Testament, Chafer contended, "It is a fair assumption that this crucial word is of divine origin being fashioned by God with a view to the elucidation of a conception which is not only foreign to the range of things human, but supreme in the range of things divine."[12] He did not venture to define the divinely created word but simply linked it to God's inspiration and upheld its central importance in the passage. The other key words in the passage, according to Chafer, were "all Scripture," and he noted that Paul had penned the epistle near the end of his life, by which time nearly the entirety of the New Testament had been written.[13] Likewise in 2 Peter, Chafer focused on the word φερω, "borne along," as the crux of God's work of inspiration, again declining to speculate exactly how God had accomplished it: "The Scriptures give abundant teaching as to the fact of inspiration but do not

---

8. Chafer, "Bibliology No. 2.1 Inspiration," 390.

9. Chafer, "Bibliology No. 2.1 Inspiration," 390.

10. Chafer, "Bibliology No. 2.1 Inspiration," 393–95.

11. Chafer, "Bibliology No. 2.1 Inspiration," 396–97.

12. Lewis Sperry Chafer, "Bibliology No. 2.2 Inspiration," *Bibliotheca Sacra* 95, no. 377 (1938): 8–9.

13. Chafer, "Bibliology No. 2.2 Inspiration," 9.

offer explanation of this phenomenon. The *how* of every miracle is wanting, and inspiration is a miracle."[14] Ultimately, Chafer concluded that evidence for inspiration rested on a "two-fold fact": "(a) That Christ so accepted the Old Testament as a whole as well as in every separate portion, and (b) that the New Testament was written at his direction and the human authors were promised superhuman ability to write according to the mind of God."[15]

The reader of the Bible could trust its canonicity as well, because God had overseen the Bible's formation just as he had inspired the writing of the individual books.[16] Chafer pointed to seven key conditions that existed during the Bible's canonization; together, these conditions attested to the trustworthiness of the process.[17] First, both the Old and New Testaments were written during a time when few writings were produced, so there was "little competition and comparatively little need of elimination." Second, the Old Testament books were written by leaders with religious authority, "Jehovah's recognized messengers." Third, the New Testament was written primarily by men appointed by Jesus himself, including the apostle Paul during his Damascus road experience. Fourth, early Christians were not engaged in the business of Bible-building but merely recognized "the living element which inspiration imparts" in the writings that would become the New Testament. Fifth, the Old Testament books shared the same inspiration, and Jesus and the apostles accepted them as such; additionally, the "closing of the New Testament Canon [was] at least intimated in Revelation 22:18." Sixth, no attempts had been made to add to the Bible's canon once the church recognized it as closed. And seventh, God brought about the formation of the canon miraculously, so that the "inerrant Word" was also "inerrantly assembled into one volume and preserved." In light of the Bible's inspiration and trustworthy canonization, it was authoritative, being used by the Holy Spirit in communication with humanity and proving true every claim about itself and its message.[18]

---

14. Chafer, "Bibliology No. 2.2 Inspiration," 13.

15. Chafer, "Bibliology No. 2.2 Inspiration," 16.

16. Lewis Sperry Chafer, "Bibliology No. 3 Canonicity and Authority," *Bibliotheca Sacra* 95, no. 378 (1938): 138. Chafer wrote that "the element of divine determination is paramount in the formation of the Canon just as it is in the dual authorship."

17. The full list of seven conditions and the quotes in the sentences that follow can be found in Chafer, "Bibliology No. 3 Canonicity and Authority," 139-43.

18. Chafer, "Bibliology No. 3 Canonicity and Authority," 153-56.

Though not all revelation was included in the Bible—Chafer mentioned the content of Joseph's dream, warning him to flee with Mary and Jesus to Egypt, which is not shared in detail in the New Testament, as well as the content of Adam's conversations with God in the garden of Eden—all Scripture was revelation from God to humanity, even if parts of the canonical writings could have been recorded by straightforward human observation.[19] Chafer contrasted revelation to reason and illumination. Reason, "paramount" in the human realm and drawn upon in systematic theology, was nonetheless "restricted to the point of insignificance" when compared to revelation.[20] Yet revelation could not have a redeeming effect apart from illumination. Chafer pointed to Balaam, King Saul, and Caiaphas as biblical examples of men who had been given revelation but had not been rescued by it; "without [revelation] none is ever able to come to personal salvation (1 Cor. 2:14), or the knowledge of God's revealed truth."[21] Ultimately, revelation could be general or specific, natural or supernatural, original or soteriological, and God could use various "modes," such as nature, providence, preservation, miracles, direct communication, the incarnation, and the Scriptures—yet the Scriptures played a special role, as the salvific revelation God had made widely available to humanity in our time.[22]

The Bible was therefore inspired, inerrant, trustworthy, authoritative, divine revelation, and supreme in every way. Chafer's theology of Scripture could venture into doxology at times, full of worshipful admiration for the Bible. Going even beyond Scripture's own description of its attributes, for instance, he wrote that it was "infinite," meaning of incomprehensible depth and worth.[23] "There is a border beyond which the human mind, basing its conclusions on experiences, cannot go; yet the human authors of the Bible do not hesitate when they reach that boundary, but move majestically on into unknown realms without intrepidity."[24]

In spite of the Bible's beauty and complexity, all dispensationalists believed it to be also perspicuous, understandable by the average reader, if

---

19. Lewis Sperry Chafer, "Bibliology: Revelation," *Bibliotheca Sacra* 94, no. 375 (1937): 264–66.
20. Chafer, "Bibliology: Revelation," 265–66.
21. Chafer, "Bibliology: Revelation," 268.
22. Chafer, "Bibliology: Revelation," 270.
23. Chafer, "Introduction to Bibliology," 133.
24. Chafer, "Introduction to Bibliology," 140.

a few principles were grasped first. Scofield noted some of these principles in the introduction to his *Scofield Reference Bible*: the Bible's unity, its meta-narrative consisting of one continuous story, its progressive revelation, its harmony, its central theme of Christ's person and work, and its testimony to a single redemption.[25] The latter principle may appear confusing in light of the covenantal eras into which dispensationalists split Scripture. Scofield noted eight such eras, starting with the Edenic and Adamic covenants, continuing through the Noahic, Abrahamic, and Mosaic covenants, the Palestinian and Davidic covenants, and ending with the new covenant in Christ.[26] Yet earlier covenants were understood by dispensationalists to be partial in scope, steps in the progressive unfolding of revelation, all pointing toward the ultimate redemption found solely in the new covenant.

The effect of dispensational bibliology was to make Scripture the only reliable grounding for all other areas of theology, as well as for thought on culture, morality, and Christian living. Arguments based on analytic the-ology or natural theology, such as those made by the great theologian of a previous generation of evangelicals, Jonathan Edwards, were not normally found among dispensationalists. Instead, a clear biblicism predominated. In addition, the dispensational understanding of eras of divine revelation, and the audiences toward which each era or dispensation was focused, could subordinate the teachings of previous covenants to their fulfillment within the new covenant. This arguably gave Old Testament passages on societal righteousness less emphasis. Both commitments, to biblicism and scriptural dispensations, impacted dispensationalism's de facto theology of cultural engagement.

SIN

Dispensationalists writing in the wake of the early twentieth-century fun-damentalist-modernist controversies were aware of the social gospel and its conception of structural sin. Walter Rauschenbusch outlined the basic prin-ciples of cultural or systemic sins in *A Theology for the Social Gospel*, published in 1917, grounding them not in the "biological channels" that transmitted

---

25. C. I. Scofield, ed., *The Scofield Reference Bible: The Holy Bible: Containing the Old and New Testaments, Authorized Version* (New York: Oxford University Press, 1945), v.

26. Scofield, *The Scofield Reference Bible*, 1297–98 (notes on Heb 8).

original sin but rather in the "channels of social tradition."[27] These "social idealizations of evil," which were caused by "super-personal forces, or composite personalities, in society"—in other words, by corrupt systems—were "the real heretical doctrines from the point of view of the Kingdom of God."[28] Rauschenbusch advocated using the tools of sociology to diagnose structural sin and to bring about its redemption.[29]

The social gospel's emphasis on structural sin cannot be found among dispensational theologians. Part of the reason was a conscious rejection of the social gospel's diminishment of personal sin and Jesus's redemption, while the other part was their bibliology summarized above. Chafer noted that "the failure of human speculation as compared to the finality of divine revelation on this theme should be familiar to all."[30] He further criticized the modernist perception of sin as a lack of moral training, because it implied that righteousness was simply a learned standard.

> If this theory were true, the cultured and civilized would be more righteous than the ignorant; a world war could not be begun by the most educated nation on earth; and Satan, who is "full of wisdom" (Ezekiel 28:12), must be as holy as he is wise. By this theory, the blame for sin is subtly transferred from man to God.[31]

From 1934 to 1936, Chafer wrote a seven-part article series on sin, notable both for what it highlighted and what it overlooked. Chafer defined sin broadly as anything opposed to God's character: "Sin is sinful because it is unlike to God."[32] Sinfulness thus included human evil, but it extended beyond humanity to the whole of the universe. As he explained, "The problem which sin creates is more than a mere conflict between good and evil in human conduct; it involves the measureless and timeless issues in the conflict between that holiness which is the substance of God's character and all that is opposed

---

27. Walter Rauschenbusch, *A Theology for the Social Gospel* (New York: Macmillan, 1917), 77–78.

28. Rauschenbusch, *A Theology for the Social Gospel*, 78.

29. Rauschenbusch, *A Theology for the Social Gospel*, 78.

30. Chafer, *Major Bible Themes*, 143.

31. Chafer, *Major Bible Themes*, 144.

32. Lewis Sperry Chafer, "The Doctrine of Sin, Part 1," *Bibliotheca Sacra* 91, no. 364 (1934): 393.

to it."[33] Sin had originated in wrong choices in both heavenly and earthly realms. Even though good and evil alike were defined by God's character—one in keeping with it and one opposed—God did not create sin; he only permitted it.[34] His reason for granting this permission remained a mystery: "The devout mind cannot but contemplate the problem of the divine permission of sin, though the sum total of all its reasonings is inadequate to form a final answer to the question."[35] Nonetheless, sin was not a surprise to God but part of his eternal plan, and Chafer offered a number of explanations to at least partially address the question of evil. These included God's desire for his own glory to "secure a company of beings" who had freely chosen victory over evil; his wish to show self-sacrificial love to those he had created, "possible only when sin is present in the world"; the opportunity for God's people to learn good experientially in contradistinction to evil, and for God to display his judgment against evil; and to demonstrate an aspect of God's character (grace) unseen before sin's entry into the world.[36] The result of humanity's first sin was death in various forms incurred by Adam.

> The penalty imposed upon Adam was that death in all its hideous reality—death *spiritual*, which he experienced the day that he sinned; death *physical*, which began at once to work in his body and was consummated when his earthly life ended; and *the second death*, in certain prospect unless through divine grace he should be redeemed from his lost estate—would be visited upon him.[37]

Additionally, Adam's sin bequeathed to all humanity original corruption and original guilt, original corruption being in itself spiritual death and original guilt resulting in physical death.[38] The fallen nature each person received from Adam was testified to by Scripture, human history, and their own conscience.[39] Chafer's conception of sin's effect on humanity could be corporate and individual, displayed in "war, inquisition, murder, prostitution, slavery,

---

33. Chafer, "The Doctrine of Sin, Part 1," 392.

34. Chafer, "The Doctrine of Sin, Part 1," 395.

35. Chafer, "The Doctrine of Sin, Part 1," 395.

36. Chafer, "The Doctrine of Sin, Part 1," 398–400.

37. Lewis Sperry Chafer, "The Doctrine of Sin, Part 2," *Bibliotheca Sacra* 92, no. 365 (1935): 16.

38. Chafer, "The Doctrine of Sin, Part 2," 19.

39. Chafer, "The Doctrine of Sin, Part 2," 20.

drunkenness, cruelty, falsehood, avarice, covetousness, pride, unbelief, and hatred of God."[40] However, he stressed personal over social sins, and the biblical solutions to sin he examined were aimed at individual wrongs. Slavery, for instance, had in the West been an international business overturned by political and cultural means, but Chafer did not venture into concepts of systemic sin or social justice that could be found in an author like Rauschenbusch.

Chafer focused instead on the spiritual aspects of humanity's current sinful condition. His third article on sin included a lengthy summary.

> Finally, the estate of unregenerate man may be summarized, (a) as being subject to death in all its forms, because of participation in Adam's sin; (b) as being born in depravity because of spiritual death and forever separated from God unless regenerated by the saving power of God; (c) as guilty of personal sins, each and every one of which is as sinful in the sight of God as the first sin of Satan or the first sin of Adam; (d) as "under sin," in which estate all—both Jew and Gentile—are now placed by divine decree and in which every human merit is disregarded to the end that the uncompromised saving grace of God may be exercised toward those who believe; and (e) as under the influence of Satan who is in authority over them, who energizes them, who blinds them concerning the gospel, and who deceives them concerning their true relation to himself.[41]

Christians continue to confront sin after coming to salvation, at least until God's consummation of his kingdom in the new heaven and new earth. This reality brings pain to the person of God: "Indeed, what Christian, waging, as all Christians do, a simultaneous battle on three fronts—the world, the flesh, and the devil, is not often, if not almost constantly, in a state of spiritual injury?"[42] Chafer listed specific consequences that sin brought to the Christian, including a number of losses, such as God's enlightening in their mind, joy, fellowship with the Father and the Son, the experience of divine love, peace, confidence in prayer, and assurance at the prospect of Jesus's

---

40. Chafer, "The Doctrine of Sin, Part 2," 21.

41. Lewis Sperry Chafer, "The Doctrine of Sin, Part 3," *Bibliotheca Sacra* 92, no. 366 (1935): 153.

42. Lewis Sperry Chafer, "The Doctrine of Sin, Part 4," *Bibliotheca Sacra* 92, no. 368 (1935): 394.

return.[43] Sin was not less offensive to God when committed by the believer, either; instead, "sin is always equally sinful and condemnable whether it be committed by the saved or the unsaved."[44] Yet God dealt differently with the sins of his own people and the sins of the unregenerate. The unsaved were called to belief and repentance; the saved to confession.[45] When the Christian turned to Christ, burdened by sin, he or she discovered a Father like the father of the prodigal son who kissed his son even before he could repent; God was predisposed in Christ to be propitious toward his children.[46] Chafer marveled at this love. "How persistent is the thought that God's heart must be softened by our tears! And, yet, how marvelous is the assurance that He is already the propitiation for our sins!"[47] In response to God's forgiveness and love, the Christian could now rely on God's Word, Christ's intercession, and the indwelling Holy Spirit to resist sin.[48]

God had further made divine provision to free Christians from the power of sin. This provision was located primarily in baptism, not baptism by water, but baptism by the Spirit, which brought about a spiritual transformation. "Christ being the righteousness of God, the believer, when thus joined to Him, is 'made' the righteousness of God *in Him* (2 Cor. 5:21) ... and by the blood of Christ is 'made nigh' (Eph. 2:13)."[49] The whole world would be freed from the power of sin in the new heaven and new earth, the initiation of which was one aspect of Christ's death on the cross; his death also brought about the defeat of principalities and powers, future national salvation of Israel, and millennial and eternal blessing of gentiles.[50]

---

43. Lewis Sperry Chafer, "The Doctrine of Sin, Part 5, Section 2," *Bibliotheca Sacra* 93, no. 370 (1936):148–49.

44. Chafer, "The Doctrine of Sin, Part 5, Section 2," 395.

45. Chafer, "The Doctrine of Sin, Part 5, Section 2," 397. Chafer also condemned in an aside the "Arminian notion" that a Christian who sinned must be saved again, an idea he said had "wrought untold injury to uncounted millions."

46. Chafer, "The Doctrine of Sin, Part 5, Section 2," 397–98.

47. Chafer, "The Doctrine of Sin, Part 5, Section 2," 398.

48. Chafer, "The Doctrine of Sin, Part 5, Section 2," 408–9.

49. Lewis Sperry Chafer, "The Doctrine of Sin, Part 5, Section 1," *Bibliotheca Sacra* 93, no. 369 (1936): 18.

50. Lewis Sperry Chafer, "The Doctrine of Sin, Part 5, Section 3," *Bibliotheca Sacra* 93, no. 371 (1936): 265.

In sum, sin was "any want of conformity to the character of God, whether it be in act, disposition, or state."[51] Sin was imputed to humanity through Adam's failure, and this original sin likewise bestowed upon every human an inborn inclination toward sin, a sin nature; all persons thus found themselves before God under a "judicial state of sin," as well as being guilty of individually committed sins.[52] Chafer did not qualify sins as more or less offensive to God based on the knowledge of the sinner, because all sins offended God's holiness equally.[53] Central to his thought was the notion sin could not be overcome at a personal or a universal level apart from God, specifically apart from Christ's death.[54]

Other dispensationalists maintained a similar view of sin and its defeat.[55] Focused primarily on individual sins, their hamartiology afforded little space for broader, social sins, even to understandings of such sins disconnected from the social gospel. Additionally, likely as a corollary to their emphasis on Christ's redemption being the sole antidote for sin, they paid little attention to the possibility of human efforts ameliorating the earthly effects of sin. Arguments for a Christian responsibility to address public ills, such as those found in Henry's later *Uneasy Conscience,* do not appear in their writings on sin. Jesus was the remedy. As a basis for social action, their hamartiology provided scant rationale for cultural engagement aimed at righting the world's wrongs.

SALVATION

Despite their emphasis on personal rather than social sins, dispensationalists were not, strictly speaking, individualistic in their theology of salvation, occupied solely by matters of personal salvation. They also wrote of earthly and cosmic aspects of Christ's redemption. As Gaebelein summarized in a

---

51. Chafer, *Major Bible Themes,* 144.

52. Chafer, *Major Bible Themes,* 144–47.

53. Chafer, *Major Bible Themes,* 148.

54. Chafer, "The Doctrine of Sin, Part 5, Section 3," 263, 265. As a practical, daily reality, however, Chafer wrote in *Major Bible Themes,* p. 151, that Christ's death achieves forgiveness for the sinner, but not the saint—forgiveness for the saint is brought about by confession: "'The Christian's sin is forgiven, not on the ground of believing unto salvation, but on the ground of confessing the sin' (1 John 1:9)."

55. See, for instance, Arno C. Gaebelein, *The Work of Christ: Past, Present and Future* (New York: Our Hope, 1913), Kindle, 11.

celebration of the effects of Christ's death, resurrection, and ongoing rule, "Every wrong will be righted on earth, and present-day evils and oppression, crime and vice, poverty and sickness will be abolished. Only He has the power to do this. ... Groaning creation is to be delivered."[56]

However, earthly aspects of salvation were not part of Christ's present work but his future work. Gaebelein reserved harsh criticism for those who thought "scientists" or "the work of man" could in any way remove the curse under which creation groaned.[57]

> There is much confusion in the minds of Christians about the present and future work of Christ. Many speak of the Lord being now the King of kings and Lord of lords, reigning over the earth. ... The church, according to this teaching, is His Kingdom, and that kingdom is gradually being enlarged under His spiritual reign until the whole world has been brought into this kingdom. All of this is wrong. The Lord Jesus Christ will reign over the earth; He will have a kingdom of glory, of righteousness and peace on this earth; the nations of the earth will have to submit to His government, but all this is still to come. It will be accomplished with His visible Return to the earth, when He will claim as the second Man the dominion of the earth. His kingly rule is future. His present work is of another nature.[58]

Dispensationalists also tend to locate earthly aspects of salvation within God's promises to Israel rather than the church. Scofield wrote, "It is perceived that just as distinctly as Israel stands connected with temporal and earthly things, so distinctly does the church stand connected with spiritual and heavenly things."[59]

The result of viewing the redemption of all creation and the temporal benefits of salvation as either future promises or promises to Israel was a restriction of Christ's present work—and the current effects of his redemptive sacrifice—to the salvation of lost souls. Chafer's theology of salvation

---

56. Gaebelein, *The Work of Christ*, 45.
57. Gaebelein, *The Work of Christ*, 45.
58. Gaebelein, *The Work of Christ*, 17.
59. C. I. Scofield, *Rightly Dividing the Word of Truth (2 Timothy 2:15): Being Ten Outline Studies of the More Important Divisions of Scripture* (Philadelphia: Philadelphia School of the Bible, 1921), Kindle, 12.

included negative and positive benefits, both focused on the individual; working together, they brought about a sinner's salvation. Negatively, Chafer wrote that Christ substituted himself for sinners, suffering for their sins and taking on himself the judgment due them.[60] Positively, he wrote that Christ imputed to sinners his righteousness, making them holy before God.[61] These two "features of salvation—the gift of eternal life and the gift of righteousness," Chafer presented as "counterparts of the one great fact of union with Christ."[62]

Furthermore, the Mosaic law was eclipsed by Christ's sacrifice because Christ was the end of the law. Yet in keeping with the dispensational view of multiple eras and covenants throughout Scripture, Chafer carefully distinguished between gentiles and Jewish people in their relationship to the law. "The law-covenant was strictly a conditional agreement which conditioned divine blessings upon human faithfulness"; for the gentile believer, it was therefore "superseded by 'grace and truth' (John 1:17)."[63] For the Jewish person, however, it would never be set aside completely.

> Nevertheless, though the legal principle is now done away—and of necessity, because of its incompatibility with the rule for conduct which grace provides—it will, when Israel returns to the land under Messiah's reign, be reestablished. ... Though it is the very law which Moses commanded that Israel will do, their situation will be altered. Christ will be on the Throne of David reigning over Israel and the whole earth; Satan will be in the abyss; and this law, rather than being merely addressed to Israel, will be written on their hearts (Jer. 31:33), but its legal character is not changed. It is the law which Moses commanded them.[64]

Christ's death brought redemption to Israel, but that redemption included the law and was not realized yet; similarly, he died to levy judgment upon fallen angels, to purify heaven, and to rescue "the whole cosmos world"—all

---

60. Lewis Sperry Chafer, "Soteriology," *Bibliotheca Sacra* 103, no. 410 (1946): 140, 142.
61. Chafer, "Soteriology," 155.
62. Chafer, "Soteriology," 155.
63. Lewis Sperry Chafer, "Soteriology, Part 2," *Bibliotheca Sacra* 103, no. 411 (1946): 261.
64. Chafer, "Soteriology, Part 2," 262.

to be experienced as future realities rather than present ones.[65] In Chafer's view, Christ's redemption of the world did not extend to the transformation of earthly societies now. Indeed, his outlook on the reconciliation of the world devoted little attention to social renewal at all, even in the future; his attention was instead occupied with the question of how Christ's death could be said to reconcile the entirety of humanity if that reconciliation was only effective for the believer.[66]

The doctrine of propitiation formed another key leg of Chafer's soteriology. He relied heavily on Scofield to define the doctrine, devoting three pages in one of his *Bibliotheca Sacra* articles to quoting Scofield's biblical exegesis of key passages.[67] Propitiation centered on God vindicating his own righteousness and law through Christ's sacrifice, and this vindication became the basis for forgiveness of sins.[68] With such an understanding of propitiation in view, Chafer objected to the idea that a sinner could cry to God for mercy. He referred to Jesus's story in Luke 18 about a tax collector to illustrate the common misunderstanding that this kind of cry would be acceptable to God. "God cannot be merciful toward the sinner in the sense of being generous or lenient, and the publican did not ask God to do such an impossible thing."[69] Instead, as an Old Testament believer, the tax collector asked for mercy on the basis of an offering, which justified him in requesting propitiation. In the current dispensation, New Testament believers were saved by trusting in the forgiveness Christ had earned. "Men are not saved by coaxing mercy out of God; they are saved when they dare to believe that God has been merciful enough to provide a Savior and that He is propitious."[70] Similarly to redemption, propitiation was brought about for the whole world, as 1 John 2:2 states, but it was effective only for the elect, and Chafer did not mention social or cultural renewal as an outcome of God's propitiation of the χοσμος (*cosmos*).[71]

---

65. Chafer, "Soteriology, Part 2," 275.
66. Chafer, "Soteriology, Part 2," 279–82.
67. Lewis Sperry Chafer, "Soteriology, Part 5," *Bibliotheca Sacra* 103, no. 412 (1946): 391–93.
68. Chafer, "Soteriology, Part 5," 391, 394.
69. Chafer, "Soteriology, Part 5," 394.
70. Chafer, "Soteriology, Part 5," 394.
71. Chafer, "Soteriology, Part 5," 394.

Related to propitiation was the judgment of the sin nature brought about by Christ's sacrifice. Such judgment did not eradicate sin altogether in the current age. "It can never be made too emphatic that this judgment does not consist in that nature being destroyed, nor is its essential power diminished."[72] Instead, the Holy Spirit was God's provision to combat the sin nature: "It is to be controlled in the believer by the superior power of the Holy Spirit."[73] Christ's death could not be expected to remove sin altogether from his people, but inasmuch as they relied on the Spirit, they could overcome it. By contrast, unbelievers remained captive to sin apart from the Spirit; any illusion of restraining sin among the unsaved or in society at large ran counter to Chafer's view of the sin nature and the current judgment upon sin brought about by Christ's death. He compared the sin nature to Satan, already doomed but still loose, and perhaps even more active than ever in this current age.[74]

The ultimate defeat of Satan would be brought about by a specific set of eschatological steps, beginning with Satan and his angels waging war against God's angels, then being confined for a thousand years, and finally being banished to the lake of fire for eternity.[75] In like manner, Christ's death offered a peace with God that could be realized now by individuals reconciled to him and peace between Jews and gentiles unified in Christ, but the peace it earned for the world would unfold in a prescribed, future program.[76]

> And, finally, there is a peace to be realized throughout the universe — foreshadowed in the thousand years under the Prince of Peace — which will be established by the judgment of Satan (Col. 2:14, 15) and of all the forces of evil. ... The program which Christ will follow is clearly predicted: first, He shall judge the nations (Matt. 25:31–46), having crushed their resistance (Ps. 2:1–3, 8, 9; Isa. 63:1–6); second, He shall put down all rule and authority, which will require a millennium of years and involve the subjection of both angelic and human spheres (1 Cor. 15:25, 26); and, third, He shall restore to God a universal

---

72. Chafer, "Soteriology, Part 5," 396.
73. Chafer, "Soteriology, Part 5," 396.
74. Chafer, "Soteriology, Part 5," 396.
75. Lewis Sperry Chafer, "Soteriology, Part 12," *Bibliotheca Sacra* 104, no. 413 (1947): 4.
76. Chafer, "Soteriology, Part 12," 6–8.

kingdom of peace in which the Son eternally reigns by the authority of the Father, and God is all in all (1 Cor. 15:27, 28).

Any longing for peace in the world today could only be temporarily and imperfectly fulfilled; perfect peace for the entire universe was a future promise of God, not a present possibility.

During the age before Christ's return (the current church age), those who were separated from God were lost, bereft of the eternal benefits granted a believer, trapped in their sin nature and living under the power of Satan.[77] God's grace to save could not be brought about by human effort but belonged to him alone to exercise.[78] In gospel presentations, Chafer therefore recommended that a minister emphasize (1) the inability of sinners to save themselves, (2) God's faithfulness to rescue any who put their trust in Jesus, (3) an individual application of the Bible's promises to the repentant sinner, (4) the glory of God made manifest in the unimportant and insignificant turning to him, (5) assurance of salvation found in trusting Jesus rather than good works, and (6) the eternal punishment of the unsaved versus the eternal blessedness of the saved.[79] Harry A. Ironside's booklet on the gospel similarly explored seven "designations" or facets of the good news, including God's grace and God's glory, and it concluded with consequences for acceptance or rejection.[80]

In sum, dispensational soteriology emphasized the sinner's standing before God, an inability to save himself or herself, and the salvation offered through the gospel. While dispensationalists acknowledged the world-transforming aspects of Christ's redemption, their theology of salvation provided no intrinsic motivation for social action, even as an implication of the gospel. Instead, Christ was the solution to worldly problems, with his resolution occurring in the future. Human efforts at fixing social ills were understood to be vain or presumptuous. In the current church age, the minister of God was to be focused on the gospel and the individual-transforming aspects of Christ's redemption.

---

77. Lewis Sperry Chafer, "The Saving Work of the Triune God, Part 2," *Bibliotheca Sacra* 105, no. 420 (1948): 394–96.

78. Chafer, "The Saving Work of the Triune God, Part 2," 397.

79. See Lewis Sperry Chafer, "Gospel Preaching," *Bibliotheca Sacra* 95, no. 379 (1938): 343–64.

80. See Harry A. Ironside, *What Is the Gospel? Understanding What It Is and What It Is Not* (Eureka, MT: Lighthouse Trails, 2016), Kindle.

ANTHROPOLOGY

Dispensationalism's view of humanity includes both creation in the image of God and the corruption of that image through the fall, but human sin and inability apart from Christ are accentuated. Indeed, humanity's relationship to God constitutes the underpinning of dispensational anthropology and is its clear preoccupation. This focus could be a strength, but arguably contributes to less attention being devoted elsewhere. Human achievements accomplished by common grace and general fulfillment of the cultural mandate in Genesis 1:28, for instance, played virtually no role in Chafer's anthropology.

Chafer took care when introducing the doctrine of anthropology to distinguish between the secular discipline and a biblical approach. There could be no genuine rapprochement between them, in his view. "The former is extra-Biblical and avoids every feature of Scripture revelation. The latter is intra-Biblical and confines itself to the Word of God and such corroborating human experience as may give confirming witness to the truth disclosed."[81] Chafer did not deny that secular, or extrabiblical anthropology could explore the "emotional and intellectual aspects of human life, or that which is psychological"; yet he saw this exploration as less significant than intrabiblical anthropology because it overlooked the "deeper realms of things moral, spiritual, and eternal." [82] Most significantly, extrabiblical anthropology overlooked God and his place in human creation and experience. While psychology could not inform intrabiblical anthropology, therefore, intrabiblical anthropology could provide sound psychological insights. The Bible was not a psychology or anthropology textbook; however, "[a] reverent study of Scripture will undoubtedly lead to the recognition of a well-defined system of psychology, on which the whole scheme of redemption is based. Great truths regarding human nature are presupposed in and accepted by the Old Testament and the New Testament."[83]

---

81. Lewis Sperry Chafer, "Anthropology," *Bibliotheca Sacra* 100, no. 398 (1943): 220.

82. Chafer, "Anthropology," 220–21.

83. Chafer, "Anthropology," 222. On p. 224, Chafer wrote further, "Over against all this, the revelation regarding man as found in the Word of God extends into many fields where a man-conceived anthropology could not enter—the true manner of creation, the original estate of man, his fall, the real cause of death in the world, the new birth, the ground of a right morality, and the resurrection of the body. Extra-Biblical anthropology will be searched in vain for any reference to these themes; yet these are realities in human life and as such become determining factors in a worthy psychology."

Chafer divided his study of anthropology into five themes: humanity's origin, the time of humanity's origin, humanity's state when created, the fall, and sin.[84] His doctrine of sin was covered above; what follows below is a summary of his thought on the other four themes.

HUMANITY'S ORIGIN

Fundamentalism's general opposition to theories of evolution, surveyed in chapter 2, shaped much of Chafer's discussion on the origin of humanity. He viewed human beginnings as the foundation upon which the framework of anthropology was built; thus, the competing visions of evolution and creation were of central importance, and he spared no respect for the system that did not require a divine hand.

> Two systems of thought—one a pure supposition, the other a reve-
> lation—purport to answer the question of man's origin. The suppo-
> sition—the evolutionary theory—is a speculation, conjecture, and
> assumption which is the best solution the unregenerate or spiritually
> unenlightened finite mind can construct. The revelation embodies a
> series of truths which are harmonious and reasonable, if the Person,
> purpose, and power of the Creator are recognized.[85]

Common antievolution arguments used by popular-level fundamentalist leaders appeared in Chafer's critique as well. He wrote that the evolutionary hypothesis offered no proof, no basis or motivation for morality, and no convincing fossil evidence: "The most unprovable items are set forth with a prejudice in favor of the evolutionary theory which is wholly detrimental to the theory advanced."[86] He also echoed the familiar concern that evolution formed humans in the image of the ape rather than that of God.[87] By contrast, God's revelation upheld that humans were created in God's likeness. Chafer did not explore the implication of the *imago Dei* in human behavior and society, but he upheld it as the more reasonable, biblical counter to evolution's diminishment of humanity.

---

84. Chafer, "Anthropology," 225–26.
85. Chafer, "Anthropology," 226.
86. Chafer, "Anthropology," 226, 228, 230.
87. Chafer, "Anthropology," 232.

THE TIME OF HUMANITY'S ORIGIN

Opposition to the doctrine of evolution further shaped Chafer's investigation of the timing of human beginnings. Scholars in various evolution-influenced fields could not agree about the time humanity came into being; thus, "what these men assert as to the age of the human family varies to such a degree that all claims of infallibility are shattered."[88] Yet Chafer was willing to grant that James Usher's chronology, placing human creation at 4004 BC, was based on an unnecessarily strict interpretation of biblical chronology and did not need to be defended as theologically necessary. Without proposing an exact date, he alluded to the potential time of creation being several thousand years earlier, and he argued this extension was sufficient to incorporate the genuine evidence for the age of humanity's existence offered by various disciplines.

> It follows that the usual reckoning may be so extended as to meet any reasonable requirement of scientific facts respecting the time of man's origin, without the perversion of any part of Scripture or the violation of any law of hermeneutics. ... The reasonable extension of human history back several thousand years beyond the dates proposed by Usher—which extension does not conflict, as before stated, with the Biblical record—allows sufficient time for all justified contentions of the historian, the geologist, the archaeologist, and the philologist.[89]

Chafer closed his consideration of the timing of humanity's origin by refuting polygenism and pre-adamitism as explanations for the diversity of human races. Instead, he contended, racial features could be formed by divine control or natural influences, but the human family remained singular and united.[90]

HUMANITY'S STATE WHEN CREATED

Chafer devoted most of his attention to the immaterial or spiritual aspects when examining the state of humanity at creation. In answer to the question of whether each human soul was created directly by God or as part of the physical procreation of a person's parents, Chafer sided with the latter,

---

88. Chafer, "Anthropology," 236.
89. Chafer, "Anthropology," 238–39.
90. Chafer, "Anthropology," 243.

traducian view. Both positions had admirable proponents, he conceded, including Charles Hodge for the former, but traducianism better explained the sin nature and better maintained Christ's full humanity.[91] Chafer also explored the dichotomous or trichotomous debate concerning humanity's being, concluding in a middle-ground manner that both were correct, because the Bible used the terms "soul" and "spirit" uniquely and synonymously. "In other words, the Bible supports both *dichotomy* and *trichotomy*. The distinction between *soul* and *spirit* is as incomprehensible as life itself, and the efforts of men to frame definitions must always be unsatisfactory."[92] He further included heart and flesh alongside spirit and soul as biblically identified immaterial aspects of humanity, with the faculties of these immaterial aspects being intellect, sensibility, will, and conscience.[93]

The responsibility of the first human Chafer simplified to one command continuing until the present day: "He did the will of God."[94] Adam's task of cultivating creation Chafer largely ignored, writing only that "aside from the task of dressing and keeping the garden" Adam's responsibility was to obey God.[95] This single-minded focus allowed Chafer to draw a direct line between Adam and all of God's people after him and to uphold the central importance of Christ's redemption. However, it undercut the importance of pursuing cultural goods or social transformation in the present day, since Adam's original task was treated as incidental rather than significant and ongoing.

THE FALL

The moment sin entered the world through Adam's disobedience, death marked humanity. Chafer identified three types of death in the Bible: spiritual death, physical death, and the second death; spiritual death occurred immediately, physical death began its process at the same time, and the prospect of second death loomed ahead.[96] Spiritual death Chafer defined

---

91. Lewis Sperry Chafer, "Anthropology, Part 3, Section 2c," *Bibliotheca Sacra* 101, no. 401 (1944): 17–18.

92. Chafer, "Anthropology, Part 3, Section 2c," 19.

93. Chafer, "Anthropology, Part 3, Section 2c," 21–29; Lewis Sperry Chafer, "Anthropology, Part 3, Section 2d," *Bibliotheca Sacra* 101, no. 402 (1944): 132–48.

94. Lewis Sperry Chafer, "Anthropology, Part 3, Section 3," *Bibliotheca Sacra* 101, no. 403 (1944): 266.

95. Chafer, "Anthropology, Part 3, Section 3," 266.

96. Lewis Sperry Chafer, "Anthropology, Part 4," *Bibliotheca Sacra* 101, no. 404 (1944): 391.

as "separation of soul and spirit from God."[97] Although Adam's descendants were born with a sin nature, Adam experienced a change in his nature after previously knowing only spiritual life, a punishment Chafer portrayed as uniquely painful.

> When Adam sinned his first sin he experienced a conversion downwards. He became degenerate and depraved. He developed within himself a fallen nature which is contrary to God and is ever prone to evil. His constitution was altered fundamentally and he thus became a wholly different being from the one God had created.[98]

Every human after Adam inherited spiritual death, but that did not mean humans had nothing good in them. People often recognized even in the worst of others some good aspects. Yet in God's outlook, humanity was depraved because it was "without merit in his sight."[99] Any honest estimation of the human experience confirmed the existence of a sinful nature, the evidence of spiritual death.[100] For both the saved and unsaved, physical death was temporary, as all would be resurrected to eternal life, but spiritual death "if not healed by redeeming grace—merges into unending second death."[101]

In sum, Chafer's dispensational anthropology upheld the image of God in humanity but did not expect to see God's goodness reflected in the unredeemed or in societies at large. Humanity was too marred by spiritual death. Little optimism about social reform efforts was afforded, as humanity's chief characteristic was the need for a right relationship with God, and righteousness apart from this relationship was futile. Even the pre-fall task of caring for creation, which could correlate with cultivating cultural goods in the present day, was downplayed. Dispensational anthropology did strongly oppose evolution—a conviction that motivated interwar fundamentalists to oppose it in public school education—yet at the same time it offered little hope that society could be convinced to adopt such a conviction apart, perhaps, from widespread revival.

---

97. Chafer, "Anthropology, Part 4," 391.
98. Chafer, "Anthropology, Part 4," 394.
99. Chafer, "Anthropology, Part 4," 396.
100. Chafer, "Anthropology, Part 4," 399.
101. Chafer, "Anthropology, Part 4," 401.

THE CHURCH AND ESCHATOLOGY

Guided by a dispensational hermeneutic, theologians like Chafer, Scofield, and others regarded the church and the end times not simply as two loci of systematic theology but, more practically, as eras of God's interaction with humanity. The church age was the present; eschatology was the future. God's work in one differed from God's work in the other, as did the group around whom his redemptive plan revolved. Understanding ecclesiology and eschatology together gave the believer a clear understanding of what to expect both now and ahead.

These dispensational theologians believed the church to be "a company of people called out from the old creation into the new, being gathered by the Spirit into one organism or body of which Christ is the Head."[102] The church was birthed at Pentecost and would continue until it was raptured before the tribulation. In response to those who might believe the church began during Jesus's life and ministry, Chafer pointed out that the Gospels only used the word "church" twice, once about a general gathering rather than Christ's body (Matt 18:17), and once prophetically about the church to come after Jesus's death and resurrection (Matt 16:18).[103] Believers were incorporated into the church by baptism, though not water baptism. Instead, it was the baptism of the Spirit, "which reaches far beyond the limits of the outward ordinance of water baptism," that united the believer to Christ.[104] Once baptized by the Spirit, every believer was a part of the church, whether or not they joined a local church—though it was understood that most normally would—and the organization and operations of physical congregations were relatively unimportant. "There is little said in the Bible regarding the organization of churches, though there is nothing written to oppose it; and, since an organization is not in view, there is nothing written in the Bible as to membership in organized churches."[105]

The most significant characteristic of the church was that it was not Israel. Three groups of people existed in the current age: Jews, gentiles, and the church. Jews were the descendants of Isaac and Jacob, the "chosen earthly

---

102. Chafer, *Major Bible Themes*, 209.
103. Chafer, *Major Bible Themes*, 210.
104. Chafer, *Major Bible Themes*, 214.
105. Chafer, *Major Bible Themes*, 210.

people of God" who rejected Jesus's kingship at his incarnation but would be reconciled to him in the future; gentiles were non-Jews with whom God had made no special covenants in the past, though he often blessed them, and the gospel was now offered to them; finally, the church was the body of believers, made up mostly of gentiles, but also of some Jews who accepted the gospel.[106] While Jews and the church were both God's people, the church was best understood as a humanly unforeseen parenthesis in God's plan.[107] When Israel rejected Jesus as their king, God created a new "heavenly people" and focused his redemptive purposes on them for a time; God's promises to his "earthly people" would yet be fulfilled, though, as his redemptive focus would return to them in the end times.[108] Jesus in his incarnation thus had, effectively, a "twofold message and purpose ... a minister to Israel to confirm the promises made to the fathers ... [and] a minister that the Gentiles might glorify God for His mercy."[109] Vastly different futures awaited Israel and the church.

In response to Christians who might object to points of dispensational interpretation, Chafer argued they, too, were actually dispensationalists. Any believer who did not practice Old Testament sacrifices or hold Old Testament expectations was a dispensationalist in his view, although not all understood the "other and deeper distinctions which do confront the careful student of the Word of God."[110]

> (1) Any person is a dispensationalist who trusts the blood of Christ rather than bringing an animal sacrifice. (2) Any person is a dispensationalist who disclaims any right or title to the land which God covenanted to Israel for an everlasting inheritance. And (3), any person is a dispensationalist who observes the first day of the week rather than the seventh. To all this it will be replied that every Christian

---

106. Chafer, *Major Bible Themes*, 210–12.

107. Lewis Sperry Chafer, "Dispensationalism." *Bibliotheca Sacra* 93, no. 372 (1936): 407. On p. 401, Chafer cited without demurral a critic's clear summation of dispensationalism's outlook on Israel and Jesus's first coming: "Christ offered the Kingdom of Israel and ... it was rejected and postponed."

108. Chafer, *Major Bible Themes*, 214.

109. C. I. Scofield, "The Return of Christ in Relation to the Jew and the Earth," *Bibliotheca Sacra* 108, no. 432 (1951): 478.

110. Chafer, "Dispensationalism," 391.

does these things, which is obviously true; and it is equally true that, to a very considerable degree, all Christians are dispensationalists.[111]

In the current age, when a Jewish person died, they went to "Abraham's bosom," as described by Jesus in Luke 16:19–31, while a Christian went to be with Christ.[112] The interim state differed because the Jews were not yet reconciled to Christ. Their reconciliation would occur after the tribulation, which they would not escape, in the millennial kingdom. The church would be spared the tribulation, caught up in the air to meet its Savior before it began. As Scofield wrote:

> If you ask me whether the church goes through the great tribulation, I ask what church you mean. ... If you mean the mass of mere profession, yes. If you mean the church of the born-again ones, baptized by the Spirit into one body, the living body of Christ, I say No. That is the blessed hope of the church.[113]

During the millennium, Christians would enjoy "the responsible and highly interesting business of governing the millennial earth,"[114] yet the era would most importantly be marked by a mass returning of the Jews to their Savior and by the fulfillment of many of God's promises to them in the Old Testament and in the Gospels.[115] Following the millennium, Jewish eschatology and Christian eschatology would continue to diverge, though both eschatologies were eternal and blessed, with Israel receiving "a transformed earth under the reign of David's Son" and Christians receiving "the glories of the redeemed in heaven."[116]

---

111. Chafer, "Dispensationalism," 391.

112. Chafer, "Dispensationalism," 421.

113. C. I. Scofield, "The Return of Christ in Relation to the Church," *Bibliotheca Sacra* 109, no. 433 (1952): 88. In support of his intricate outline of end-times events, Scofield contested on p. 79 that the book of Revelation communicated clearly: "Let me say, once for all, that every symbol in the Revelation has either been used already in the Bible, where the meaning of it becomes familiar, or it is explained in the Revelation, in the immediate context."

114. Scofield, "Return of Christ in Relation to the Church," 88.

115. For an example of a promise in the Gospels being applied to Israel rather than the church, see Scofield, "Return of Christ in Relation to the Church," 84, where Scofield writes that Jesus's promise of going to prepare mansions is for Jews who will follow him rather than Christians: "Dear friends, let us not talk about our going to the *mansions* any more. They are not for us."

116. Chafer, "Dispensationalism," 425–26.

Although nothing in dispensationalism's theology of the church and the end times explicitly discouraged social action in the current age, much could implicitly deter it. Dispensationalists' designation of the church as God's "heavenly people" with a heavenly future, for instance, turned attention away from earthly concerns. The earth belonged to God's other people, the Jews. Nor could Christian principles be detected in any current earthly government. Scofield declaimed such a conception strongly during World War I.

> They have never governed for one fraction of a second under the Christian ideal—never once. There has been no such thing as a Christian nation. I used to have to argue that. I do not have to argue it now. I have but to point to the fact that in the scene where the gospel has been longest preached and where the civilization of which we have been so proud has won its greatest triumphs—right there the passions of men are let loose and they are murdering each other in hecatombs. ... The civilization of which we have been so proud has ended in bloodshed.[117]

Dispensational theology also views participation in the church more as a spiritual reality than an embodied practice. Believers are called to exercise the spiritual gifts imparted to them and to share the gospel, yet the church itself has no worldly responsibility. Chafer summarized: "Strictly speaking, the Church has no mission; for God has never commissioned her as a corporate body to undertake any task whatsoever."[118] With its lack of attention to the organization and mission of the church, dispensational ecclesiology might appear thin to some, but dispensationalists view it as a revitalized doctrine, brought to fresh life by a better understanding of the divisions of Scripture: "It was given to Martin Luther in the sixteenth century to reinstate the doctrine of salvation through faith alone, and, in the last century, it was given to J. N. Darby of England to reinstate the doctrine of the church."[119]

---

117. C. I. Scofield, "The Course and End of the Age," *Bibliotheca Sacra* 108, no. 429 (1951): 105–6.
118. Chafer, *Major Bible Themes*, 216.
119. Chafer, *Major Bible Themes*, 209.

A FUNDAMENTALIST THEOLOGY
OF SOCIAL ACTION

Now to the question at hand: were fundamentalist efforts to redeem society inconsistent with their dispensational theology? As the sections above have demonstrated, the answer to this question is both yes and no, because fundamentalist social action was partly consistent with dispensational theology and partly inconsistent: consistent by operating within a dispensational understanding of the Bible, sin, and salvation, but inconsistent by pushing against dispensational views of anthropology, the church, and eschatology. Fundamentalist social action also charted new ground theologically. Whereas dispensational theologians had an underdeveloped theology of culture and cultural engagement, dispensational activists began to chart a practical theology of cultural engagement at the grassroots level by entering the public fray.

Dispensational fundamentalists did not oppose evolutionism or alcohol in identical ways, but when viewed as a group in newspaper reporting on their activities, commonalities arise. Their outlook was consistently shaped by the Bible's teachings; they were alarmed by social movements that undermined those teachings; and paradoxically, they rarely argued from the Bible itself in support of their positions. Occasionally they accused opponents of undermining Scripture or religion, both of which they viewed as benefits to society, but more often they presented religion-free arguments—essentially, "secular" arguments based on reason, social consequences, and the common good. Most commonly of all, fundamentalist activists argued that the teaching of evolution and the legal sale of alcohol frayed the country's moral fiber, leading to negative consequences for the nation and its citizens.

When comparing the antievolution and pro-Prohibition campaigns of dispensational activists to formal dispensational theology, some elements align better than others. Overall, fundamentalist activists were faithful to the dispensational doctrine of Scripture. Though they framed arguments in terms of social outcomes, they held their positions based on biblical conviction. The Bible taught creation and denounced drunkenness; no one doubted that was why they cared about those issues. Fundamentalists also knew well that theological liberals, who questioned the inspiration and inerrancy of Scripture, supported evolution and some opposed Prohibition; organizing against both stances was, by proxy, a way to affirm Scripture. Additionally, in keeping with the dispensational divisions of Scripture, fundamentalists tended to avoid recourse to Old Testament verses about social righteousness in support of their positions. They worked to promote uprightness but not with arguments that ran counter to a dispensational view of the Bible.

Fundamentalist activism also accorded well with the dispensational doctrines of sin and salvation. While fundamentalists fought battles at the state and national levels, they believed the sin issues underlying those battles were personal. Specifically, fundamentalists did not see systemic sin at work in the teaching of evolution or in efforts to repeal Prohibition; rather, they saw sin and its mind-clouding effect harming and misleading individuals. Nor did they believe righteousness could be achieved by legislation, as proponents of the social gospel did. Instead, they believed good laws might mute sinfulness. The gospel defeated it. Activists like McPherson stressed that salvation provided the power to overcome drunkenness. Furthermore, salvation transformed individuals, but it did not transform the earth; worldly salvation was intended for the Jewish people in the end times. Fundamentalists never proposed an earthly utopia as the end goal of their activism.

Despite general alignment between dispensational fundamentalists' social efforts and dispensational theology, some discordance is evident in the areas of anthropology, ecclesiology, and eschatology. Opposition to evolution marked dispensational anthropology and fueled fundamentalist activism, but dispensational anthropology paid little attention to humanity's role in cultivating creation and societies and in bringing about cultural goods. Fundamentalists may have perceived a responsibility to pass laws that upheld biblical truth and values, but that responsibility was inadequately grounded in their anthropology. Additionally, dispensationalism viewed the reign of spiritual death over unredeemed humanity as complete, allowing no prospect for genuine righteousness. While the unbeliever might do good deeds occasionally, those deeds were incomplete in God's eyes and achieved no spiritual benefits. Could they therefore be expected to achieve social benefits? Even fundamentalists' modest hope that good laws might mitigate sin found little support in dispensational anthropology.

Similarly, the fundamentalists surveyed in this book maintained a clear distinction between Israel and the church, and between this age and the age to come; however, they also aimed for political achievements and social goods that extended beyond what their eschatology upheld as possible. Nothing in the premillennial dispensational vision implied that a nation in the present day could be convinced to legislate against immorality or that school districts could be moved to promote a biblical view of human origins. Such expectations fit the millennium perhaps, but not the church age. Even longing for widespread revival to bring about social change was friendlier to a postmillennial optimism than to dispensational eschatology. Furthermore, dispensational ecclesiology offered the church no role in world transformation and included no conception of the church and society mutually benefitting each other, such as that which a twentieth-century Reformed thinker like Abraham Kuyper could propose. Yet fundamentalists regularly used their churches to host political talks and rallies.

If fundamentalists' social action aligned only unevenly with their dispensational theology, then Henry's critique of fundamentalist disengagement aligned unevenly as well. Henry was aware of interwar fundamentalists' concern for select cultural issues, such as alcohol and alcoholism, so it is possible he grouped dispensational activists together with formal dispensational theologians as a rhetorical strategy, overstating his case to make a point. Aspects of Chafer's thought did, after all, explicitly discourage cultural engagement.

However, as chapters 2 and 3 of this study have demonstrated, dispensational activists skirted such limitations. By engaging in social action that conflicted with aspects of their own doctrine, they in effect began to chart a new theology of cultural engagement, developed by themselves rather than by professional theologians like Chafer. This theology was dispensational at its core and somewhat incoherent because it weakened core beams in dispensationalism's theological structure. Yet it did promote a Christian responsibility to oppose sin and disbelief using political means. In sum, this working theology of cultural engagement looked to the gospel alone for transformation but argued pragmatically for social restraints on evil. It placed ultimate hope in Christ's return but believed the world could, perhaps, be made a little better in the here and now. Contrary to criticisms that fundamentalists were disengaged or pessimistic, the interwar leaders who created this cultural theology became deeply involved in public issues, alternating between expectations of victory and fears about the consequences of defeat.

5

CONCLUSION

The central question this book sought to answer is whether interwar fundamentalists reflected evangelicalism's activist impulse, which David Bebbington defines to include both social and spiritual concerns, or whether they abandoned cultural engagement. More specifically, it investigated early interwar fundamentalists for evidence of disengagement from social concerns following the 1925 Scopes Trial. Did fundamentalists retreat, possibly due to the public shame of the trial, or did they continue to wield influence in the public square, particularly in support of Prohibition and in opposition to the teaching of evolution?

When viewed through the lens of newspaper reporting, the answer to this question is that fundamentalists continued in their social aims after the Scopes Trial. No hint of retreat can be found in newspaper articles published in New York, Pennsylvania, Illinois, and Ohio between 1920 and 1933. Nor was the trial portrayed as an embarrassment for conservative Christians. Though some columnists, such as critic H. L. Mencken, depicted much about fundamentalists in such a manner, the trial itself attracted mostly balanced coverage. Additionally, fundamentalists appeared to exit the trial with renewed motivation to continue the fight. New organizations formed, and old and new leaders emerged with rekindled energy to oppose the godless teaching of human evolution in public schools. Overall, both sides of the debate appeared to view the Scopes Trial as an introductory battle in a longer war, rather than a decisive skirmish.

A couple of further observations may be made. First, what the Scopes Trial failed to accomplish in deterring the social aims of interwar fundamentalists, the deaths of key fundamentalist leaders may have hastened. The sudden passing of William Jennings Bryan in the days after the Scopes Trial, followed by John Roach Straton a few years later, limited fundamentalists' ability to generate headlines. Although the deaths probably did not undermine grassroots opposition to evolutionism or support for Prohibition, the loss of both men did diminish fundamentalism's public voice. Bryan and Straton were followed by reporters on the national stage, making news around the country, and their social causes were well-known. By contrast, Billy Sunday's career was fading in the early interwar period, and though Aimee Semple McPherson's popularity was rising, she was not as closely associated in the national media with social causes. William Jennings Bryan, in particular, was irreplaceable. When he spoke on an issue, reporters tended to cover it. The deaths of Bryan, a presidential-level political figure, and Straton, a big-city New York pastor, likely slowed fundamentalism's momentum on public issues. No other leaders would prove capable of taking their places in the early interwar period.

Second, fundamentalism did not possess a coherent theology of cultural engagement. Dispensationalism was ascendant among fundamentalists, yet crucial aspects of its anthropology, ecclesiology, and eschatology undermined social efforts. In particular, dispensationalism included no cultural mandate stemming from Genesis 1:28, afforded the church no clear worldly responsibilities, and dismissed the prospect of social transformation in the current age. Christians had no earthly goals at all, strictly speaking, in the framework of dispensationalism, as heaven was the future home of believers. The earth was Israel's home. Although fundamentalist activists upheld dispensationalism's bibliology and hamartiology, which fueled their opposition to evolutionism and alcohol, they sought to bring about social change on these issues in a manner that was inconsistent with dispensationalism's organizing principle that God's purposes vary in different eras. The grassroots theology of cultural engagement they developed by their actions was therefore incoherent in key respects. Whether fundamentalist social efforts would have been more successful with a firmer theological grounding remains an open question.

This study raised a couple of other questions as well. As mentioned in the introduction, one question is how to understand Carl Henry's critique of fundamentalist disengagement. No definitive resolution will be offered here, just a couple of possible interpretations.

First, it is possible Henry overstated his case and downplayed fundamentalists' social concerns as a rhetorical strategy. After all, Henry himself had written a book on the Pacific Garden Mission in Chicago a few years before *The Uneasy Conscience of Modern Fundamentalism* was published. He was aware of the mission's fundamentalist history and its outreach ministry amid poverty and alcoholism. Seen in this light, Henry's critique was one of degree rather than of existence—fundamentalists engaged with some cultural issues, in his view, but not many and with insufficient emphasis.

A second, alternative possibility is that Henry viewed fundamentalists' social concerns as limited. His vision reached beyond a few hot-button cultural issues and evangelistic social outreach to education, government, the arts, and every aspect of civil society. It also included stances that were not rigidly conservative, such as cooperating with theological opponents to bring about the common good. Seen in this light, Henry's critique was one of focus—fundamentalists engaged with some issues, in his view, but their scope was too narrow and their posture too unyieldingly separatist.

Another question left unresolved by this study was whether fundamentalists withdrew from social action later in the interwar period or became further marginalized by its end. If either occurred, was the change sudden or a gradual shift? Based on newspaper reporting between 1920 and 1933, a gradual shift would seem more likely, but a study of reporting on fundamentalist cultural engagement between 1934 and the neo-evangelical emergence in the mid-1940s would do much to complete the picture. As with the question of Henry's critique, more research and analysis remain to be done.

One clear takeaway may be gleaned from this study, however: The Scopes Trial did nothing to dissuade fundamentalists from seeking to legislate against the social ills of evolutionism and alcohol. The trial was a significant event, but not a conclusive one, and was more energizing to both sides than disillusioning. Any interpretation of the Scopes Trial that sees a fundamentalist retreat in its wake must be viewed as inaccurate, which casts doubt on the larger, accompanying narrative about fundamentalism's peculiarity within evangelical history. Was the fundamentalist era truly an anomaly, a period when conservative Christians neglected the social activism that had otherwise marked evangelicals since the Great Awakening? Early interwar newspaper reporting suggests otherwise, as the observer can see in it a fundamentalist movement that continued to care deeply about positive cultural change. The primary conclusion to this study, therefore, is that interwar fundamentalists were just as thoroughly evangelical as the Moody-era revivalists before them and the neo-evangelical thought leaders after them, marked by biblicism, crucicentrism, conversionism—and activism.

For better and worse, evangelicals have always been marked by a desire to "enforce the ethics of the gospel" in the world. Interwar fundamentalists before and after the Scopes Trial were no different.

APPENDIX

—

ALPHABETICAL LISTING OF NEWSPAPERS

An alphabetical listing of newspapers included in the newspaperarchive.com database, 1920–1933, for the states of Illinois, New York, Ohio, and Pennsylvania.

ILLINOIS			
City	Newspaper	First issue	Last issue
Albany	Albany Review	09/20/1928	05/01/1930
Alton	Alton Daily Telegraph	01/03/1853	09/04/1962
Alton	Alton Evening Telegraph	02/01/1883	11/18/1995
Alton	Alton Grundy County Labor News	05/18/1889	12/11/1958
Alton	Alton Pioneer	10/20/1924	05/29/1925
Alton	Alton Shurtleff Pioneer	09/16/1925	03/21/1951
Alton	Alton Telegraph	03/09/1836	10/31/2012
Alton	Alton Telegraph and Democratic Review	06/08/1849	04/06/1987
Alton	Alton Weekly Telegraph	05/05/1851	10/03/1987
Amboy	Amboy Lee County Farm News	06/06/1922	12/19/1922
Arlington Heights	Arlington Heights Cook County Herald	01/12/1901	04/03/1970
Arlington Heights	Arlington Heights Daily Herald Suburban Chicago	01/05/1901	11/12/2019
Arlington Heights	Arlington Heights Herald	09/13/1912	09/09/1977
Arlington Heights	Arlington Heights Sunday Herald	08/22/1930	08/22/1930
Ashton	Ashton Gazette	07/14/1904	12/21/1922

Beardstown	*Beardstown Illinoian Star*	01/20/1902	12/29/1977
Beardstown	*Beardstown Weekly Enterprise*	01/24/1913	01/04/1924
Bensenville	*Bensenville DuPage County Register*	12/12/1903	12/28/1970
Blue Island	*Blue Island Suburban Star*	08/29/1930	12/28/1934
Blue Island	*Blue Island Sun Standard*	04/04/1913	09/29/1977
Blue Island	*Sun Standard*	11/08/1928	12/29/1977
Bowen	*Bowen Chronicle*	09/20/1900	12/30/1937
Brimfield	*Brimfield News*	04/06/1888	12/04/1975
Brookfield	*Brookfield Suburban Magnet*	07/05/1913	08/09/1945
Calumet City	*Calumet City Pointer*	06/13/1924	06/18/2000
Calumet City	*Calumet City Times*	05/28/1928	02/11/1999
Carbondale	*Carbondale Daily Free Press*	10/12/1903	07/11/1953
Carbondale	*Carbondale Free Press*	01/07/1899	06/30/1949
Centralia	*Centralia Daily Sentinel*	10/12/1869	08/24/1953
Centralia	*Centralia Evening Sentinel*	11/01/1906	12/31/1975
Centralia	*Centralia Sentinel*	05/28/1863	03/13/1967
Chadwick	*Chadwick Review*	01/02/1930	10/18/1945
Champaign	*Champaign Banker Farmer*	12/01/1913	03/01/1926
Chicago	*ADA News*	04/07/1932	12/26/1977
Chicago	*Chicago Auburn Community Booster*	09/22/1921	07/22/1950
Chicago	*Chicago Auburn Parker*	01/21/1932	12/19/1951
Chicago	*Chicago Austin News*	06/30/1932	08/26/1976
Chicago	*Chicago Better Farming*	05/01/1913	03/01/1925
Chicago	*Chicago Collyers Eye*	04/06/1918	12/30/1922
Chicago	*Chicago Daily Illini*	10/07/1898	12/13/1975
Chicago	*Chicago Daily National Hotel Reporter*	01/02/1918	12/30/1922
Chicago	*Chicago Daily News*	10/09/1879	08/15/1945
Chicago	*Chicago Daily Tribune*	03/01/1878	08/15/1945
Chicago	*Chicago Dziennik Chicagoski*	07/27/1899	06/23/1922
Chicago	*Chicago Englewood Economist*	09/11/1906	02/06/1924
Chicago	*Chicago Englewood Times*	01/20/1905	12/28/1928
Chicago	*Chicago Express*	05/20/1882	05/18/1966
Chicago	*Chicago Farmers Wife*	01/01/1906	04/01/1939

Chicago	*Chicago Heights Star*	07/13/1911	04/23/2000
Chicago	*Chicago Merchants Telegram*	11/12/1919	07/12/1923
Chicago	*Chicago Packer*	04/13/1907	06/17/1939
Chicago	*Chicago Prairie Farmer*	01/01/1841	12/29/1923
Chicago	*Chicago Sentinel*	01/14/1911	01/13/1949
Chicago	*Chicago South End Reporter*	12/31/1929	12/28/1978
Chicago	*Chicago Star Publications*	04/19/1906	04/07/1971
Chicago	*Chicago Suburban Star*	01/29/1925	05/13/1932
Chicago	*Chicago Sullivans Englewood Times*	11/17/1922	12/26/1924
Chicago	*Chicago Tribune*	04/23/1849	12/31/1977
Chicago	*News Journal*	01/10/1923	12/29/1977
Chicago	*Southend Reporter*	12/06/1912	12/29/1977
Chicago	*Southtown Economist*	01/07/1921	02/26/1964
Chicago	*Suburbanite Economist*	04/28/1905	12/31/1975
Chicago Heights	*Chicago Heights Star*	04/12/1901	06/29/2000
Christopher	*Christopher Progress*	01/03/1929	12/28/1977
Collinsville	*Collinsville Advertiser*	03/02/1918	02/25/1922
DePue	*De Pue Leader*	01/05/1917	12/28/1945
Decatur	*Decatur Daily Review*	01/22/1876	08/31/1931
Decatur	*Decatur Evening Herald*	01/01/1927	08/31/1931
Decatur	*Decatur Herald*	07/11/1885	07/31/1931
Decatur	*Decatur Review*	10/02/1878	08/03/1930
Decatur	*Decatur Review Advertiser*	03/13/1931	08/21/1931
Deer Creek	*Deer Creek Progress*	04/24/1919	09/15/1921
Deerfield	*Deerfield Lake County Township Records*	01/01/1850	04/13/1976
Deerfield	*Deerfield Township Atlas and Plat Book*	09/26/1926	09/26/1926
Deerfield	*Deerfield Township Auditors Record*	06/12/1889	03/26/1974
Deerfield	*Deerfield Township Clerk Miscellaneous Files*	01/01/1856	06/23/1959
Deerfield	*Deerfield Township Election Papers*	10/16/1868	04/04/1926
Deerfield	*Deerfield Township Highway Commissioners Record*	04/16/1889	04/19/1962

DeKalb	*DeKalb Daily Chronicle*	01/02/1918	12/31/1930
Dixon	*Dixon Evening Telegraph*	03/31/1885	12/31/1977
Downers Grove	*Downers Grove Reporter*	01/18/1895	12/29/1922
Earlville	*Earlville Leader*	01/04/1883	12/29/1977
East St. Louis	*East St. Louis Daily Journal*	10/01/1920	12/31/1934
East St. Louis	*East St. Louis Daily Livestock Reporter*	12/01/1916	12/10/1960
East St. Louis	*East St. Louis Daily National Live Stock Reporter*	12/01/1916	09/13/1957
East St. Louis	*East St. Louis Journal*	08/05/1917	04/11/1941
Edwardsville	*Edwardsville Intelligencer*	11/18/1869	12/31/1977
Evanston	*Evanston Lake Shore News*	05/08/1912	09/28/1923
Flora	*Flora Journal Record*	01/06/1921	12/30/1926
Flora	*Flora Record*	01/01/1920	12/30/1920
Forest Park	*Forest Park Review*	10/20/1917	12/28/1977
Forrest	*Forrest Corn Belt News*	08/17/1933	12/29/1938
Franklin Grove	*Franklin Grove Franklin Reporter*	03/22/1906	12/28/1922
Franklin Park	*Franklin Park Beacon*	06/23/1922	04/13/1928
Freeburg	*Freeburg Tribune*	01/09/1904	12/29/1977
Freeport	*Freeport Journal Standard*	01/03/1916	11/17/2016
Galesburg	*Galesburg Evening Mail*	02/14/1927	02/14/1927
Galesburg	*Galesburg Republican Register*	06/11/1903	09/30/1925
Galva	*Galva News*	01/05/1916	12/29/1977
Geneseo	*Geneseo Republic*	01/27/1893	12/25/1938
Gillespie	*Gillespie Record*	01/06/1926	05/26/1927
Harrisburg	*Harrisburg Daily Register*	12/22/1919	08/31/1993
Harvard	*Harvard Herald*	12/23/1887	12/30/1977
Harvard	*Harvard Herald And Independent*	12/11/1924	01/18/1940
Harvard	*Harvard Herald Independent*	10/23/1924	12/04/1924
Harvey	*Harvey Tribune*	01/03/1930	06/28/1973
Henry	*Henry Current News*	12/02/1920	06/02/1921
Henry	*Henry News Republican*	06/09/1921	06/08/1977
Henry	*Henry Republican*	10/07/1869	06/02/1921
Herrin	*Herrin Daily Journal*	02/28/1918	11/19/1951
Highland Park	*Highland Park Press*	08/08/1912	09/13/1951

Hillsdale	*Hillsdale Tri Village Review*	01/02/1930	05/01/1930
Industry	*Industry Press*	03/23/1916	12/29/1921
Jacksonville	*Jacksonville Courier*	07/09/1890	10/18/2013
Jacksonville	*Jacksonville Daily Journal*	04/01/1891	12/31/1982
Jacksonville	*Jacksonville Illinois Daily Courier*	03/05/1883	03/31/1982
Jacksonville	*Jacksonville Journal*	06/22/1875	02/08/1977
Jacksonville	*Jacksonville Sentinel*	02/17/1871	10/29/1978
Joliet	*Joliet Farmers Weekly Review*	04/24/1929	12/29/1977
La Harpe	*La Harpe Quill*	10/13/1898	04/12/1932
Lacon	*Lacon Home Journal*	01/26/1910	12/29/1921
Ladd	*Ladd Journal*	01/10/1929	12/31/1942
Lanark	*Lanark Gazette*	01/06/1892	02/21/1923
Lawrenceville	*Lawrenceville Lawrence County News*	01/07/1909	12/27/1922
Liberty	*Liberty Bee*	01/11/1933	12/27/1933
Libertyville	*Libertyville Independent*	04/28/1916	08/02/1923
Macomb	*Macomb Daily By Stander*	07/01/1920	07/07/1922
Marion	*Marion Daily Republican*	06/01/1925	06/01/1925
Marion	*Marion Evening Post*	06/02/1925	08/01/1941
Marion	*Marion Semi Weekly Leader*	01/18/1916	12/29/1922
Marshall	*Marshall Clark County Democrat*	12/12/1917	12/29/1977
Marshall	*Marshall Herald*	08/19/1908	12/12/1975
Mason City	*Mason City Banner Times*	03/19/1925	08/16/1928
Mattoon	*Mattoon Journal*	05/11/1878	07/15/1966
McHenry	*McHenry Plaindealer*	08/11/1875	06/01/1933
Midlothian	*Midlothian Bremen Messenger*	11/07/1930	04/21/1977
Midlothian	*Midlothian Messenger*	11/07/1930	03/14/1947
Moline	*Moline Daily Dispatch*	07/08/1896	12/31/1969
Monmouth	*Monmouth College Catalog*	06/25/1857	01/01/2009
Monmouth	*Monmouth College Newspaper Courier*	11/01/1867	05/07/2010
Monmouth	*Monmouth College Newspaper Oracle*	06/01/1897	11/20/1998
Monmouth	*Monmouth College Ravelings*	01/01/1853	01/01/1977
Monmouth	*Monmouth College Society Catalogue 1856 to 1880*	06/01/1880	05/01/1924

Monmouth	Monmouth College Yearbook Ravelings	01/01/1892	01/01/2002
Monmouth	Monmouth Daily Atlas	07/01/1905	12/31/1923
Monmouth	Monmouth Daily Review	01/03/1921	03/31/1921
Monmouth	Monmouth Republican Atlas	06/14/1895	10/16/1924
Monmouth	Monmouth Review	12/08/1871	10/15/1924
Monmouth	Monmouth Review Atlas	03/04/1904	12/31/1924
Morgan Park	Morgan Park Suburban Star	01/03/1924	07/05/1929
Morgan Park	Suburban Star	07/17/1924	10/07/1926
Mount Carmel	Mount Carmel Register	12/11/1844	08/31/2016
Mount Prospect	Mount Prospect Daily Herald	07/18/1930	01/23/1931
Mount Prospect	Mount Prospect Herald	01/03/1930	04/11/1969
Mount Prospect	Mount Prospect Review	12/14/1932	01/14/1942
Mount Vernon	Mount Vernon Register News	07/28/1863	12/31/1977
Mount Vernon	Mount Vernon Daily Herald	06/10/1929	06/10/1929
Mount Vernon	Mount Vernon Daily News	03/14/1892	03/20/1920
Mount Vernon	Mount Vernon Register News	01/03/1921	10/31/1977
Murphysboro	Murphysboro Daily Independent	07/02/1923	10/31/1949
Oak Park	Oak Park Directory	01/01/1886	01/01/1930
Oak Park	Oak Park Oak Leaves	01/24/1902	12/28/1977
Oak Park	Oak Park Oak Parker	04/21/1923	03/26/1954
Oak Park	Oak Park Review	06/29/1901	09/10/1967
Oak Park	Oak Park Telephone Directory	01/01/1909	08/01/1977
Palatine	Palatine Enterprise	01/05/1901	12/23/1968
Palatine	Palatine Herald	03/21/1873	04/12/1975
Patoka	Patoka Register	09/28/1903	11/24/1966
Polo	Polo Ogle County Farmer	09/28/1922	06/12/1941
Princeton	Princeton Bureau County Tribune	01/01/1892	04/03/1975
Quincy	Quincy Daily Herald	08/02/1853	05/30/1926
Quincy	Quincy Morning Whig Journal	01/02/1926	05/30/1926
Quincy	Quincy Whig	05/12/1838	05/30/1920
Quincy	Quincy Whig Journal	06/01/1920	10/15/1925
Riverdale	Riverdale Pointer	06/07/1907	08/28/1974
Rockton	Rockton Herald	04/27/1877	12/29/1977

Saint Anne	*Saint Anne Record*	10/20/1905	12/27/1951
Sandoval	*Sandoval Times*	08/02/1929	01/24/1930
Shawneetown	*Shawneetown Gallatin Democrat*	03/01/1906	12/25/1986
South Holland	*South Holland Tribune*	12/31/1890	11/08/1977
Spring Valley	*Spring Valley Gazette*	01/31/1918	12/31/1925
Springfield	*Springfield Berkshire World and Cornbelt Stockman*	01/01/1910	01/01/1926
Springfield	*SpringField Farm Home*	08/01/1899	06/01/1920
Sterling	*Sterling Blue And Gold News*	03/22/1927	04/20/1927
Sterling	*Sterling Daily Gazette*	05/24/1915	02/29/1980
Sterling	*Sterling Daily Standard*	12/04/1893	12/06/1978
Sterling	*Sterling Standard*	01/04/1872	12/31/1928
Sycamore	*Sycamore True Republican*	10/01/1898	12/31/1968
Tampico	*Tampico Tornado*	11/21/1871	03/17/1966
Thomas	*Thomas Review*	01/25/1929	02/20/1930
Thomson	*Thomson Review*	05/11/1911	04/30/1970
Tinley Park	*Tinley Park Star Herald*	11/14/1926	04/01/1982
Toluca	*Toluca Star Herald*	01/10/1913	11/12/1920
Toulon	*Toulon Stark County News*	03/17/1859	12/29/1977
Troy	*Troy Call*	01/01/1900	09/19/1947
Urbana	*Urbana Daily Courier*	03/01/1903	12/31/1935
Wilmette	*Wilmette Life*	01/04/1924	02/01/1940
Woodhull	*Woodhull Dispatch*	06/06/1889	12/31/1970
Wyoming	*Wyoming Daily Post Herald*	09/09/1885	02/04/1948
Wyoming	*Wyoming Post Herald*	12/07/1872	12/28/1977

NEW YORK			
City	**Newspaper**	**First issue**	**Last issue**
Altamont	*Altamont Enterprise*	07/21/1888	03/28/1958
Arcade	*Arcade Herald*	10/14/1927	12/29/1960
Au Sable Forks	*Adirondack Record*	01/16/1913	11/19/1920
Au Sable Forks	*Au Sable Forks Adirondack Record*	03/06/1908	11/19/1920
Au Sable Forks	*Au Sable Forks Adirondack Record Elizabethtown Post*	11/26/1920	12/23/1971

Auburn	Auburn Weekly American	02/07/1855	10/06/1958
Bolivar	Bolivar Breeze	08/27/1892	10/14/1965
Brewster	Brewster Standard	11/05/1870	12/29/1977
Brockport	Brockport Republic	10/17/1856	06/25/1925
Brockport	Brockport Republic and Brockport Democrat	07/02/1925	12/30/1954
Bronxville	Bronxville Press	02/20/1925	04/01/1937
Bronxville	Bronxville Review	01/30/1902	04/01/1937
Brookfield	Brookfield Courier	03/13/1889	11/07/1935
Buffalo	Buffalo Bee	03/09/1912	10/20/1950
Buffalo	Buffalo Canisian	05/25/1929	03/03/1933
Buffalo	Buffalo Dziennik Dla Wszystkich	03/16/1914	01/24/1921
Buffalo	Buffalo Dziennik Dla Wszystkich Polish Everybody's Daily	01/17/1911	01/30/1920
Buffalo	Buffalo Morning Express	01/15/1849	08/11/1964
Canandaigua	Canandaigua Daily Messenger	01/03/1922	12/30/1977
Canton	Canton Aggie Observer	03/08/1923	03/01/1925
Canton	Canton Commercial Advertiser	10/02/1797	03/25/1952
Canton	Canton Hill News	05/22/1911	12/08/1977
Cape Vincent	Cape Vincent Eagle	05/02/1872	09/06/1951
Cattaraugus	Cattaraugus Times	11/05/1903	03/19/1920
Cazenovia	Cazenovia Republican	05/03/1854	12/21/1977
Chateaugay	Chateaugay Record and Franklin County Democrat	01/13/1893	12/29/1977
Chatham	Chatham Courier	03/06/1862	03/24/1927
Cobleskill	Cobleskill Index	05/05/1869	12/27/1945
Dansville	Dansville Advertiser	08/02/1860	06/26/1931
Dansville	Dansville Express	06/07/1877	01/23/1931
Dansville	Dansville Express and Advertiser	07/03/1931	12/04/1931
Dunkirk	Dunkirk Evening Observer	12/04/1882	09/30/1989
Dunkirk	Dunkirk Observer	10/26/1885	04/30/2007
East Hampton	East Hampton Star	07/31/1886	12/26/1968
Elizabethtown	Elizabethtown Post	10/31/1851	11/18/1920
Endicott	Endicott Bulletin	08/20/1914	10/28/1950

Endicott	*Endicott Times*	12/04/1930	12/26/1935
Fayetteville	*Fayetteville Eagle Bulletin*	08/03/1933	02/17/1977
Freeport	*Freeport Daily Review*	03/07/1921	01/14/1926
Geneva	*Geneva Herald*	10/01/1886	12/15/1977
Geneva	*Geneva Hobart Herald*	03/01/1879	02/25/1932
Hammond	*Hammond Advertiser*	04/29/1886	04/21/1949
Haverstraw	*Haverstraw Rockland County Times*	01/06/1894	12/30/1971
Heuvelton	*Heuvelton Bee*	03/09/1912	08/25/1923
Honeoye Falls	*Honeoye Falls Times*	06/01/1893	04/02/1964
Hudson	*Hudson Columbia Republican*	01/06/1887	06/26/1923
Irvington	*Irvington Gazette*	10/18/1907	08/28/1969
Ithaca	*Ithaca Cornell Daily Sun*	09/16/1880	05/10/1974
Ithaca	*Ithaca Ithacan*	10/15/1926	12/08/1977
Jamestown	*Jamestown Morning Post*	01/01/1930	03/31/1930
Keeseville	*Keeseville Essex County Republican*	05/08/1844	12/29/1973
Kingston	*Kingston Daily Freeman*	04/01/1872	12/30/1977
Little Valley	*Little Valley Cattaraugus Republican*	09/20/1901	04/20/1922
Lowville	*Lowville Black River Democrat*	01/11/1913	07/01/1943
Lowville	*Lowville Black River Gazette*	10/19/1825	03/23/1922
Margaretville	*Margaretville Catskill Mountain News*	07/03/1902	12/27/1973
Middletown	*Central Valley Post*	01/06/1927	03/24/1927
Middletown	*Chester Press*	01/06/1927	03/24/1927
Middletown	*Daily Herald*	12/18/1925	12/31/1926
Middletown	*Daily Herald Middletown Times Press*	04/16/1901	10/31/1927
Middletown	*Florida Journal*	01/06/1927	03/24/1927
Middletown	*Highland Falls Standard*	01/06/1927	03/24/1927
Middletown	*Highland Mills Star*	01/06/1927	03/24/1927
Middletown	*Lake Region Reporter*	01/13/1927	03/24/1927
Middletown	*Maybrook Enterprise*	01/06/1927	03/24/1927
Middletown	*Middletown Daily Argus*	01/27/1876	01/15/1992
Middletown	*Middletown Daily Herald*	06/02/1919	12/15/1925
Middletown	*Middletown Daily Herald and Times Press*	01/03/1927	12/01/1927

Middletown	Middletown Daily Times Press	06/21/1906	10/30/1926
Middletown	Middletown Highland Mills Star	01/06/1927	03/24/1927
Middletown	Middletown Maybrook Enterprise	01/06/1927	10/17/1929
Middletown	Middletown Orange County Independent	04/02/1915	12/26/1929
Middletown	Middletown Orange County Press	11/02/1900	11/21/1929
Middletown	Middletown Orange County Star Eagle	11/14/1929	12/17/1942
Middletown	Middletown Orange County Times	01/02/1900	08/11/1925
Middletown	Middletown Orange County Times Press	02/02/1906	12/29/1925
Middletown	Middletown Record	05/25/1923	05/27/1973
Middletown	Middletown Times Herald	10/02/1927	12/24/1957
Middletown	Orange County Independent	03/31/1927	12/26/1929
Middletown	Orange County Record	01/06/1927	03/17/1927
Middletown	Orange County Times Press	02/05/1907	03/24/1927
Middletown	Storm King Sentinel	01/06/1927	03/24/1927
New York	Barnard Bulletin	01/07/1901	12/05/1977
New York	New York Ameerika Eestlane Hariduslik Ja Informatsiooni Ajakiri	03/26/1925	11/05/1925
New York	New York Clipper	10/01/1898	07/12/1924
New York	New York Columbia Spectator	05/01/1877	12/08/1977
New York	New York Commercial Advertiser	10/02/1797	03/25/1952
New York	New York Herald	01/01/1836	05/14/1922
New York	New York Stars and Stripes	03/14/1852	08/09/1945
New York	New York Vaudeville News	04/16/1920	06/08/1929
Ogdensburg	Ogdensburg Advance News	03/21/1933	05/30/1971
Olean	Olean Evening Herald	08/26/1883	12/31/1931
Olean	Olean Times	02/01/1909	03/22/1941
Olean	Times Evening Herald	01/02/1932	06/11/1935
Oneonta	Oneonta Daily Star	11/01/1916	12/31/1934
Penn Yan	Penn Yan Chronicle Express	01/06/1926	12/29/1977
Plattsburgh	Plattsburgh Cardinal Points	05/12/1905	12/15/1977
Port Jervis	Port Jervis Evening Gazette	11/06/1832	12/13/2013

Potsdam	*Potsdam Clarkson Integrator*	02/01/1920	12/06/1977
Potsdam	*Potsdam Courier and Freeman*	09/18/1861	12/27/1977
Poughkeepsie	*Poughkeepsie Miscellany News*	08/08/1888	12/02/1977
Poughkeepsie	*Poughkeepsie Vassar Alumnae Quarterly*	11/01/1917	09/01/1977
Riverhead	*Riverhead County Review*	09/16/1904	07/20/1950
Rochester	*Rochester Catholic Courier*	01/06/1933	03/22/1945
Rochester	*Rochester Catholic Courier and Journal*	03/15/1929	12/05/1952
Rochester	*Rochester Catholic Journal*	10/05/1880	03/08/1929
Rushford	*Rushford Spectator*	11/11/1880	12/23/1932
Saint Regis Falls	*Saint Regis Falls Adirondack News*	03/12/1887	04/29/1933
Salamanca	*Salamanca Cattaraugus Republican*	09/20/1901	12/28/1938
Salamanca	*Salamanca Republican Press*	10/25/1909	12/31/1949
Saranac Lake	*Saranac Lake Adirondack Daily Enterprise*	02/21/1895	12/30/1977
Scarsdale	*Scarsdale Inquirer*	07/04/1901	12/29/1977
Schenectady	*Schenectady Concordiensis*	11/01/1877	11/16/1977
Syracuse	*Syracuse Evening Telegram*	05/14/1923	02/18/1924
Syracuse	*Syracuse Herald*	01/16/1881	09/21/1986
Syracuse	*Syracuse Journal*	07/02/1850	03/03/1940
Syracuse	*Syracuse Post Standard*	01/01/1875	11/12/2019
Syracuse	*Syracuse Standard*	01/04/1875	06/26/2013
Wellsville	*Spectator*	04/23/1910	10/29/1972
Wellsville	*Wellsville Allegany County Reporter*	09/08/1881	04/13/1920
Wellsville	*Wellsville Daily Reporter*	04/13/1804	12/30/1977
White Plains	*White Plains Daily Press*	04/01/1929	03/22/1930

OHIO			
City	**Newspaper**	**First issue**	**Last issue**
Athens	*Athens Daily Messenger*	11/25/1905	05/25/1976
Athens	*Athens Messenger*	01/18/1850	04/28/2017
Athens	*Athens Messenger and Herald*	07/09/1891	02/23/1959
Athens	*Athens Sunday Messenger*	10/01/1922	04/23/2017

Cambridge	Cambridge Daily Jeffersonian	05/23/1912	10/31/1977
Canton	Canton Daily News	03/17/1913	07/03/1930
Canton	Canton Junior News	12/18/1921	10/28/1923
Canton	Canton Morning News	07/02/1906	12/01/1923
Canton	Canton News	11/26/1924	06/21/1926
Canton	Canton Sunday News	01/07/1923	11/04/1923
Carey	Carey Times	09/19/1888	12/30/1970
Cincinnati	Cincinnati Catholic Telegraph	04/01/1847	12/01/2012
Cincinnati	Cincinnati Catholic Telegraph Register	01/04/1894	06/29/1962
Cincinnati	Cincinnati Commercial Tribune	07/01/1896	12/03/1930
Circleville	Circleville Daily Union Herald	01/01/1919	12/05/1927
Circleville	Circleville Herald	06/01/1926	12/31/1977
Cleveland	Cleveland America	03/05/1918	11/02/1922
Cleveland	Cleveland Gazette	08/25/1883	12/29/1923
Cleveland	Cleveland Ohio Farmer	01/05/1907	12/30/1922
Cleveland	Cleveland Svet World	08/01/1922	07/31/1924
Columbus	Columbus Evening Dispatch	12/14/1877	02/10/1969
Coshocton	Coshocton County Democrat	06/15/1859	10/31/1956
Coshocton	Coshocton Tribune	10/21/1863	12/31/1977
Defiance	Defiance Crescent News	03/31/1898	04/30/2007
Defiance	Defiance Daily Crescent News	01/02/1895	05/27/1972
Defiance	Defiance Daily Express	05/07/1894	09/30/1986
Delphos	Delphos Courant	01/14/1928	02/23/1962
Delphos	Delphos Daily Herald	09/30/1869	12/31/1977
Delphos	Delphos Herald	05/20/1869	07/12/1977
Dover	Dover Daily Reporter	03/21/1917	06/13/2013
Dover	Dover Daily Times	04/18/1906	10/19/1967
East Liverpool	East Liverpool Evening News Review	08/29/1892	06/23/1986
East Liverpool	East Liverpool Evening Review	06/16/1885	08/31/1994
East Liverpool	East Liverpool Review	09/16/1913	01/29/1975
East Liverpool	East Liverpool Review Tribune	10/01/1924	01/28/1994
East Liverpool	East Liverpool Saturday Review	11/01/1879	06/25/1994
East Liverpool	East Liverpool Weekly Crisis	06/29/1905	01/08/1994

Elyria	*Elyria Chronicle*	08/31/1853	07/31/2014
Elyria	*Elyria Chronicle Telegram*	07/01/1919	04/30/2019
Elyria	*Elyria Constitution*	03/25/1875	02/20/2014
Elyria	*Elyria Reporter*	12/02/1898	02/28/1990
Elyria	*Elyria Sunday Times Signal*	07/25/1926	07/26/1926
Findlay	*Findlay Courier*	03/05/1923	12/31/1977
Findlay	*Findlay Morning Republican*	10/13/1921	09/29/1954
Findlay	*Findlay Republican Courier*	02/23/1923	12/31/1975
Gambier	*Gambier Kenyon Collegian*	01/01/1856	12/08/1977
Granville	*Granville Denisonian*	09/23/1898	05/02/1958
Granville	*Granville Licking Pioneers Minutes and Isaac Smucker Scrapbooks*	05/01/1867	09/01/1926
Granville	*Granville Times*	06/11/1880	06/24/1987
Hamilton	*Butler County Democrat*	01/20/1876	10/19/1922
Hamilton	*Hamilton Daily News*	12/20/1881	02/04/1933
Hamilton	*Hamilton Daily News Journal*	02/07/1933	10/27/1971
Hamilton	*Hamilton Evening Journal*	04/17/1908	04/25/1941
Kent	*Kent Tribune*	11/15/1917	09/05/1929
Lancaster	*Lancaster Daily Eagle*	01/02/1915	04/30/1963
Lancaster	*Lancaster Daily Gazette*	01/24/1915	05/16/1929
Lancaster	*Lancaster Eagle Gazette*	09/01/1927	07/30/1974
Lima	*Lima Daily News*	06/07/1889	11/28/2004
Lima	*Lima News*	05/09/1898	07/31/2019
Lima	*Lima Times Democrat*	04/04/1860	07/06/1948
Logan	*Logan Democrat Sentinel*	01/13/1910	05/30/1935
Logan	*Logan Hocking County Sentinel*	08/01/1850	12/22/1970
Mansfield	*Mansfield News*	04/02/1895	03/31/1977
Mansfield	*Mansfield News Journal*	05/13/1908	02/29/1976
Marion	*Marion Daily Star*	07/24/1878	05/27/1975
Marion	*Marion Star*	01/01/1889	10/31/1975
Marysville	*Evening Tribune*	10/01/1932	11/11/1933
Marysville	*Marysville Evening Journal Tribune*	03/14/1912	05/10/1958
Marysville	*Marysville Evening Tribune*	11/30/1821	06/30/1936
Marysville	*Marysville Journal Tribune*	05/01/1928	08/07/1971

Marysville	*Marysville Union County Journal*	01/08/1878	03/01/1951
Massillon	*Evening Independent*	01/01/1907	12/31/1976
Mechanicsburg	*Mechanicsburg Daily Telegram*	10/17/1917	08/31/1938
Mechanicsburg	*Mechanicsburg Morning Telegram*	10/21/1903	01/23/1936
Mechanicsburg	*Mechanicsburg News Item*	10/15/1903	03/30/1922
Medina	*Medina County Gazette*	01/07/1870	05/31/1979
Medina	*Medina Sentinel*	09/07/1899	05/12/1978
Middletown	*Middletown Friday Noon*	09/13/1929	12/20/1929
New Philadelphia	*New Philadelphia Daily Times*	10/31/1903	03/02/1968
New Philadelphia	*New Philadelphia Ohio Democrat and Times*	03/29/1900	12/31/1925
New Philadelphia	*New Philadelphia Times*	01/07/1886	10/10/1921
New Philadelphia	*New Philadelphia Times Reporter*	07/04/1889	03/27/1998
Newark	*Newark Advocate*	07/01/1901	07/30/1977
Newark	*Newark American Tribune*	12/14/1926	12/31/1926
Norwalk	*Norwalk Reflector*	01/21/1862	08/31/1979
Norwalk	*Norwalk Reflector Herald*	01/27/1913	06/04/1964
Oberlin	*Oberlin Review*	02/24/1875	12/09/1977
Orrville	*Orrville Courier Crescent*	11/18/1904	12/29/1977
Orrville	*Orrville Crescent*	05/31/1870	03/11/1976
Oxford	*Oxford Western Roundup*	04/11/1931	04/01/1971
Piqua	*Piqua Daily Call*	01/01/1885	12/15/1977
Piqua	*Piqua Daily Call and Piqua Press Dispatch*	03/31/1922	06/16/1927
Piqua	*Piqua Press Dispatch*	05/27/1921	06/18/1921
Portsmouth	*Portsmouth Daily Times*	03/27/1894	04/10/1963
Portsmouth	*Portsmouth Morning Sun*	06/13/1922	02/28/1930
Portsmouth	*Portsmouth Sunday Sun*	04/06/1930	04/06/1930
Portsmouth	*Portsmouth Sunday Times*	04/12/1930	06/28/1936
Portsmouth	*Portsmouth Times*	09/28/1858	12/31/1977
Portsmouth	*Portsmouth Weekly Times*	01/09/1915	01/07/1921
Richwood	*Richwood Bulletin*	08/23/1868	12/26/1929
Richwood	*Richwood Gazette*	11/21/1872	12/28/1978

Salem	*Salem News*	12/20/1905	12/31/1977
Sandusky	*Sandusky Daily Sanduskian*	06/01/1849	09/23/1950
Sandusky	*Sandusky Register*	04/23/1894	07/31/2014
Sandusky	*Sandusky Star Journal*	12/20/1901	10/31/1963
Sandusky	*Sandusky Sunday Register*	01/04/1885	06/10/2012
Sandusky	*Sunday Register*	04/03/1911	04/23/2006
Springfield	*Springfield News Sun*	07/05/1931	07/05/1931
Springfield	*Springfield Sunday News*	05/25/1919	05/25/1919
Steubenville	*Herald Star*	07/27/1863	12/31/1977
Steubenville	*Steubenville Daily Herald and News*	01/07/1875	10/30/1875
Steubenville	*Steubenville Herald*	01/03/1890	12/04/1924
Steubenville	*Steubenville Herald Star*	09/02/1899	10/31/1977
Van Wert	*Van Wert Daily Bulletin*	03/14/1855	05/16/1936
Van Wert	*Van Wert Times*	09/05/1884	05/16/1936
Van Wert	*Van Wert Times Bulletin*	09/04/1928	12/31/1977
Washington Court House	*Washington C H Daily Herald*	02/06/1911	03/11/1941
Washington Court House	*Washington C H Herald*	12/21/1916	02/02/1937
Washington Court House	*Washington C H Record Herald*	11/05/1912	12/26/1974
Washington Court House	*Washington Court House Herald*	04/24/1913	09/30/1977
Washington Court House	*Washington Court House Record Herald*	01/09/1911	12/31/1977
Westerville	*Westerville American Issue*	07/05/1912	05/01/1932
Wilmington	*Wilmington News Journal*	07/02/1930	11/23/1977
Xenia	*Morning Republican*	05/10/1919	12/22/1926
Xenia	*Xenia Daily Gazette*	11/23/1881	11/21/2007
Xenia	*Xenia Evening Gazette*	03/19/1918	12/30/1944
Xenia	*Xenia Morning Republican*	03/26/1923	12/22/1926
Zanesville	*Sunday Times Signal*	10/07/1928	11/29/1959
Zanesville	*Times Signal*	12/07/1924	03/27/1959
Zanesville	*Zanesville News*	08/24/1865	01/21/1946

Zanesville	Zanesville Signal	12/13/1923	09/30/1959
Zanesville	Zanesville Times Recorder	05/31/1923	12/31/1977
Zanesville	Zanesville Times Signal	03/02/1924	02/07/1927

PENNYSLVANIA			
City	**Newspaper**	**First issue**	**Last issue**
Altoona	Altoona Evening Mirror	06/15/1927	12/30/1974
Altoona	Altoona Mirror	12/02/1876	03/31/2019
Bedford	Bedford Gazette	06/23/1854	03/31/2016
Bedford	Bedford Inquirer	11/27/1857	09/29/2012
Bellwood	Bellwood Bulletin	11/22/1889	05/29/1946
Bradford	Bradford Era	05/10/1879	12/31/1977
Bradford	Bradford Evening Star and Daily Record	07/01/1922	11/14/1922
Bradford	Bradford Star Record	07/01/1922	09/30/1922
Bristol	Bristol Bucks County Gazette	08/14/1873	12/31/1926
Bristol	Bristol Bucks County Independent	04/29/1921	02/05/1932
Bristol	Bristol Courier	12/15/1920	06/04/1956
Bristol	Bristol Courier Times	06/19/1925	07/17/1965
Bristol	Bristol Daily Courier	06/14/1916	01/15/1966
Charleroi	Charleroi Mail	03/30/1908	08/31/1960
Chester	Chester Daily Times	09/07/1876	10/14/1977
Chester	Chester Evening Times	06/19/1886	09/15/1964
Chester	Chester Times	04/18/1882	12/26/1961
Clearfield	Clearfield Progress	06/18/1913	08/31/2016
Connellsville	Connellsville Courier	06/08/1888	08/28/1972
Connellsville	Connellsville Daily Courier	11/10/1902	12/31/1977
Connellsville	Connellsville Weekly Courier	06/02/1905	07/11/1929
Conshohocken	Conshohocken Recorder	04/26/1879	12/29/1964
Delta	Delta Herald and Times	12/05/1884	06/25/1920
Delta	Delta Herald Times	12/29/1899	09/27/1934
Doylestown	Doylestown Intelligencer	07/01/1932	02/28/2017
DuBois	DuBois Courier	12/25/1884	01/05/1987
DuBois	DuBois Courier Express	01/26/1932	12/31/1993

DuBois	*DuBois Daily Courier*	03/26/1888	09/08/1955
DuBois	*DuBois Daily Express*	11/11/1918	08/29/1944
DuBois	*DuBois Morning Courier*	12/05/1888	09/28/1923
DuBois	*DuBois Morning Journal*	06/23/1905	09/12/1935
East Berlin	*East Berlin News*	09/18/1925	04/12/1935
East Berlin	*East Berlin News and Biglerville News*	03/12/1926	06/18/1926
East Berlin	*East Berlin News Comet*	09/18/1925	03/03/1983
East Berlin	*News Comet*	06/20/1930	08/29/1952
Easton	*Easton Lafayette*	10/01/1884	12/09/1977
Gettysburg	*Gettysburg Compiler*	05/18/1857	07/01/1950
Gettysburg	*Gettysburg Star and Sentinel*	05/29/1867	12/26/1953
Gettysburg	*Gettysburg Times*	01/01/1909	12/31/2018
Gettysburg	*Gettysburg Weekly Gettysburgian*	10/05/1898	11/18/1977
Greenville	*Greenville Evening Record*	11/01/1897	12/31/1923
Greenville	*Greenville Record Argus*	01/02/1924	12/31/1994
Hanover	*Hanover Evening Sun*	04/29/1915	03/31/1994
Hershey	*Hershey Press*	09/03/1909	12/30/1926
Huntingdon	*Huntingdon Daily News*	02/01/1922	02/28/2018
Indiana	*Indiana Democrat*	05/07/1862	04/28/1937
Indiana	*Indiana Evening Gazette*	09/09/1904	11/28/1981
Indiana	*Indiana Patriot*	08/08/1914	10/22/1921
Indiana	*Indiana Progress*	01/21/1870	12/29/1937
Indiana	*Indiana Weekly Messenger*	12/02/1874	12/29/1938
Kittanning	*Kittanning Simpson Leader Times*	01/02/1915	12/31/1977
Kittanning	*Kittanning Simpsons Daily Leader Times*	01/02/1920	12/30/1961
Kutztown	*Kutztown Patriot*	11/01/1890	12/25/1958
Lebanon	*Lebanon Daily News*	10/04/1872	12/31/1977
Lebanon	*Lebanon Daily News and Lebanon Daily Times*	06/13/1927	06/15/1927
Lebanon	*Lebanon Daily News and the Lebanon Daily Times*	09/21/1925	10/30/1931
Lebanon	*Lebanon Semi Weekly News*	11/01/1894	08/31/1961
Lincoln University	*Lincoln University Lincoln News*	11/01/1925	10/16/1946

Lititz	*Lititz Record*	02/08/1878	06/10/1937
Lock Haven	*Lock Haven Express*	03/02/1889	12/31/1977
Monessen	*Monessen Daily Independent*	11/08/1902	12/17/2003
Monessen	*Monessen Valley Independent*	04/22/1926	12/31/2015
Narberth	*Narberth Our Town*	10/29/1914	12/29/1948
Nazareth	*Nazareth Item*	12/02/1926	05/09/1940
New Castle	*New Castle Daily City News*	01/01/1886	05/29/2008
New Castle	*New Castle News*	12/15/1880	09/30/2017
New Castle	*New Castle Weekly News*	01/12/1881	04/16/2011
New Holland	*New Holland Clarion*	01/18/1873	12/29/1950
New Oxford	*New Oxford Item*	01/04/1889	02/23/1967
Oil City	*Blizzard*	06/30/1896	03/30/1956
Oil City	*Derrick*	09/11/1871	12/31/1977
Oil City	*Oil City Blizzard*	04/01/1896	03/30/1956
Oil City	*Oil City Daily Derrick*	07/09/1872	07/11/1951
Oil City	*Oil City Derrick*	09/11/1871	12/31/1977
Oil City	*Weekly Derrick*	01/01/1891	09/07/1933
Philadelphia	*Checkerboard*	07/08/1795	11/01/1977
Philadelphia	*Philadelphia Daily Pennsylvanian*	07/01/1796	12/14/1977
Philadelphia	*Philadelphia Evening Public Ledger*	09/14/1914	12/30/1922
Philadelphia	*Philadelphia Inquirer*	11/07/1860	12/31/1923
Philadelphia	*Philadelphia Jewish Exponent*	04/15/1887	12/30/1977
Philadelphia	*Philadelphia La Libera Parola*	04/20/1918	12/23/1922
Philadelphia	*Philadelphia Tribune*	01/06/1912	01/12/1924
Pittsburgh	*Pittsburgh Catholic*	04/13/1844	03/07/1957
Reading	*Reading Eagle*	12/19/1868	07/15/1949
Smethport	*McKean County Democrat*	03/17/1859	07/15/1971
Smethport	*McKean County Miner*	12/04/1873	12/22/1977
Smethport	*McKean Democrat*	04/24/1919	06/28/1928
Smethport	*Smethport McKean County Democrat*	01/06/1859	07/15/1971
Smethport	*Smethport McKean Democrat*	06/20/1890	10/13/1927
Somerset	*Somerset Daily Herald*	07/01/1929	02/27/1937
State College	*State College Penn State Collegian*	09/28/1911	05/30/1940

Swarthmore	*Swarthmore News*	05/02/1914	09/02/1921
Swarthmore	*Swarthmore Swarthmorean*	07/18/1914	06/05/1953
Titusville	*Titusville Herald*	06/14/1865	08/31/2017
Towanda	*Towanda Daily Review*	12/13/1879	09/30/1987
Tyrone	*Tyrone Daily Herald*	04/06/1858	02/28/2018
Uniontown	*Daily News Standard*	06/17/1896	05/15/1941
Uniontown	*Uniontown Evening Genius*	08/25/1913	08/19/1930
Uniontown	*Uniontown Evening Standard*	12/17/1888	12/31/1977
Uniontown	*Uniontown Morning Herald*	01/31/1808	12/31/1977
Warren	*Warren Allegheny Mail*	04/13/1836	1946/03/11
Warren	*Warren Morning Mirror*	1922/01/12	06/30/1928
Warren	*Warren Times Mirror*	10/01/1929	11/26/1973
Warren	*Warren Tribune*	04/01/1927	11/03/1928
Waynesboro	*Waynesboro Record Herald*	11/11/1918	12/31/1977
Wellsboro	*Wellsboro Agitator*	07/13/1854	12/26/1963
Wellsboro	*Wellsboro Gazette*	06/09/1874	12/30/2015
Wilkes Barre	*Wilkes Barre Sunday Independent*	07/02/1933	04/27/1958
Williamsport	*Daily Gazette and Bulletin*	12/02/1870	04/21/1923
Williamsport	*Gazette and Bulletin*	12/23/1869	09/10/1955
Williamsport	*Williamsport Sun Gazette*	04/18/1929	11/01/1973

BIBLIOGRAPHY
—

PRIMARY SOURCES:
BOOKS, CHAPTERS, AND JOURNAL ARTICLES

Anonymous. "Evolution in the Pulpit." Pages 27–36 in *The Fundamentals*. Vol. 8. Chicago: Testimony Publishing, 1910.

Chafer, Lewis Sperry. "Anthropology." *Bibliotheca Sacra* 100, no. 398 (1943): 220–43.

———. "Anthropology, Part 3." *Bibliotheca Sacra* 100, no. 400. (1943): 479–96.

———. "Anthropology, Part 3, Section 2c." *Bibliotheca Sacra* 101, no. 401 (1944): 8–29.

———. "Anthropology, Part 3, Section 2d." *Bibliotheca Sacra* 101, no. 402 (1944): 132–48.

———. "Anthropology, Part 3, Section 3." *Bibliotheca Sacra* 101, no. 403 (1944): 264–82.

———. "Anthropology, Part 4." *Bibliotheca Sacra* 101, no. 404 (1944): 391–402.

———. "Bibliology No 2.1 Inspiration." *Bibliotheca Sacra* 94, no. 376 (1937): 389–408.

———. "Bibliology No. 2.2 Inspiration." *Bibliotheca Sacra* 95, no. 377 (1938): 7–21.

———. "Bibliology No. 3 Canonicity and Authority." *Bibliotheca Sacra* 95, no. 378 (1938): 137–56.

———. "Bibliology: Revelation." *Bibliotheca Sacra* 94, no. 375 (1937): 264–80.

———. "Dispensationalism." *Bibliotheca Sacra* 93, no. 372 (1936): 390–449.

———. *Dispensationalism*. Fort Worth, TX: Exegetica Publishing & Biblical Resources, 2015.

———. "Evils Resulting from an Abridged Systematic Theology." *Bibliotheca Sacra* 91, no. 362 (1934): 134–54.

———. "For Whom Did Christ Die?" *Bibliotheca Sacra* 105, no. 417 (1948): 7–35.

———. "Gospel Preaching." *Bibliotheca Sacra* 95, no. 379 (1938): 343–64.

———. "Introduction to Bibliology." *Bibliotheca Sacra* 94, no. 374 (1937): 132–52.

———. *Major Bible Themes: Presenting Forty-Nine Vital Doctrines of the Scriptures, Abbreviated and Simplified for Popular Use, Including Suggestive Questions on Each Chapter, with Topical and Textual Indices.* Chicago, IL: Moody Bible Institute, 1926. Google e-book edition.

———. *Salvation.* Grand Rapids: Kregel, 2004.

———. "Soteriology." *Bibliotheca Sacra* 103, no. 410 (1946): 140–60.

———. "Soteriology, Part 2." *Bibliotheca Sacra* 103, no. 411 (1946): 261–82.

———. "Soteriology, Part 5." *Bibliotheca Sacra* 103, no. 412 (1946): 391–410.

———. "Soteriology, Part 12." *Bibliotheca Sacra* 104, no. 413 (1947): 3–24.

———. *Systematic Theology.* Grand Rapids: Kregel, 1993.

———. "The Doctrine of Sin, Part 1." *Bibliotheca Sacra* 91, no. 364 (1934): 390–408.

———. "The Doctrine of Sin, Part 2." *Bibliotheca Sacra* 92, no. 365 (1935): 7–25.

———. "The Doctrine of Sin, Part 3." *Bibliotheca Sacra* 92, no. 366 (1935): 134–53.

———. "The Doctrine of Sin, Part 4." *Bibliotheca Sacra* 92, no. 368 (1935): 394–411.

———. "The Doctrine of Sin, Part 5, Section 1." *Bibliotheca Sacra* 93, no. 369 (1936): 5–25.

———. "The Doctrine of Sin, Part 5, Section 2." *Bibliotheca Sacra* 93, no. 370 (1936): 133–61.

———. "The Doctrine of Sin, Part 5, Section 3." *Bibliotheca Sacra* 93, no. 371 (1936): 263–88.

———. "The Saving Work of the Triune God, Part 2." *Bibliotheca Sacra* 105, no. 420 (1948): 387–403.

———. "The Saving Work of the Triune God, Part 4." *Bibliotheca Sacra* 106, no. 422 (April 1949): 133–48.

———. "Trinitarianism, Part 4." *Bibliotheca Sacra* 97, no. 388 (1940): 390–409.

———. "Trinitarianism, Part 5." *Bibliotheca Sacra* 98, no. 389 (1941): 7–28.

———. "Unabridged Systematic Theology." *Bibliotheca Sacra* 91, no. 361 (1934): 8–23.

Darrow, Clarence, and William Jennings Bryan. *The World's Most Famous Court Trial: A Complete Stenographic Report of the Famous Court Test of the Tennessee Anti-Evolution Act, at Dayton, July 10 to 21, 1925,*

Including Speeches and Arguments of Attorneys. Cincinnati, OH: National Book Company, 1925.

Edwards, Jonathan. *The Works of Jonathan Edwards Online*. Jonathan Edwards Center at Yale University, http://edwards.yale.edu.

Fey, Harold Edward. "Baptists Ask Ban on War Liquor: Cleveland Convention Endorses National Prohibition—Refuses to Change Prewar Position on War." *The Christian Century* 59, no. 23 (June 10, 1942): 762–63.

Gaebelein, Arno C. *The Work of Christ: Past, Present and Future*. New York: Our Hope, 1913. Kindle edition.

———. *Things to Come*. Seventh edition. New York: Our Hope, n.d.

Hankins, Barry, ed. *Evangelicalism and Fundamentalism: A Documentary Reader*. New York: New York University Press, 2008.

Henry, Carl F. H. *The Uneasy Conscience of Modern Fundamentalism*. Grand Rapids: Eerdmans, 1947.

———. *Pacific Garden Mission: A Doorway to Heaven*. Grand Rapids: Zondervan, 1942.

Himes, Andrew. *Sword of the Lord: The Roots of Fundamentalism in an American Family*. Self-published, 2011.

Hodge, Charles. *What Is Atheism?* New York: Scribner, Armstrong, and Company, 1874.

Ironside, Harry A. *What Is the Gospel?: Understanding What It Is and What It Is Not*. Eureka, MT: Lighthouse Trails, 2016. Kindle edition.

Jacobsen, Douglas. *Reader in Pentecostal Theology: Voices from the First Generation*. Bloomington, IN: Indiana University Press, 2006.

Machen, J. Gresham. *Christianity and Liberalism*. Grand Rapids: Eerdmans, 1923.

Macintosh, Douglas Clyde. "After Prohibition and Repeal, What." *Religion in Life* 8, no. 3 (1939): 323–38.

McPherson, Aimee Semple. *This is That: Personal Experiences, Sermons, and Writings*. Los Angeles: Bridal Call, 1919.

———. "Aimee McPherson Says Goodbye: California's noted preacher leaves for Holy Land with a parting word on Prohibition." Hearst Metrotone News, early 1930s.

Packer, J. I. *"Fundamentalism" and the Word of God*. Grand Rapids: Eerdmans, 1958.

Rauschenbusch, Walter. *A Theology for the Social Gospel*. New York: Macmillan, 1917.

Riley, William Bell. *The Antievolution Pamphlets of William Bell Riley*. New York: Taylor & Francis, 1995.

Rodeheaver, Homer A. *Twenty Years with Billy Sunday*. Nashville, TN: Cokesbury Press, 1936.

Ryrie, Charles C. *Dispensationalism*. Revised, Expanded edition. Chicago: Moody Publishers, 1995.

Savage, Minot J. *Evolution & Religion; from the Standpoint of One Who Believes in Both*. Philadelphia: G. H. Buchanan and Company, 1886.

Scofield, C. I. *Rightly Dividing the Word of Truth (2 Timothy 2:15): Being Ten Outline Studies of the More Important Divisions of Scripture*. Philadelphia: Philadelphia School of the Bible, 1921. Kindle edition.

———. "Tested by Grace." *Bibliotheca Sacra* 107, no. 428 (1950): 488–96.

———. "The Course and End of the Age." *Bibliotheca Sacra* 108, no. 429 (1951): 105–16.

———. "The Last World Empire and Armageddon." *Bibliotheca Sacra* 108, no. 431 (1951): 355–62.

———. "The Return of Christ in Relation to the Church." *Bibliotheca Sacra* 109, no. 433 (1952): 77–89.

———. "The Return of Christ in Relation to the Jew and the Earth," *Bibliotheca Sacra* 108, no. 432 (1951): 477–87.

———, ed. *The Scofield Reference Bible. The Holy Bible: Containing the Old and New Testaments. Authorized Version*. New and improved edition. New York: Oxford University Press, 1945.

———. "The Times of the Gentiles." *Bibliotheca Sacra* 107, no. 427 (1950): 343–55.

Sunday, William A. *The Sawdust Trail: Billy Sunday in His Own Words*. Iowa City, IA: University of Iowa Press, 2005.

———. "The Famous 'Booze' Sermon." *Criswell Theological Review* 5, no. 2 (2008): 71–98.

U.S. Bureau of the Census. *Historical Statistics of the United States: Colonial Times to 1970, Part 1*. By William Lerner. Washington, DC, 1975.

Walvoord, John F., and Lewis Sperry Chafer. *Major Bible Themes: 52 Vital Doctrines of the Scripture Simplified and Explained*. Revised edition. Grand Rapids.: Zondervan, 1974.

SECONDARY SOURCES: BOOKS

Allen, Frederick Lewis. *Only Yesterday: An Informal History of the 1920s.*
Perennial Classics edition. New York: Harper Perennial, 2010.

Baker, David Weston, ed. *Looking into the Future: Evangelical Studies in
Eschatology.* Grand Rapids: Baker Academic, 2001.

Balmer, Randall. *The Making of Evangelicalism: From Revivalism to Politics,
and Beyond.* Waco, TX: Baylor University Press, 2010.

Barfoot, Chas. H. *Aimee Semple McPherson and the Making of Modern
Pentecostalism, 1890–1926.* London: Equinox, 2011.

Beale, David O. *In Pursuit of Purity: American Fundamentalism Since 1850.*
Greenville, SC: Unusual Publications, 1986.

Bebbington, David W. *The Dominance of Evangelicalism: The Age of Spurgeon
and Moody.* Downers Grove, IL: IVP Academic, 2005.

———. *Evangelicalism in Modern Britain: A History from the 1730s to the 1930s.*
Grand Rapids: Baker Books, 1992.

Blumhofer, Edith. *Aimee Semple McPherson: Everybody's Sister.* Grand
Rapids: Eerdmans, 1993.

Bruns, Roger A. *Preacher: Billy Sunday and Big-Time American Evangelism.*
Urbana, IL: University of Illinois Press, 1992.

Carpenter, Joel A. *Revive Us Again: The Reawakening of American
Fundamentalism.* New York: Oxford University Press, 1997.

Carter, Heath W., and Laura Rominger Porter, eds. *Turning Points in the
History of American Evangelicalism.* Grand Rapids: Eerdmans, 2017.

Caudill, Edward. *Intelligently Designed: How Creationists Built the Campaign
against Evolution.* Urbana, IL: University of Illinois Press, 2013.

Chatraw, Joshua D., and Karen Swallow Prior. *Cultural Engagement: A Crash
Course in Contemporary Issues.* Grand Rapids: Zondervan Academic,
2019.

Coker, Joe L. *Liquor in the Land of the Lost Cause: Southern White Evangelicals
and the Prohibition Movement.* Lexington, KY: University Press of
Kentucky, 2007.

Cole, Stewart G. *The History of Fundamentalism.* Westport, CT: Greenwood
Press, 1931.

Collins, Kenneth J. *Power, Politics, and the Fragmentation of Evangelicalism:
From the Scopes Trial to the Obama Administration.* Downers Grove,
IL: IVP Academic, 2012.

DeWitt, Dale Sumner. *Dispensational Theology in America during the Twentieth Century: Theological Development and Cultural Context.* Grand Rapids: Grace Bible College, 2002.

Dochuk, Darren. *From Bible Belt to Sunbelt: Plain-Folk Religion, Grassroots Politics, and the Rise of Evangelical Conservatism.* New York: Norton, 2011.

Dochuk, Darren, Thomas S. Kidd, and Kurt W. Peterson. *American Evangelicalism: George Marsden and the State of American Religious History.* South Bend, IN: University of Notre Dame Press, 2016.

Dollar, George W. *A History of Fundamentalism in America.* Greenville, SC: Bob Jones University Press, 1973.

Dorsett, Lyle. *Billy Sunday and the Redemption of Urban America.* Grand Rapids: Eerdmans, 1991.

Eskridge, Larry, and Mark A. Noll, eds. *More Money, More Ministry: Money and Evangelicals in Recent North American History.* Grand Rapids: Eerdmans, 2000.

Frank, Douglas. *Less Than Conquerors: How Evangelicals Entered the Twentieth Century.* Grand Rapids: Eerdmans, 1986.

———. *God's Rascal: J. Frank Norris and the Beginnings of Southern Fundamentalism.* Lexington, KY: University Press of Kentucky, 1996.

Furniss, Norman F. *The Fundamentalist Controversy, 1918–1931.* Hamden, CT: Archon Books, 1963.

Gasper, Louis. *The Fundamentalist Movement.* Paris: Mouton, 1963.

Gatewood, Willard B., Jr. *Controversy in the Twenties; Fundamentalism, Modernism, and Evolution.* Nashville, TN: Vanderbilt University Press, 1969.

Gloege, Timothy. *Guaranteed Pure: The Moody Bible Institute, Business, and the Making of Modern Evangelicalism.* Durham, NC: University of North Carolina Press, 2015.

Hankins, Barry. *Jesus and Gin: Evangelicalism, the Roaring Twenties and Today's Culture Wars.* New York: Macmillan, 2010.

Hart, D. G. *That Old-Time Religion in Modern America: Evangelical Protestantism in the Twentieth Century.* Chicago, IL: Ivan R. Dee, 2002.

Hatch, Nathan. *The Democratization of American Christianity.* New Haven: Yale University Press, 1989.

Hindmarsh, Bruce. *The Spirit of Early Evangelicalism: True Religion in a Modern World*. New York: Oxford University Press, 2018.

Hutchinson, Mark, and John Wolffe. *A Short History of Global Evangelicalism*. New York: Cambridge University Press, 2012.

Kidd, Thomas. *The Great Awakening: A Brief History with Documents*. Boston: Bedford/St. Martin's, 2008.

———. *Who Is an Evangelical?* New Haven: Yale University Press, 2019.

King, Gerald W. *Disfellowshiped: Pentecostal Responses to Fundamentalism in the United States, 1906–1943*. Eugene, OR: Pickwick, 2011.

Krapohl, Robert H., and Charles H. Lippy. *The Evangelicals: A Historical, Thematic, and Biographical Guide*. Westport, CT: Greenwood Press, 1999.

Kraus, C. Norman. *Dispensationalism in America*. Richmond, VA: John Knox Press, 1958.

Lantzer, Jason S. *"Prohibition Is Here to Stay": The Reverend Edward S. Shumaker and the Dry Crusade in America*. Notre Dame, IN: University of Notre Dame Press, 2009.

Larson, Edward J. *Summer for the Gods: The Scopes Trial and America's Continuing Debate over Science and Religion*. New York: Basic Books, 1997.

Lienesch, Michael. *In the Beginning: Fundamentalism, the Scopes Trial, and the Making of the Antievolution Movement*. H. Eugene and Lillian Youngs Lehman Series. Chapel Hill: University of North Carolina Press, 2007.

McAlister, Melani. *The Kingdom of God Has No Borders: A Global History of American Evangelicals*. New York: Oxford University Press, 2018.

Marsden, George M. *Fundamentalism and American Culture: The Shaping of Twentieth-Century Evangelicalism, 1870–1925*. New York: Oxford University Press, 1980.

———. *Reforming Fundamentalism: Fuller Seminary and the New Evangelicalism*. New edition. Grand Rapids: Eerdmans, 1995.

———. *The Outrageous Idea of Christian Scholarship*. New York: Oxford University Press, 1997.

———. *Understanding Fundamentalism and Evangelicalism*. Grand Rapids: Eerdmans, 1991.

Martin, Robert Francis. *Hero of the Heartland: Billy Sunday and the Transformation of American Society, 1862–1935*. Bloomington: Indiana University Press, 2002.

Marty, Martin E., and R. Scott Appleby, eds. *The Fundamentalism Project*, 5 volumes. Chicago: University of Chicago Press, 1991–1995.

Mathews, Mary Beth Swetnam. *Doctrine and Race: African American Evangelicals and Fundamentalism between the Wars*. Tuscaloosa, AL: University of Alabama Press, 2018.

Moran, Jeffrey P. *The Scopes Trial: A Brief History with Documents*. The Bedford Series in History and Culture. New York: Palgrave, 2002.

Noll, Mark A. *American Evangelical Christianity: An Introduction*. Malden, MA: Blackwell, 2001.

———. *America's God: From Jonathan Edwards to Abraham Lincoln*. New York: Oxford University Press, 2002.

———. *The Rise of Evangelicalism: The Age of Edwards, Whitefield, and the Wesleys*. Downers Grove, IL: InterVarsity Press, 2003.

Noll, Mark, and David N. Livingstone, eds. *B.B. Warfield: Evolution, Science, and Scripture, Selected Writings*. Grand Rapids: Baker Books, 2000.

Okrent, Daniel. *Last Call: The Rise and Fall of Prohibition*. New York: Scribner, 2010.

Olson, Roger E. *Pocket History of Evangelical Theology*. Downers Grove, IL: InterVarsity Press, 2007.

———. *The Story of Christian Theology: Twenty Centuries of Tradition Reform*. Downers Grove, IL: IVP Academic, 1999.

Richards, Jeffrey J. *The Promise of Dawn: The Eschatology of Lewis Sperry Chafer*. Eugene, OR: Wipf & Stock, 2002.

Ruotsila, Markku. *Fighting Fundamentalist: Carl McIntire and the Politicization of American Fundamentalism*. New York: Oxford University Press, 2015.

———. *The Origins of Christian Anti-Internationalism: Conservative Evangelicals and the League of Nations*. Washington, DC: Georgetown University Press, 2008.

Russell, C. Allyn. *Voices of American Fundamentalism: Seven Biographical Studies*. Louisville, KY: Westminster Press, 1976.

Ruthven, Malise. *Fundamentalism: A Very Short Introduction*. New York: Oxford University Press, 2007.

Sandeen, Ernest R. *The Roots of Fundamentalism, British and American Millenarianism: 1800-1930*. Grand Rapids: Baker Books, 1978.

Scott, Eugenie C. *Evolution vs. Creationism: An Introduction*. Westport, CT: Greenwood, 2004.

Singham, Mano. *God vs. Darwin: The War between Evolution and Creationism in the Classroom*. Lanham, MD: Rowman & Littlefield, 2009.

Stanley, Brian. *The Global Diffusion of Evangelicalism: The Age of Billy Graham and John Stott*. Downers Grove, IL: IVP Academic, 2013.

Steensland, Brian, and Philip Goff, eds. *The New Evangelical Social Engagement*. New York: Oxford University Press, 2014.

Sutton, Matthew Avery. *American Apocalypse: A History of Modern Evangelicalism*. Cambridge: Harvard University Press, 2014.

———. *Aimee Semple McPherson and the Resurrection of Christian America*. Cambridge: Harvard University Press, 2007.

Sweeney, Douglas A. *The American Evangelical Story: A History of the Movement*. Grand Rapids: Baker Academic, 2005.

Treloar, Geoffrey R. *The Disruption of Evangelicalism: The Age of Torrey, Mott, McPherson and Hammond*. Downers Grove, IL: IVP Academic, 2017.

Trollinger, William V., Jr. *God's Empire: William Bell Riley and Midwestern Fundamentalism*. Madison, WI: University of Wisconsin Press, 1991.

Walls, Andrew. *The Missionary Movement in Christian History: Studies in the Transmission of Faith*. Maryknoll, NY: Orbis Books, 1996.

Wenger, Robert E. *Social Thought in American Fundamentalism, 1918-1933*. Eugene, OR: Wipf and Stock, 2007.

Williams, Daniel K. *God's Own Party: The Making of the Christian Right*. New York: Oxford University Press, 2010.

Wills, Garry. *Head and Heart: A History of Christianity in America*. New York: Penguin Books, 2007.

Wolffe, John. *The Expansion of Evangelicalism: The Age of Wilberforce, More, Chalmers and Finney*. Downers Grove, IL: IVP Academic, 2007.

SECONDARY SOURCES:
CHAPTERS, ARTICLES, AND DISSERTATIONS

Abbott, Gary L Sr. "Southern Comfort: Indulgence and Abstinence in the South." Pages 195-207 in *Religion & Alcohol: Sobering Thoughts*. New York: Peter Lang, 2004.

Alsdurf, Phyllis E. "The Founding of *Christianity Today* Magazine and the Construction of an American Evangelical Identity." *Journal of Religious & Theological Information* 9, nos. 1/2 (2010): 20–43.

Baer, Jonathan R. "American Dispensationalism's Perpetually Imminent End Times." *The Journal of Religion* 87, no. 2 (April 2007): 248–64.

Cornwall, Robert. "Primitivism and the Redefinition of Dispensationalism in the Theology of Aimee Semple McPherson." *Pneuma* 14, no. 1 (January 1, 1992): 23–42.

Curtis, Heather D. "'God Is Not Affected by the Depression': Pentecostal Missions During the 1930s." *Church History* 80, no. 3 (September 2011): 579–89.

Davies, John. "Science and the Sacred: The Evolution Controversy at Baylor, 1920–1929." *East Texas Historical Journal* 29, no.2 (October 1991): 41–53.

Ellis, William E. "Edgar Young Mullins and the Crisis of Moderate Southern Baptist Leadership." *Foundations* 19, no. 2 (April 1976): 171–85.

Fuller, Daniel P. "The Hermeneutics of Dispensationalism." PhD diss., Northern Baptist Theological Seminary, 1957.

George, Timothy. "Inventing Evangelicalism: No One Was More Pivotal to the Emerging Movement Than Carl F. H. Henry." *Christianity Today* 48, no. 3 (March 2004): 48–51.

———. "If I'm an Evangelical, What Am I?" *Christianity Today* 43, no. 8 (August 1999): 9.

Greene, Alison Collis. "The End of 'The Protestant Era'?" *Church History* 80, no. 3 (September 2011): 600–10.

Gribben, Crawford. "Wrongly Dividing the Word of Truth: The Uncertain Soteriology of the Scofield Reference Bible." *The Evangelical Quarterly* 74, no. 1 (January 2002): 3–25.

Hankins, Barry. "The (Worst) Year of the Evangelical: 1926 and the Demise of American Fundamentalism." *Fides et Historia* 43, no. 1 (2011): 1–14.

Harper, Brad. "The Scopes Trial, Fundamentalism, and the Creation of an Anti-Culture Culture: Can Evangelical Christians Transcend Their History in the Culture Wars?" *Cultural Encounters* 3, no. 1 (2006): 7–16.

Harrell, David Edwin, Jr. "The Roots of the Moral Majority: Fundamentalism Revisited." *Currents in Theology and Mission* 9, no. 2 (April 1982): 67–92.

Harrington, Carroll Edwin. "The Fundamentalist Movement in America,
    1870-1920." PhD diss., University of California, Berkeley, 1959.
Herzog, Jonathan. "America's Spiritual-Industrial Complex and the Policy
    of Revival in the Early Cold War." *The Journal of Policy History* 22, no. 3
    (2010): 337-65.
House, Paul R. "Remaking the Modern Mind: Revisiting Carl Henry's
    Theological Vision." *Southern Baptist Journal of Theology* 84 (Winter
    2004), 4-24.
Jones, Bartlett C. "Prohibition and Christianity, 1920-1933." *The Journal of
    Religious Thought* 19, no. 1 (1962): 39-57.
Keas, Michael N. "Darwinism, Fundamentalism, and R. A. Torrey."
    Perspectives on Science and Christian Faith 62, no. 1 (March 2010): 25-51.
Livingstone, David N. "The Idea of Design: The Vicissitudes of a Key
    Concept in the Princeton Response to Darwin." *Scottish Journal of
    Theology* 37, no. 3 (1984): 329-57.
McBirnie, Robert Sheldon. "Basic Issues in the Fundamentalism of
    William Bell Riley." PhD diss., State University of Iowa, 1952.
McDannell, Colleen. "Christianity in the United States during the Inter-
    war Years." *The Cambridge History of Christianity*, volume 9. Edited
    by Hugh McLeod. New York: Cambridge University Press, 2006.
Marsden, George M. "The Rise of Fundamentalism." Pages 133-53 in
    Turning Points in the History of American Evangelicalism. Edited
    by Heath W. Carter and Laura Rominger Porter. Grand Rapids:
    Eerdmans, 2017.
Miller, Robert Moats. "A Footnote to the Role of the Protestant Churches in
    the Election of 1928." *Church History* 25, no. 2 (June 1956): 145-59.
Nebeker, Gary L. "The Theme of Hope in Dispensationalism." *Bibliotheca
    Sacra* 158, no. 629 (January 2001): 3-20.
Nelson, Roland. "Fundamentalism in the Northern Baptist Convention."
    PhD diss., University of Chicago, 1964.
Pennock, Pamela E. "'The Number One Social Problem of Our Time':
    American Protestants and Temperance Politics in the 1950s." *Journal
    of Church and State* 54, no. 3 (September 2011): 375-405.
Perry, Everett L. "The Role of Socio-Economic Factors in the Rise and
    Development of American Fundamentalism." PhD diss., University
    of Chicago, 1959.

Peterson, Kurt W. "Minnesota's Norwegian-American Lutherans and the Question of Anti-Evolution Legislation." *Journal of the Lutheran Historical Conference* 2 (2012): 26–48.

Pietsch, B. M. "Lyman Stewart and Early Fundamentalism." *Church History* 82, no. 3 (September 2013): 617–46.

Rausch, David A. "Our Hope: An American Fundamentalist Journal and the Holocaust, 1937–1945." *Fides et Historia* 12, no. 2 (1980): 89–103.

Rogers, Mark. "End Times Innovator: Paul Rader and Evangelical Missions." *International Bulletin of Missionary Research* 37, no. 1 (January 2013): 17–24.

Ruotsila, Markku. "Carl McIntire and the Fundamentalist Origins of the Christian Right." *Church History* 81, no. 2 (June 2012), 378–407.

Russell, C. Allen. "William Bell Riley: Architect of Fundamentalism." *Foundations* 18, no. 1 (January 1975): 26–52.

Sheppard, Gerald T. "Pentecostals and the Hermeneutics of Dispensationalism: The Anatomy of an Uneasy Relationship." *Pneuma* 6, no. 1 (Fall 1984): 5–33.

Shields, Jon A. "Framing the Christian Right: How Progressives and Post-War Liberals Constructed the Religious Right." *Journal of Church and State* 53, no. 4 (May 2011): 635–55.

Sindell, Gail Ann. "Gerald B. Winrod and the Defender." PhD diss., University of Michigan, 1973.

Straton, Hillyer H. "John Roach Straton: The Great Evolution Debate." *Foundations* 10, no. 2 (April 1967): 137–49.

Sutton, Matthew Avery. "'Between the Refrigerator and the Wildfire': Aimee Semple McPherson, Pentecostalism, and the Fundamentalist-Modernist Controversy." *Church History* 72, no. 1 (March 2003): 158–88.

Sweeney, Douglas A. "The Essential Evangelicalism Dialectic: The Historiography of the Early Neo-Evangelical Movement and the Observer-Participant Dilemma." *Church History* 60, vol. 1 (March 1991): 70–84.

Taylor, Thomas T. "Tennessee v. Scopes versus Inherit the Wind: The Trial in the Play and the Film." *Fides et Historia* 37, no. 2 (2005): 165–75.

Waggoner, Paul M. "The Historiography of the Scopes Trial: A Critical Re-Evaluation." *Trinity Journal* 5, no. 5 (1984): 155–74.

Wedel, Rachael. "Prohibition and Religion: Mennonite Brethren and the Temperance Movement, 1900–1940s." *Mennonite Life (Online)* 69 (May 2015).

Weeks, David L. "Carl F. H. Henry's Moral Arguments for Evangelical Political Activism." *Journal of Church and State* 40, no. 1 (Winter 1998): 83–106.

———. "The Political Thought of Carl F. H. Henry." PhD diss., Loyola University of Chicago, 1991.

SUBJECT & AUTHOR INDEX

—